PRAISE FOR *NO CHOICE*

"A powerful, necessary, absolutely captivating account of abortion in America, situating the fight for this fundamental human right inside a much broader landscape of reproductive injustice. Anchored in richly rendered individual stories—told with grace, nuance, and compassion—*No Choice* is required reading for the terrifying post-*Roe* reality in which we find ourselves. This is a book full of the history of resistance and resilience we need to understand and mobilize [for] the fight to come."

—**Leslie Jamison**, author of *The Empathy Exams*
and *Make It Scream, Make It Burn*

"Highly informative, a compassionate look not just at history and current events around reproductive rights, but also the future. *No Choice* offers an invaluable contribution to the discourse and a reminder that abortion has a history that spans centuries. It has always happened and will always happen, even if it is not safe and legal. A post-*Roe* world is not a world without abortion, instead it is a world where more people die from lack of access to reproductive healthcare. This book reminds us that we have seen this in the past and we do not need to return to those horrors. The way forward is policy that centers the living and their needs, not the ideologies of those who cannot conceive of change."

—**Mikki Kendall**, author of *Hood Feminism*

"Andrews' thoughtful and eye-opening original reporting chronicles one of the most definitive moments of our generation through the eyes of the people who lived and breathed it every day. Her thoughtfully crafted narrative tells the stories of all who've had and provide abortions with unflinching love and clear-eyed honesty. *No Choice* is the story of how we lost *Roe*, who was closest to the pain when it happened, and whose lives were forever changed because of it."

—**Renee Bracey Sherman**, founder and
executive director of We Testify

NO
CHOICE

NO
CHOICE

**The Destruction of *Roe v. Wade*
and the Fight to Protect a
Fundamental American Right**

BECCA ANDREWS

PUBLICAFFAIRS
New York

PublicAffairs
Hachette Book Group
1290 Avenue of the Americas, New York, NY 10104
www.publicaffairsbooks.com
@Public_Affairs

Printed in the United States of America

First Edition: October 2022

Published by PublicAffairs, an imprint of Perseus Books, LLC, a subsidiary of
Hachette Book Group, Inc. The PublicAffairs name and logo is a trademark of
the Hachette Book Group.

The Hachette Speakers Bureau provides a wide range of authors for speaking events.
To find out more, go to www.hachettespeakersbureau.com or call (866) 376-6591.

The publisher is not responsible for websites (or their content) that are not owned by
the publisher.

Editorial production by Christine Marra, *Marra*thon Production Services.
www.marrathoneditorial.org
Print book interior design by Jane Raese.
Set in 12-point Minion

Library of Congress Cataloging-in-Publication Data has been applied for.

ISBNs: 978-1-5417-6839-0 (hardcover), 978-1-5417-6308-1 (ebook)

LSC-C

Printing 1, 2022

To everyone who has overcome barriers—
practical, cultural, or otherwise—to get abortion care.
Even if you don't find your precise experience
in these pages, your story matters.

Contents

PART THREE
Post-*Roe*

NO
CHOICE

Introduction

FOR **TWENTY-THREE YEARS,** I was vehemently antiabortion. My parents raised my sister and me in a tiny evangelical Methodist church in our West Tennessee farming community, the sort of place where casseroles and cakes appear when something bad befalls anyone within the county lines. Our church was white but not because the community itself was—the halls of worship in our county were always segregated. I remember the first time I heard the word *abortion* spoken there; I must have been thirteen, maybe fourteen years old. It happened in my Sunday school class, held in a recently constructed annex to our church that felt stark and bare compared to the warm, worn wood and ethereal stained-glass glow of the original structure. I always felt more exposed there, away from the dim, cozy sanctuary, partly due to my teenage awkwardness, partly due to the acrid smell of new paint, the blinding whiteness of barely used dry-erase boards, and the cold of the uncomfortable metal folding chairs we perched on for class. The air-conditioning, blasting against the weighty humidity of summertime in the South, licked at my bare legs and arms until my limbs were covered in gooseflesh. My family was one of a handful that were considered "new" members of the church, even though we'd been attending for years and were devoted members, present every Sunday and well trained in the tasks that accompanied annual events, like frying pies for the fall BBQ fund-raiser. Everyone else could trace their lineage in the church back decades, in some cases centuries. The last names of the deceased, inscribed upon the pews and the windows, belonged to most of the living congregants as well.

The lesson that day was being taught by a man who had always treated my family with kindness, greeting us with unrestrained warmth, a ruddy-complected young father who seemed to always be laughing or tossing his little boys in the air to make them shriek with joy. He pressed us to consider evil and harm we had never fathomed in our adolescence. It was the first time I'd been asked to consider the nuances of abortion. We were high schoolers—nearly grown. Some of our peers were having their first children, after all. It was time to start talking to us as adults. What did we think of abortion? I have a hazy recollection of one of my classmates declaring that the act is a murderous one. What about for victims of rape? he pressed gently. Incest? Unease bloomed in my stomach; until that moment I had never considered that anyone would get an abortion for any reason other than pure selfishness—when we are teenagers, we are at the height of our ego, and it's difficult to comprehend much beyond our narrow interpretation of the world. I don't really recall him offering up a hard and fast opinion; I think his point was to show us that the world is a complex place, and the more you learn about it, the harder it is to apply the lessons taught in the protective halls of church or Sunday school or youth group. He was right about that.

For me, this was where the religion I grew up fervently believing in first got thorny, catching not only on my empathy but also my pragmatism. As of that morning in Sunday school, I was an abso-lutist, declaring that God could make any evil beautiful if a woman would simply devote her faith and her body to him. Childbirth would somehow, in my underexamined ideology, mean that all would be well. Still, something tugged at me, a knowledge that it couldn't be so simple, that life was not so straightforward, a sense that there was more to the story. Even then I understood something of the magni-tude of growing another person inside oneself, of giving birth, the mechanics of which seemed truly horrifying, and of raising a child without the means and the stalwart desire to do so—out of simply having no other choice. Over the years, that sense that there had to be more to this grew until I could no longer ignore it. Some of my fading certainty came out of pure stubbornness: I never could stand being told I couldn't do something, certainly not on the basis of my gender, no matter the plans of a paternalistic god I could neither see nor hear. As my world grew, as I learned to let in more people who were unlike me, I could no longer find reasons to justify my worldview as it had been formed in the halls of that country church. My upbringing, which imbued an inherently female responsibility in me to keep the peace above all else, is not fully dissolved. Even now, when relatives or acquaintances whose politics I cannot immediately identify ask me what my book is about, or what I cover as a reporter, I reply with something vague like "health care" or "women's health," just to err on the side of preserving peace and to avoid igniting a fire I know I cannot muster the energy to put out.

When I think about that day in Sunday school, I recall more about the emotion in the room than what was said. I remember the fear, the uncertainty, the strange thrill of talking about a subject that was taboo. I remember the way the word *abortion* sounded from the mouth of a God-fearing man, more like a demonic ritual than a medical procedure. It's understandable that so many of the women I've spoken with for this book have wished to avoid it, even when they do want to tell their stories. Over the three years I spent interviewing people, many who have sought abortion care told me that they had kept their abortions secret from those around them and had also quietly locked the memory away inside themselves for decades, not wanting to confront the internalized stigma that they had subconsciously absorbed. In the beginning, I expected to hear that sentiment only from women who were able to get illegal abortions before the Supreme Court's ruling of *Roe v. Wade* in 1973, which legalized the procedure nationwide. And it's true that the vast majority of those women, now in their seventies and eighties, were never able to bring themselves to tell their families or friends about their choice until they decided to tell their stories here. Even so, most of them chose to disguise their identities.

But now, I thought, people must be more likely to be vocal about their abortion experiences. Renee Bracey Sherman, who has been called "the Beyoncé of abortion storytelling," created and organized a nonprofit called We Testify that is devoted to giving people from all backgrounds a space to describe their abortion experiences on their own terms. There are social media campaigns like Lindy West, Amelia Bonow, and Kimberly Morrison's "Shout Your Abortion" project. Abortion rights groups use storytellers to normalize the medical procedure on Instagram and Facebook. Gen Z activists take to TikTok to cobble together micro poems in video form about their pro-choice convictions. But to my surprise, things haven't actually changed so much. Abortion is still often whispered about, if it's discussed at all, especially in states governed by antiabortion legislatures. Those states have been existing in a post-*Roe* status for a long time, years before the Supreme Court overturned the *Roe v. Wade* ruling, which cemented the constitutional right to abortion for nearly fifty years.

"[Abortion is] unfortunately a word that society has come to associate with negative things," said Susan Dodd, who ran the Knoxville Center for Reproductive Health from 2009 to 2021, the Tennessee city's sole independent clinic that offers surgical abortion as well as medication abortion. "I think we need another word." In the foreword to Diane Schulder and Florynce Kennedy's 1971 book *Abortion Rap*, a compilation of women's testimonies about the necessity of legalized abortion in the first legal challenge on behalf of patients to the constitutionality of abortion statutes, *Abramowicz v. Lefkowitz*, then congresswoman Shirley Chisholm expresses a similar thought: "There are many ways to avoid the negative associations and connotations that surround the word. We could, for example, borrow the term advanced by the British when they recently rewrote their laws—'pregnancy termination' . . . If we view the issue in this perspective we are at what one might call 'ground zero.'"

Language has been a point of contention in the reproductive health sphere for decades. In December 1972, Jimmye Kimmey, a white woman who was the executive director of the Association for the Study of Abortion, proposed the word *choice* as the antonym to *life*, the rallying cry of the growing antiabortion movement, and has been credited with coming up with the term *pro-choice*. "Right to life is short, catchy, composed of monosyllabic words—an important consideration in English," she wrote in a memorandum. "We need something comparable. Right to choose would seem to do the job. And . . . choice has to do with action, and it's action that we're concerned with."

So, too, is there a distinction between action and agency, and that intention shows up in the push to reclaim the word *abortion* to normalize the procedure and erase stigma rather than hide behind a vague idea of choice. "Hi I'm Laurie Bertram Roberts, I'm not pro-choice, I'm a #ReproductiveJustice activist and I'm pro-abortion," tweeted Bertram Roberts, a Black grassroots organizer in Mississippi. Even before the procedure was legalized, many women were quite forthright about their need for an abortion, though they used coded language to discuss terminating a pregnancy: instead of the clinical coolness of the word *abortion,* they preferred to say they wished to be "fixed up," or they needed to "bring [their] courses on" or "be brought around." It was more of an "open secret" than oppressed silence. The metaphor of women being "silenced" about abortion is a reductive stereotype of helplessness that limits recognition of agency. The importance of being able to talk about abortion freely is in its power to normalize what it is—a very safe medical procedure. (Fourteen times safer than childbirth, in fact.)

As of the most recent estimations, about one out of every four women in the United States will have an abortion in her lifetime; many of those women do not turn around and become advocates for abortion access. They shouldn't have to. They should have the freedom to be able to get the health care they need and go on to live their lives. Except the right to abortion isn't considered as intrinsic as the one to gall bladder surgery. It has been constantly in danger. The ceaseless attack on abortion don't just limit who can have one; it shrouds the entire process under a layer of projected immorality that isn't easy to cast off, particularly if you grew up anywhere other than a coastal metropolitan area.

I have never had an abortion. I became pro-choice through the slow realization as I came into adulthood that, by design, I knew very little about my own body, like the women I grew up alongside. I know grown women who have never been to see a gynecologist, and still others who did not know what a pelvic exam was long after they became sexually active. Their churches and their schools' abstinence-only sex education do not discuss women's health, and in so many conservative homes, the subject of women's bodies is steeped in fear of premature sex to such a degree that the need for knowledge and care is drowned out. Many simply do not have access to reproductive health care or contraception—full stop—for all sorts of reasons: lack of a nearby gynecologist, lack of affordable birth control options, lack of health care because their state chose to not expand Medicaid, making routine check-ups an out-of-reach luxury. In the summer of 2022, the federal protections to the right to an abortion, too, were obliterated. How can we hold people accountable for seeking abortion care when we do not equip them to have basic control over their own reproductive lives?

Still, I remember vividly what it was like to hold a conviction as visceral and ironclad as the one that abortion is murder. It's not my belief anymore, but it is that of millions of people, and that belief, wrong though I believe it to be, has shaped American politics in a powerful way, launching a societal clash that has inspired more war metaphors than anyone ever thought the English language could produce. Boiling down the issue of abortion care to equate to murder has taken an unquestionable toll on the American societal psyche, and now, we are paying the price. This is why so many women had never shared their stories before I asked, and even then, they were clearly afraid. And while this was the case most often in pre-*Roe* abortion stories, and for those who live in post-*Roe* states, it is by no means exclusive to them. Liberal women in progressive areas also struggle to talk about their abortions because the antiabortion arguments have penetrated so deeply into our society and culture.

Even so, I don't dismiss people who identify as antiabortion or even pro-life (though I cannot abide the "pro-life" label because it begs the question of whose life, precisely, is valued). I understand the gripping certainty that accompanies it. My hope is that readers from all kinds of backgrounds and belief systems will come to this text willing to engage with the stories of the people who have opened themselves up for this book.

This book will lay out the costs of "the war on women," as it has been called: from the obvious, intended consequences, like the steady narrowing of access to abortion care and its ultimate demise as a constitutional right, to the more insidious costs in health education, in the legal system, and in the medical profession. But most of all, *No Choice* is about those who have made decisions about their reproductive agency and about how those decisions have affected them and their families. I believe deeply in the power of narratives told by those who have faced the obstacles created from the struggle over reproductive rights—and the people who have risked so much to help them overcome. Many of them asked me to hide their identities for fear of being recognized in these pages by family members, friends, or coworkers, and I obliged. Their words are most important.

*Author's note: It is crucial to acknowledge that abortion care is necessary health care for all birthing people, including transgender men and nonbinary people. Throughout this book, I try to be specific about who I am talking about. You'll notice in the pre-*Roe *years I talk about women collectively, and post-*Roe, *I speak more about pregnant people, people with uteruses, and birthing bodies, referring to women only when I am talking about people who use that specific gender identity. This is in an imperfect effort to be as inclusive and as accurate as possible.*

PART ONE

Before *Roe*

CHAPTER 1

Women's Business

HER NAME WAS Phaenarete.
    Not much is known about her, beyond the fact that she was the mother of Socrates. But Phaenarete was a midwife who provided abortion care as part of her full-spectrum reproductive health repertoire, and her work is referenced, briefly, in the philosopher Plato's *Theaetetus*. I imagine her as powerful, tall and strong and connected to the earth like the cypress tree, which is said to exist between the worlds of life and death. Midwives tread that threshold, working in the in-between, that liminal space of pregnancy and birth, potential for life and life itself, and also potential for death. It takes bravery to labor in that space, physical and emotional fortitude, and mental acuity. Phaenarete was what we would now call an obstetrician. She was a pharmacist, a priestess, a wise woman. Language, to her and other midwives of her time, was healing medicine to be prescribed with the same weight as herbal remedies. I like to think of her walking the streets of Athens, among the ridged stone columns, head held high, being warmly greeted by friends and neighbors—some of whom she had guided through childbirth, others of whom she

tended through abortion. This, to me, is an image of reproductive health utopia. Community based, stigma free, and respected.

Though I am a journalist, I am also a human being with her own values and, as some would call them, biases, so I should disclose up front that abortion rights as discussed in this book are grounded in the belief that all people deserve the freedom to choose whether they wish to reproduce and how to manage their families on their own terms. This is known as the reproductive justice framework, and it was founded by a group of Black women in 1994 who sought to fill in the gaps for the lives of low-income women and women of color in the abortion rights movement, which was largely led by upper-middle-class white women.

For as long as people could get pregnant, they have sought ways to control their reproductive lives with contraceptive practices and abortion care. It's impossible to imagine a society without abortion: it's an experience that spans communities, continents, civilizations. Academics and anthropologists say that induced abortion is likely "a universal cultural phenomenon," and there are hundreds of tribal writings that mention abortion practices. Even so, power dynamics in modern society deeply affect abortion—from knowledge of the procedure, to whose story gets told and in what way, and who gets what kind of care. So, too, have those dynamics existed throughout time—men have traditionally controlled women's bodies, whiteness has been privileged as somehow more worthy of care, some strains of religion attract more money and influence than others—and none of it has any basis in science or even fuzzier standards like worthiness. It's all made up, a fiction, perhaps even a lie. For this reason, laying out the history of reproductive care practices and the forces that have influenced the distribution of those practices is crucial.

In Euripides's classic Greek tragedy *Medea*, first produced in 431 BCE, a key declaration is delivered by the play's namesake: "I would rather stand three times with a shield in battle than give birth once." This sentiment seems utterly reasonable in context. Death in childbirth was routine, sometimes from exhaustion and uncontrollable hemorrhaging and babies in breech, occasionally from infection. Still, there doesn't seem to be much recorded history of abortion in ancient Greece, though women did certainly seek out ways to manage their fertility, and records of abortive methods exist. In the first century, the physician and pharmacologist Dioscorides wrote a series of books called *De materia medica* (Materials of Medicine) that included a wide range of recommended oral contraceptives and fourteen forms of abortifacients or emmenagogues, which are herbs that are used to encourage menstrual flow. Plato mentions contraception, pain management in birthing, and abortion in his writings. He also recommended abortion, though he was open to infanticide, for all women older than forty. (He also was an early eugenicist, advocating for government-controlled selective breeding in order to create a clear social order: the intelligent and well bred would be rulers while the least intelligent or those with the least desirable traits would be workers.) In *Theaetetus,* in which Plato meditates on the nature of knowledge, Socrates, who is traditionally regarded as Plato's teacher, said: "And furthermore, the midwives, by means of drugs and incantations, are able to arouse the pangs of labor, and, if they wish, to make them milder, and to cause those to bear who have difficulty in bearing; and they cause miscarriages if they think them desirable." Not much is discussed regarding the morality or immorality of abortion, but Aristotle concluded that a male fetus's soul bloomed into existence after forty days. Plato maintained that life began at birth and not before.

Ancient Greek medicine also often attributed female maladies to an idle womb. If one's wife was not having sex frequently enough, it was said that inactivity could dry her uterus into lightness, and it might float up inside her body to seek moisture from other organs, resulting in some sort of hysteria. This theory led the Greeks to their word for hysteria: *hystera* is the Greek word for "womb." It should be apparent here who is wielding the power in this situation, and this sort of ideology also serves to present women as disempowered, helpless even when it comes to their own bodies. It's a pattern we see play out over and over again throughout time—one party presents another party as incapable of autonomy, when, in fact, the former is simply seeking a means to control the latter. To that end, it appears that abortion was acceptable in particular cases in which a woman was enslaved by someone who felt a pregnancy detracted from her material worth, which would in turn jeopardize a source of revenue for her owner; one example in the Hippocratic texts involves a "valuable singing girl." Because successful pregnancies that resulted in a live childbirth were precious in ancient Greek and Roman society, the abortion methods mentioned in the Hippocratic text were likely used for spontaneous miscarriage in instances where the pregnancy was clearly abnormal.

For the ancient Romans, meaning roughly from the eighth century BCE to the fifth century CE, as in modern America, it appears class was a major factor in who was able to control their reproductive circumstances—not surprising, given that economic power has also been a force that has bent and twisted the course of history. Though abortion was legal in both the republic and, later, the empire, wealthy Romans seem to have borne fewer children; literature from that time portrays such women as disinclined toward childbirth and more prone to seeking abortions, sometimes to maintain vanity (though all the texts were written by men, so take it with a pillar, not a grain, of salt). Another factor was economic. For those upper-class families, if a girl was born, she came into the world, pink and squalling and unaware of the expectation that her parents would provide a substantial dowry when she was to be married. Ultimately, men were able to exercise power over the women they married because their status as the legal heads of the family gave them ownership over any pregnancy. If a man were to exert his authority over the fate of a pregnancy, the fetus was understood to be his property; the discussion was not centered on morality. (The Old Testament of the Bible assumes a similar stance.)

Soranus of Ephesus, an esteemed Greek physician who practiced in Rome, penned detailed instructions on the conditions that demanded abortion care rather than birth, such as a contracted pelvis and swelling and fissures in the uterus that could complicate delivery. The Romans were also interested in ways to prevent unwanted pregnancy, and the contraceptive methods of the time are entertaining, though they also call for skepticism. One ritual involved splitting open the head of a hairy spider, extracting the worms that habitate therein, and then wrapping those worms in strips of deer flesh to be worn as an amulet by the woman. We have Pliny the Elder to thank for this visual, one of the many medical remedies recorded in his thirty-seven-book series *Natural History*, which is considered the oldest surviving scientific encyclopedia and perhaps the most complete picture of cultural knowledge that exists from ancient Rome. By today's standards, it is of deeply dubious scientific accuracy in its medicinal and biological suggestions, meaning, don't try this at home. The Greeks, Romans, and Egyptians all produced records of pregnancy termination. Some inserted papyrus and dry sponges into the uterus in an effort to cause it to expel its contents along with the foreign substances; others used herbal irritants, like laurel and peppers. Vaginal instruments, perhaps used for early abortion care, have been uncovered within the ruins of Pompeii.

In ancient Egypt, the Ebers Papyrus, which details herbal remedies and medicines and dates back to circa 1550 BCE, lists an impressive series of abortion methods. Some of those ingredients described are still used in the Middle East and North Africa. Egyptian historical materials share a great deal of commonality with the Greek Hippocratic texts, too much to be coincidental, some scholars say, but there is no documented evidence that connects them.

The massive growth of Christianity brought a change in attitude regarding abortion, and of course, the Christian church in all its forms has, for centuries, played a part in how society discusses ending pregnancy. Jewish traditions, by contrast, have consistently prioritized the life of the pregnant person over that of an embryo or fetus. The first known Christian writings conflict with Roman cultural attitudes about abortion. The *Didache*, one of the earliest known Christian texts, which is also known as the *Lord's Teachings Through the Twelve Apostles to the Nations*, comes out against intentionally ending a pregnancy. (Still, it has ultimately not been accepted into the canon of the New Testament.) While there is an Old Testament passage regarding fetal life in the Bible, there are no explicit mentions of abortion and no moral judgment cast upon shedding a pregnancy by choice. The aforementioned passage is in Exodus, where biblical laws over who is owed damages in the instance of a miscarriage caused by outside violence are detailed. The Hebrew translation states: "When people who are fighting injure a pregnant woman so that there is a miscarriage, but no other harm occurs," financial compensation to the family affected is in order. In the Greek translation, however, there's more emphasis on the fetus: "If two men fight and strike a pregnant woman and her child come forth not fully formed, he (the striker) will be punished with a fine." According to the Rabbi Danya Ruttenberg and the Rev. Katey Zeh, when the Hebrew Bible began to be translated into the Greek Septuagint, the Hebrew word *ason*, meaning "harm," "damage," or "disaster," became the Greek *exeikonismenon*, which is more like "from the image." As a result, the passage from Exodus becomes: "When men fight, and one of them pushes a pregnant woman and miscarriage occurs, but it is not in the form." Ruttenberg and Zeh say the original "harm" in Hebrew refers to the death of the pregnant person, which means the Greek Septuagint takes away the emphasis of harm to the pregnant person and places it instead on the fetus and its developmental stage. Some scholars also understand this change to have happened in the cultural context of the Greco-Roman period.

This translation has raised questions for evangelicals about where the line is in gestational development. What is considered fully formed, a true life, and what is simply potential? Many early theologians fell somewhat in line with Aristotle's theory that there were three stages to the development of the soul: the vegetable soul very early in pregnancy, the animal soul, and, finally, the human soul, which is imbued when the fetus begins to move in the womb. Augustine of Hippo, an early Christian theologian whose work deeply influenced the development of early Western Christianity, deferred to Aristotle, and was horrified that people were having sex for more than just procreative purposes, which he deemed to be sinful. So, too, in his eyes, was abortion at any stage.

Despite the pattern of oppression, women throughout time have passed along knowledge and remedies to take care of "women's business." As Barbara Ehrenreich and Deirdre English wrote in their first edition of *Witches, Midwives, and Nurses: A History of Women Healers*: "Women have always been healers . . . they were called 'wise women' by the people, witches or charlatans by the authorities. Medicine is part of our heritage as women, our history, our birthright." Goddesses in ancient Greece and Egypt were worshipped for their curative powers. Isis was the goddess of medicine, and Athena, Hera, and Leto were known as healers, too. While many of the civilizations mentioned here were built to favor male leadership, women found power in their own ways, even if they were not often allowed the authority to chronicle the cultures they created.

People indigenous to America have a long, intimate knowledge of which herbs can help a woman control her body. Stoneseed and dogbane, which have natural contraceptive properties, were used by the Shoshone peoples and the Bodéwadmi to prevent pregnancy. Studies of indigenous cultures also turn up evidence of commonplace abortion practices. A South American matrilocal native tribe known as the Wichí reportedly abort the first pregnancy of any member as a matter of routine, to make the childbirths that follow easier. American native tribes also have documented abortion practices that prioritize the health and well-being of the person carrying the fetus and their quality of life. Abortion rights advocate Lawrence Lader writes that in such communities, "abortion is so commonplace that . . . guilt and psychic damage [are] virtually unknown," an assertion that bears out in more recent research.

The most powerful path to reproductive autonomy has historically come from outside the medical establishment. In more recent history, women have banded together to provide medical care for one another and their communities—and were widely punished for it. In the Middle Ages, the number of female surgeons dwindled as male church and state leaders began to deem women the inferior sex, and formal education was reserved generally for males. By the mid-fourteenth century, laws were passed to regulate how surgery could be practiced and by whom, which further pushed women out of medicine. The creation of professionalized medicine was instigated by a desire to shift power and authority from women to men, while keeping the (unpaid) domestic expectations of women fully intact. During the Middle Ages, the health of the household remained a responsibility that was gendered female in Europe. Women were also hunted as witches for providing medical care, including obstetrical services, across Europe and what is now the United States from the fourteenth century to the seventeenth century. So-called witches were persecuted for any perceived sexual sin, including vague accusations of "lewdness," but the medieval Catholic Church and the burgeoning Protestant Church also took great offense to the way female healers were core providers of reproductive health care, which encompassed contraception and abortion. Though abortion itself was not considered a crime by law, it certainly was seen as such in the eyes of the church, which doled out its own punishments accordingly. A fear of female sexuality was at the heart of the witch-hunt fervor, since witches were believed to have been seduced by Satan. One of the best-known treatises on the evils of witchcraft, *Malleus Maleficarum,* was written by Heinrich Kramer, a Catholic clergyman, who described women as inherently weak and deceptive: "Since [women] are feebler both in mind and body, it is not surprising that they should come more under the spell of witchcraft. For as regards intellect, of the understanding of spiritual things, they seem to be of a different nature than men. . . . But the natural reason is that she is more carnal than a man, as is clear from her many carnal abominations. And it should be noted that there was a defect in the formation of the first woman, since she was formed from a bent rib, that is, a rib of the breast, which is bent as it were in a contrary direction to a man. And since through this defect she is an imperfect animal, she always deceives."

That fear is recognizable in the United States today. Our entire culture has been shaped by it, our laws and policies molded by would-be witch hunters. Even so, women continued to seek control over their reproductive agency in the face of patriarchal values, and in some ways, they were at an advantage given the lack of knowledge and fear held by men regarding their bodies. In the early nineteenth century and before, women shared ways to "restore the menses," relying on drugs and herbal concoctions to bring forth what had been blocked by a pregnancy. It was seen as a simple solution to a disruption in bodily function and a way to bring the body back into balance. For example, to ward off pregnancy, a colonial Maryland woman said that she had "twice taken Savin; once boyled in milk and the other time strayned through a Cloath." Savin, derived from juniper bushes, was often used because of its wide availability, given that the plant was native to the area. Colonial women also used herbs like pennyroyal, tansy, ergot, and Seneca snakeroot to expel the contents of the uterus.

Broadly, abortion wasn't considered a matter for the legal sphere in the United States until shortly before the Civil War. Common law accepted abortion as fairly routine up until "quickening," when the fetus can be felt moving within the uterus. The concept of quickening dates back to Aristotle, who said male fetuses quickened—that is, began to move—in the womb after forty days, while female fetuses take somewhere around eighty to ninety days to do the same. No one seems sure of where Aristotle's idea came from, or how fetal gender was determined with any sort of accuracy during pregnancy, but the word itself comes from the root word *quick*, which was once a synonym for living. And no one is certain who first took up Aristotle's idea as a viable way to view the subject of abortion in modern times, but states in the nineteenth century adopted quickening as the bright line up to which abortion was perfectly acceptable, and the courts hewed to the concept for most of that time. Decreeing abortion as acceptable up until quickening is, in a way, evidence that pregnant people were trusted in those times. After all, no one can tell that the fetus has quickened except the person carrying it.

Still, this is the point at which abortion began to be regulated. The General Assembly of Connecticut was the first to criminalize abortion, enacting a law in 1821 that banned abortion after quickening, though it specified cases where poison was used to induce a miscarriage. (The law was modeled after legislation passed in British Parliament in 1803.) Then came Missouri. Then Illinois. And New York. Sound familiar? More states followed. All this legislation was written and enacted by men.

The advent of so-called professionalized medicine in the twentieth century brought political and economic motivation for powerful people to frame abortion as an evil comparable to murder. The American Medical Association—which, until 1876, was exclusively white and male—launched its fight against abortion in 1859. Though some AMA-affiliated doctors may have been motivated morally, they were also threatened by the financial competition posed by midwives and healers, building on the momentum of the witch-hunt fervor of the Middle Ages that still simmered in the background. It wasn't just men; as Alicia Gutierrez-Romine notes in her book, *From the Back Alley to the Border.* "Because women physicians tried desperately to distance themselves from midwives after the professionaliza-tion of medicine, many took a staunchly conservative anti-abortion stance. Female physicians often spearheaded anti-abortion and anti-midwife campaigns so that they would not appear tolerant, weak, or unprofessional." The antiabortion movement in the United States was set in motion.

As winter was beginning to cede to spring in 1873, Congress passed a new law that has become known as the Comstock Act. The legislation was a symptom of a growing societal moral panic, par-ticularly among middle-class Christians, and it, too, was led into being by a man. (After all, men have the most to lose in the decay of the patriarchal family structure.) The story of Anthony Comstock is almost cliché: small-town New England white boy makes it to big, bad New York City to find it absolutely *teeming* with obscenity that threatens his worldview. Haunted by the knowledge that sex can be pleasurable for all parties involved, not just those with penises, and that sex can even be had in the name of fun, not just reproduction, he pledged to do what he could to make sure the word didn't get out. As a well-connected political insider, he used his influence to persuade Congress to pass "An Act for the Suppression of Trade In, and Cir-culation of, Obscene Literature and Articles of Immoral Use." This mouthful of a title eventually became known as the Comstock Act. While the law failed to clearly define what it meant by "obscenity," it outlawed the distribution of "obscene, lewd or lascivious," "im-moral," or "indecent" materials through the mail, which included information about contraception and abortion. (Emma Goldman, the white anarchist political writer who fought for women's rights and gay rights, was not impressed, and she referred to Comstock as one of a cohort of "Puritanic eunuchs" in an essay, "The Hypocrisy of Puritanism," published in the early 1900s.) Comstock was also a prolific book burner; he likely would have felt right at home in our modern Republican Party.

It's no coincidence that abortion became heavily scrutinized and regulated in the nineteenth century, as women like Goldman were beginning to assert their own political power. As the twentieth century began, and women also declared their rights to sexual freedom, the attacks on reproductive autonomy escalated.

CHAPTER 2

Unfit

WE CANNOT CONSIDER ways women have worked to harness their own reproductive power without exploring the ways that power has been wielded against them, particularly for Black and brown women. Abortion rights are inextricably bound with reproductive justice, defined as "the human right to maintain personal bodily autonomy, have children, not have children, and parent the children we have in safe and sustainable communities," by SisterSong, the collective of Black women who coined the term. Enslaved Black women in the United States were not afforded a straightforward personal ideology of whether or not they wanted children, or how they wished to experience motherhood. "For slave women, procreation had little to do with liberty," writes Dorothy Roberts in *Killing the Black Body*. "To the contrary, Black women's childbearing in bondage was largely a product of oppression rather than an expression of self-definition and personhood." Black enslaved women were often denied the dignity of choosing their sexual partners. Some enslavers forced enslaved people to "breed," like livestock, based on favorable attributes that they thought might manifest in future laborers. Even mothers' milk was not sacred: Black women were often expected to serve as wet nurses for their enslavers' offspring, nurturing another generation of oppressors with their bodies. Further, enslaved Black women's bodies were experimented on, notably by a white man named James Marion Sims, known as the "father of modern gynecology." He did not use anesthetics on his victims. Under the brutality of the white gaze, Black bodies were reduced to chattel, a mere means to an end, and Black women were stripped of any sense of agency, their emotions and desires not taken into account.

Some enslaved Black women used sexual abstinence or herbal abortifacients as a form of rebellion, including "the infusion or decoction of tansy, rue, roots and seed of the cotton plant, pennyroyal, cedar gum, and camphor," according to one 1860 medical record from a white physician in Tennessee. Care was rooted in community: enslaved women shared medical knowledge with one another and preserved that knowledge through generations. Dorothy Roberts writes that herbal skill was likely brought over from Africa and passed down through oral tradition by midwives who had been captured and taken to America to live out their lives in bondage. A refusal to bear children was a powerful statement for enslaved women; in doing so, they also denied their enslavers economic gains. In another common scenario, an enslaved woman raped by a white man might seek abortifacients in part to avoid the misplaced rage of her rapist's wife. Still, these women were forced to consider their long-term survival. Some enslaved women were told they would be freed if they gave birth to a certain number of healthy children. As Loretta Ross and Rickie Solinger note in their book *Reproductive Justice: An Introduction*, all decisions made by Black enslaved women regarding their reproductive lives that were outside their enslavers' wishes "constituted a woman's claim of full personhood—her linkage of her reproductive life to human freedom." In some cases, a woman would kill her newborn out of desperation to not cede her child to the horrors of slavery, which would likely mean an eventual loss of the child anyway. Nearly one in three Black babies living in the Upper South in 1820 were sold off to enslavers who whisked them away from their families either further south or westward. We should also consider the labor done by Black enslaved women in their own households, in their devotion to their own families, as "a form of resistance, directly benefiting Black people rather than their white masters alone," Roberts notes. "Further, although a slave woman's act of giving birth enhanced the master's workforce, it just as surely ensured the life of the slave community." Black motherhood, too, was and remains an important liberty and rebellion against white supremacy. Black motherhood and grief has brought forth powerful grassroots efforts against racially motivated police brutality.

But if an enslaved woman did not produce children, her value decreased, and the potential for brutal abuse as punishment for her infertility increased, as did the risk that she could be sold off and separated from those she loved. That's not to say that women were protected from abuse during pregnancy. Roberts writes vividly of the horrifying acts that sprung from the imaginations of white slaveholders who were driven by bloodlust. A Black woman, facedown in the dirt, a hole dug for her swollen belly so that the fetus inside her would be protected by the earth, while she was mercilessly flayed for some crime that could never stand up to reason. She was only a vessel; her soon-to-be child was the slave master's economic interest. She was thoroughly dehumanized.

Unfortunately, because these women were abused and silenced, it is almost impossible to know the full extent of how and under what circumstances they chose to exercise their limited control over their reproductive lives. In researching this book, this barrier to the voices of these women has come up again and again: those who may have sought to end their pregnancy but were denied the means, in the name of patriarchy or white supremacy or both, also had few avenues to tell their stories.

When colonizers came to the Americas and stole land from the natives, they showed little hesitation toward committing mass genocide along the way. Andrew Jackson, the seventh president of the United States of America, once wrote that "the whole Cherokee Nation ought to be scourged," and his actions reflected that abhorrent belief. He signed the Indian Removal Act in 1830, which led to the forcible removal of tribes from the Southeastern United States, along what is known as the "Trail of Tears." Jackson led massacres of Native peoples, and consistently gave orders to kill women and children who were hiding, in his pursuit of total annihilation. When indigenous people were mostly either dead or corralled on government-controlled reservations, the colonizers also insisted on forcing them to assimilate to their Eurocentric culture, meaning indigenous languages, traditions, and ways of life were also stolen through erasure. This violent whitewashing has not only meant the loss of treasured knowledge and identity for Native Americans but also that Native bodies were subjected to "professionalized medicine," beginning as early as the 1830s, when the Ho-Chunk peoples (also called the Winnebago) were coerced into a treaty that exchanged land in what became Wisconsin for the promise of health services. This marked the early beginnings of the federal Indian Health Service (IHS), officially founded in 1955, which, scholar Jane Lawrence observes, approached the Native people it was meant to serve as though they were less than human in their intelligence and morality. Though these health services were effective at treating disease and lowering infant mortality, the ideology that regarded Native peoples as "less than" led to egregious human rights abuses. "Some of [the IHS doctors] did not believe that American Indian and other minority women had the intelligence to use other methods of birth control effectively and that there were already too many minority individuals causing problems in the nation," writes Lawrence. Forced sterilization of Native women began in the 1960s. The procedure was often done surreptitiously, under the guise of an appendectomy or directly after a woman had given birth, without her knowledge. A Government Accountability Office (GAO) report found that 3,406 Native women were sterilized without proper consent between 1973 and 1976 among IHS hospitals and IHS contract facilities in four regions. There were twelve IHS program areas, and there were reportedly some 165,000 Native women of childbearing age in the country. An estimated 25 percent of them had been sterilized, though some experts say the number is likely higher, as the GAO report was not comprehensive.

Two fifteen-year-old Cheyenne girls were robbed of their reproductive capabilities during what they were told was an appendectomy. A woman suffering from severe headaches was prescribed a hysterectomy, as a physician chalked up her pain to "female problems." Eventually, it was discovered that she had a brain tumor. Another woman wrestling with alcoholism went to seek medical help for her affliction, and the IHS doctor sterilized her, telling her she could have a "womb transplant" later, when she was ready to have children. When she recovered and became engaged, she went to another doctor to request the transplant so she and her future husband could build a family. She was distraught when she was told there was no such thing as a womb transplant.

When Native women did bear children, the state interfered. Those who were thought to have too many children were threatened with loss of welfare benefits, which they would not have needed if their land had not been stolen in the first place. Children were taken from their families and put in foster care for absurd, sometimes made-up infractions; Native kids were also funneled into government-run boarding schools, where they were not allowed to wear their Native dress, speak their language, or worship any god other than the Christian god. Many were not allowed to visit home for at least three years, if they got to go back at all. Thousands of children died in the schools, buried in unmarked graves. For the most part, these injustices were ignored by the burgeoning feminist movement of the time, which meant Native women broadly regarded self-proclaimed feminists with distrust and wariness.

To be sure, Black women's bodies and fertility were under siege by white supremacist forces even after slavery was abolished. Then, the dynamic changed. Since Black people were no longer legally understood as property, Black babies were no longer considered a commodity by the white people who oversaw the economic interests of the United States. Instead, they were seen as a threat, a potential demographic force that could upend white control. Under the racist, so-called science of eugenics—which sought to build a strong Aryan nation in the United States and eliminate social ills through planned reproduction—the majority of the country had adopted proeugenics legislation by 1935. This resulted in the sterilization of women of color, immigrants, poor white people, and disabled people. The movement stemmed largely from xenophobia and economic shifts that no longer favored men as their own employers or even as primary workers; women were becoming more educated and, consequently, began working outside the home. Unfortunately, many white women who were advocating for contraception as a means of furthering their own autonomy did not appear to mind partnering with the eugenics movement to further their agenda. (Margaret Sanger, a white woman who founded Planned Parenthood, most famously chose this alliance.)

Economic responsibility and power were the bedrock of masculinity, and without it, men feared a loss of identity. bell hooks, the Black feminist scholar and writer, said it best when she wrote about white patriarchal value systems: "Capitalism has taught him that, at all costs, his property can and must be protected. Patriarchy has taught him that his masculinity has to be proved by the willingness to conquer fear through aggression."

As women and people of color became a greater economic force, and as female sexuality revolved less and less around reproduction and male satisfaction, men in power responded to these perceived threats with laws. In 1962, the American Law Institute published the Model Penal Code, standardizing criminal law and attempting to expand medical access to abortion care, while still relying on the power structures in place. A "policy of cautious expansion," as it has been described, gave doctors more justification for therapeutic abortion care by taking mental health into consideration, but it did not empower patients to be involved in their own medical decisions. The final verdict remained firmly in the hands of doctors and medical staff.

Women were forced to justify their need for abortion care by proving severe mental distress, to perform their hysteria to the satisfaction of men. If the doctor didn't buy it, then his patient was forced to give birth.

Around the same time, in 1960, the beginnings of the grassroots antiabortion movement were forming in response to state legislatures that were considering legalizing the procedure. The meetings were small and humble and began as conversations among friends and neighbors, generally middle-class Americans who were prone to the idea that their country was starting to resemble Sodom and Gomorrah, the cities in the Bible's Book of Genesis that were eventually destroyed by God as a result of their irredeemable wicked nature. Moral panic, brought on by women's liberation and sexual freedom, was taking hold among those who felt their power was being threatened by cultural change. The wheel turns again.

CHAPTER 3

With a Little Help

IN 1968, SHERRY was done with San Francisco. The Haight had lost the carefree, anything-goes air that had drawn her into the city in the first place, and now it was infected with a stench of addiction and death that was wearing on her. She was tired of hearing about friends overdosing, sick of the fear that the drugs that were supposed to transport her, unscathed, to another world could be laced with something that would end her. She had a child to think about—a son, whom she adored. Plus, the guy she was living with at that time had just gotten busted for marijuana possession and taken to a prison in Chino, at the other end of the state, to serve out a short sentence. She was twenty-three or twenty-four, and she was, in her own words, young and crazy and alone. *Why not?* she thought. So she followed him, settling in Los Angeles so that she could visit him from time to time; maybe, she thought, they could find a new life together when he got out.

Sherry, a white woman, had no money to speak of; she carefully measured out a living for herself and her two-year-old son on welfare. After rent, she had about a hundred dollars a month to work with. She tried to sustain the electricity of being in a new city, but the spark kept getting stamped out by her loneliness. She met a girl, about her own age, who lived in the same apartment building and recognized that she was hemmed in. "You need a night out," the girl insisted. It did sound nice—the promise of a new friendship, an evening among the city lights rather than looking out at them from a distance, a break from the constant stress of what comes next. A neighbor she had come to trust promised to look after her little boy, and so it was decided. She kissed her son and left, still wearing her daily uniform of jeans and a T-shirt; nothing fancy for a casual night out in a new city with new people. She wasn't trying to impress anyone; she only wanted to breathe and stretch and *be*.

From there, she remembers only that she was raped.

When she says it out loud, the tone of her voice is matter-of-fact. It is what it is; it happened. She never saw him again; she doesn't know his name. He had some connection to the girl and her boyfriend, who she never spoke to after she was raped; it was too much to look at them, much less tell them what had happened to her, and besides, what would be the point? She only knows that she said no, and he did not care. When she missed her period, she knew deep down that she was pregnant, but the trauma of being raped was too heavy and fresh. She couldn't let herself believe this was now happening to her, too. Weeks went by, and she would try to explain away the changes in her body as simply hormonal, as symptoms of post-traumatic stress, and all the while the pregnancy grew inside her as time ticked by, ever louder, insisting that she *do* something.

The expanse of LA was overwhelming, and it was hard to imagine there was anyone in the never-ending city of millions who she could talk to. She certainly couldn't tell her family or any friends. The only person she truly trusted nearby was in prison, and she couldn't wrap her head around a way to tell him what had happened. But then she remembered an acquaintance, her roommate's friend who had worked registering voters in Mississippi and had ridden with the Freedom Riders. She knew he came from a progressive family in LA, and she desperately wanted to talk to another woman about her predicament. When she had mentioned she was moving there, he had given her his mother's phone number and told her to use it if she needed anything. Now she did. She didn't say what was wrong on the phone, only that she had a problem, and would Cynthia please come over so they could talk.

Cynthia pulled into the apartment complex parking lot a few hours later. It was awkward at first. How do you tell a complete stranger that you were raped, and then you were ensnared in the resulting trauma, and now you need an abortion? She doesn't remember exactly how she managed to get the words out, but together, they came up with a plan. Cynthia found what was known as "the list"—compiled and meticulously updated by abortion rights activists. The list was essentially a directory of abortion providers in Japan, Sweden, and Mexico. Sherry recalls that the only condition to use the list was to one day share your abortion story, an obligation she says she was not ready to fulfill until she spoke to me for this book. "I'm almost eighty now," she told me. "And before I die, I have to talk about this, I really do."

It was decided; she would go to Ciudad Juárez to have an abortion, but it would cost her. She had to borrow $500 from Cynthia, since she was quickly approaching the third trimester, and she had to prepare for a four-day stay and an unfamiliar medical procedure in a country that was not her own. By the time the plans were made, a tentative bond had formed between the two women, and Sherry left her son with Cynthia, telling him that she was going to visit her mother and she would be back in a few days. "I don't know what I would have done without her," Sherry says.

On the plane to El Paso, she tried not to think too much about what she was about to do and instead focused on the feeling that she would soon be able to move on. The hospital sent a car to pick her up from the airport. They drove across the Rio Grande into Juárez, wordlessly, and directly to the clinic, which was a section of a larger hospital. The $500 covered not only the procedure itself but also her hospital stay and her travel to and from the clinic all the way from Los Angeles; she recalls the medical practice providing a sort of travel service with the procedure. When she arrived, she settled into a waiting area, where she sat for hours among a gaggle of young women, who looked to be in high school or college, and their mothers. Most of them seemed to be from the Midwest, and she was surprised to find that everyone she spoke to was soundly against legalizing abortion. "I think it was, 'It's OK for people who can afford to do this, but it's not OK for anybody else,'" she recalls. "It was very bizarre—they were all white." Most of them came and went: because their pregnancies were in earlier stages, they needed to be at the clinic for only four hours or so. But because Sherry was approaching her sixth month, she would have a much longer stay. The trip itself was put together out of desperation, and Sherry hadn't known what exactly to expect because she had never been to Mexico or had an abortion, but she had heard tales of dirty, greedy Mexican men who had no business providing any sort of medical care. Now, the racism that lurks behind the prevailing stereotype is more evident, but then, she was relieved to find that the clinic was bright and clean, and the nurses were friendly, warm women who helped her order food in Spanish from the restaurant next door. She doesn't remember much about going into the abortion or what it felt like to wake up from the anesthesia—everything is lost in a daze of apprehension that gave way to relief. She still felt slightly off when she got into the car to cross back into Texas, but she dismissed it; surely it would lift with time. She was hot and uncomfortable, but she had to get home to her son. She grabbed her bag and trudged from the car into the airport, but she was soon overwhelmed with dizziness, and she lost consciousness momentarily. She came back around and desperately shook just enough fog from her mind to stumble to a pay phone and call the clinic. They brought her back to the hospital to treat the infection that was causing her body to burn with fever and her muscles to shake. She stayed in Juarez for an extra day, hooked up to an antibiotic IV drip that eased her temperature back down.

When she returned home, her life regained its former shape. She found she could begin to move forward. She made friends, she learned to love Southern California, and she continued to be active in the antiwar movement. She went on to help start a center to care for women with mental health issues, and after that, she became a labor organizer. For the next several decades, she lived precisely the rich, full life she had hoped for. She didn't dwell on her abortion—it did not define her—but it did make possible the world she ultimately built for herself.

SHERRY IS ONE of thousands of women who the Society for Humane Abortion (SHA) reportedly helped connect to vetted abortion providers outside the United States by the end of the 1960s. Patricia Maginnis, Rowena Gurner, and Lana Phelan, a group of white women known as the Army of Three, dedicated themselves to aiding people seeking abortion care by making the list that helped Sherry, teaching classes on self-managing abortions, and creating and distributing leaflets with information about abortion. For them, the women they served took top priority, and the well-being of their clients was more pressing than any political fight or struggle. Later, they also founded ARAL, the Association to Repeal Abortion Laws, as the legal arm of SHA. Their California roots, too, are significant. As of 1935, the state law regarding abortion was thus: "Every person who provides, supplies, or administers to any woman, or procures any woman to take any medicine, drug, or substance, or uses or employs any instrument or other means whatever, with intent thereby to procure the miscarriage of such woman, unless the same is necessary to preserve her life, is punishable by imprisonment in the State prison not less than two nor more than five years."

SHA, founded in 1962, was one of the earliest forms of grassroots feminist abortion rights organizing. As SHA's leader and founding member, Pat Maginnis was a far cry from your coiffed politico with prepared remarks. She was known to dress in clothes she had either bought at a thrift store or simply found on the street, and she said what was on her mind, to hell with propriety, which she considered only to be a speed bump to meaningful progress. Of course, some of that sense of urgency came from her own experiences.

She was born into a Catholic family, the fifth of seven children, during the Great Depression, and her mother continued to give birth even after a doctor advised her that it was no longer safe; her faith, adopted from her husband, forbade contraception. The physical and mental toll that resulted made a deep impression on Pat, though she clarifies that her mother would never admit to anything other than fulfillment from their large family. Still, two miscarriages and two childbirths with only a year in between drained her mother of energy and patience, which was already in low supply. Pat's family moved from New York to Okarche, Oklahoma, in 1930 to follow her father's pioneering dreams. Once there, food and resources had to be carefully stretched as the family grew from seven to nine. The patriarch of the family worked as a veterinarian, caring for livestock in all seasons, while Pat's mother did the bookkeeping for the family, as well as overall care for the household; she had a particular knack for carpentry. She installed kitchen cabinets in the three-room, tar-paper shack and took on home improvement projects when inspiration struck.

Pat's paternal grandmother's life, too, had been derailed by an inability to control her reproductive capabilities: she was beginning to gain traction as an opera star when she became pregnant, out of wedlock, with Pat's father. Pat has described her family as abusive, and her relationship with them was strained. She recalls a specific rebellion as a teenager, when she fashioned a halter out of her satiny pink bedspread, studded with flowers, and ran out the front door to wave at a truck full of soldiers who were passing by on Highway 81. When her parents' car rolled down the driveway, her heart dropped into her stomach. They said nothing, but she could see their dismay. They simply pulled her out of the local Catholic school and transferred her to a convent to continue her education. The incident was, according to Pat, an example of how ill suited she was to her family's expectations.

Pat decided early on in her life that she did not wish to have children and that she would live her life firmly on her own terms. She rejected the faith she has been raised in, describing the Catholic Church as a place that reduced women to incubators. Acknowledging the cliché of "Catholic guilt," she made clear that not a whisper of such emotion remained in her body; instead, she found slow-burning, sustained rage. As a young woman, she joined the Women's Army Corps in 1951, where she trained to become a surgical technician. She was sent to Panama for two years, but instead of assisting with surgeries, she was relegated to the pediatric and obstetric wards. There, she watched the consequences of illegal abortion and religious stigma play out. Women were suffering from botched abortions—some self-managed, some sloppily performed by strangers who had promised they knew what they were doing. There were women giving birth against their will, or giving birth despite extreme risk to their lives. There were infants born with severe maladies and abnormalities. For the rest of her life, Pat was unable to forget the suffering of one particular woman. She was Colombian, married to a Puerto Rican soldier, and she had recently gone home to Colombia to visit family, where she became pregnant by a man who was not her husband. Pieces are missing from the story because Pat learned it through her limited perspective as a white English speaker stationed at Panama's Fort Clayton, but one thing is clear: this woman did not want to be pregnant. She feared her husband's wrath, and she dreaded his return to the base from Korea. In her terror, she had been forced into a straitjacket and held at the hospital like an animal, captive in a cage constructed of chain-link fence, a simple bed in the center. She didn't speak any English, but that didn't stop the army physicians from shouting at her to "shut up!" whenever she began to wail. Nurses' aids, like Pat, were forbidden from engaging with her despair. "This woman just cried and and begged and pleaded for mercy and help," Pat says. She watched, silently wishing for some intervention in the form of a miscarriage.

The sight of a woman who was literally imprisoned for her sexual expression made Pat feel queasy and unsteady, like she had survived a sort of physical impact that left her reeling. When she finished her stint with the Women's Army Corps, she moved to New York City in 1953 to process all that she had seen and to try and understand who she was outside the confines of strict institutions like the Catholic Church and the military. The agony on the Colombian woman's face etched itself indelibly into her, and Pat told her New York roommates and other women she encountered of the tale, over and over, as if reciting an incantation that was keeping her alive. The woman's plight stayed with Pat after she left New York City about a year later to attend classes at San Jose State University, where she became pregnant for the first time, despite using a diaphragm. She asked around, and in her recollections—she's vague on the details, making oblique references like "by various indirect communications"—she made her way to Tijuana to a doctor who called himself Dr. Serolongi. She was steeled for whatever might come; she had no way of knowing for sure whether the clinic would be clean or if the physician would be competent or if she would survive this gamble at all, but she knew she could not be a mother. Two men attended to her: a Mexican man, who did all the talking, and a man who appeared to be American and reminded her of a football player. The latter performed the procedure. After it was over, a taxi picked her up to take her to the bus station so she could begin her journey home. He smiled at her in the rearview mirror. "*Tenga un plato de menudo, flaquita,*" he said, not unkindly. Have a plate of *menudo*, skinny girl. She chuckled wearily, grateful for his kindness, but she was too tired to think of food. Later, her stomach rumbled.

The indignity of having to leave her country to seek the procedure ignited a fire that had been smoldering for years. As she processed all that she had been through—the quiet conversations with trusted friends, the travel, the fear and uncertainty—she swore she would not travel beyond the borders again to exercise basic reproductive autonomy, nor would she stand by and allow the status quo for women to remain as such. The following Christmas, she discovered she was pregnant once more, and she decided it was time to take control of her own body. She remembered that she still had a catheter lying around from her time as an army nurse, and she knew enough about the reproductive system to carefully move it up into her uterus. She felt an unpleasant pop and a stabbing pain—she had only managed to puncture the placenta. "I didn't understand that I could introduce a fluid which would have been an abortifacient, or I could have used a suction idea," she explained in an interview decades later. She leaked amniotic fluid constantly, and at six months' gestation, she went into hard labor in the middle of one of her college classes. The contractions came on swiftly and took her by surprise. She started to double over in pain, but she caught herself and breathed through it, grasping the sides of her desk. Once she was able to stand, she silently left the room and staggered home. By the time she made it, the contractions were nearly ten minutes apart.

For the next sixteen hours, she endured the pain as best she could, but around two o'clock the next morning, she was nearly out of her mind with agony. She was up front with the county hospital staff, telling them plainly that the abortion was self-induced rather than spontaneous. The nurses were horrified, and she was shoved into an exam room to finish the process alone and without pain medication. There, she delivered a fetus. The doctor, who was Catholic, came into the room and asked if he could baptize the fetus. "Well, please make it Buddhist," she retorted. Later, a doctor returned to inform her that the fetus had not survived and asked her what she wanted to do with it. She asked if it could be donated to science, and he told her that places in the area already had what they needed and weren't accepting any more specimens. Pat shrugged. "Well, bury it." The doctor left, and a hospital administrator came down. She glowered at Pat. "You have to name it," she informed Pat tersely.

"I don't," Pat countered.

"You do."

"I'm not going to name that . . . that fetus. It's nothing to me, and I'm not going to name it."

The circular argument continued in this vein until Pat's exasperation won out. "Fine," she said. "Name it Pat Maginnis."

"So, somewhere in Santa Clara County, under holy ground, there is a pine box, which of course you and I know is just a misuse of pine boxes, but the undertakers have a law that fetuses over 500 grams have to have a burial service," she recalled.

The next year, in 1959, "sure enough, my great Catholic uterus with all its Catholic eggs, managed to put out another pregnancy," she says. This time, she and her partner had been relying on withdrawal as a form of contraception, which, she says, is akin to "Vatican roulette." She tried injecting a mild Lysol solution into her cervix. Nothing happened. Unsure of what else to try, she did the only thing she could think of in the moment: she shoved an unwashed finger as far into her vagina as it would go. As a result, she got a serious infection, and her fever skyrocketed so that she sought treatment at San Francisco General Hospital, as she had recently moved to the city by the Bay. As before, she announced that she had attempted to self-manage her abortion, and as before, she was met with revulsion. Nurses filed in and out of her room, pleading with her to carry to term, insisting that once she had a beautiful, bouncy baby, she would love it, and all would be well. Motherhood would settle over her, quietly and easily, and she would find herself wrapped in bliss. But Pat, with her steely certainty, knew herself better than that and was familiar with all the parts of motherhood they were glossing over. That night, she aborted in the bathroom of her hospital room. The following day, she was interrogated, alone, by two plainclothes inspectors from the homicide detail about the circumstances of her medical state. "We understand you've had an abortion," one said to her, waiting for her denial.

Pat gave a humorless smile. "Yes, I induced it myself."

The inspectors' mouths hung open. After a beat, the short one sputtered, "Well, what are you, some kind of contortionist?"

She kept her composure, adopting a bored tone to counter the fear that was beginning to vibrate through her. "Well no, I just took a catheter, and I'll be very glad to show you what I did if you like. I'll be happy to demonstrate."

"You're going to court," the larger inspector growled. "We're going to haul you before a grand jury."

"Well, I'll be glad to show them in court what I did."

The interrogation slipped into irrelevant biographical detail from there—where her parents were, her schooling, her familiarity with the city of San Francisco. They left her with instructions to call them once she was released from the hospital. "OK," she said uncertainly. She spent another week in the hospital recovering from the infection. She never found herself pregnant again. A few days later, the inspectors called her at her home, and she curtly informed them that she was under no obligation to answer their questions, acting on advice given to her by an ACLU attorney, and hung up. It was the last she heard of them.

She passed the next six months or so living in San Francisco, but she felt the draw to finish her degree and returned to San Jose State. While finishing up requirements to graduate, she began to experiment with reproductive freedom activism. Her first major foray into organizing was catalyzed by a newspaper article she spotted in 1961. The headline promised a new California bill to legalize abortion, brought forth by Assemblyman John T. Knox. The proposed law struck her as insulting and meek: it legalized the procedure specifically in hospitals and only when the continuance of the pregnancy involves "substantial risk that mother or child will suffer grave and irremediable impairment of physical or mental health," or in cases of rape or incest. Still, the paper declared it the most major proposed change to the state's abortion laws in eighty-nine years, and she fished around in a drawer for a pair of scissors and clipped out the story.

Change was often incremental, and all she knew was that she wanted to be part of the path forward. She took the clipping, hastily sketched a petition to legalize abortion, and flew out the door to start talking to people on the sidewalks. For two years, Pat traversed the city, hitting up students on campus and stay-at-home mothers in wealthy parts of town and people who were experiencing homelessness. Meanwhile, the bill died quietly in committee, and she made her way back to San Francisco to continue her work gathering public opinion on abortion rights.

Grainy black-and-white footage shows Pat as a slight young woman, her face set with determination, bandied about by the San Francisco winds while she stands resolute on a sidewalk. A local television reporter asks if she believes in abortion rights for any reason; she doesn't blink, even as her hair floats, Medusa-like, around her head. "Some 100,000 women—this is California women alone—subject themselves to improper or illegal abortions," she patiently explains. "I think that in itself is a rather staggering figure, and I feel great indignation as a woman to think that women have to subject themselves to second-rate medical care for a safe surgical procedure." In 1962, she began the first iteration of the Society for Humane Abortion.

ROWENA GURNER HADN'T been settled in Palo Alto long when she was thumbing through an issue of the *New Republic* and she stopped short at an advertisement for a published lecture, titled "Abortion and Human Dignity." The lecture had been penned by Garrett Hardin, an ecologist whose writings about population control eventually developed a white nationalist bent, but at the time, the lecture had struck Pat Maginnis as significant in comparison to the watery suggestions of other men in power, and she put out an ad to distribute copies of it. Rowena had also had an illegal abortion: she became pregnant after her diaphragm failed. The ob-gyn who fitted it for her did not bother to explain to her how she should check to make sure it was placed correctly over the cervix. She had traveled to Puerto Rico, like thousands of others in the 1960s, and paid twice what she had been told to expect. Her boss threatened to fire her should she return from her "vacation" any later than planned, and she found scant kindness or comfort in her ordeal. She, too, was angered by the lengths she had to go to get her abortion. She vowed that someday, somehow, someone would pay for what she had been put through.

Roughly a year after her abortion, Rowena decided she needed a change, so she hopped on her three-speed bicycle with very little beyond a pack of clothes, a sleeping bag, and a flyswatter, riding for four months from New York until she reached the Bay Area. A new friend knew of Pat and suggested that Rowena introduce herself, handing her a telephone number. Rowena procrastinated a bit on reaching out—"I am not a joiner," she admitted in an interview in the 1980s—but eventually she called Pat and met her at her small, cluttered apartment. She saw the chaos Pat was operating in—this woman was brilliant but not especially known for order and coordination—and went to work answering letters from women who needed help. Rowena was famously responsible for giving the group structure. She bought clothes for Pat to wear for speaking engagements; she worked to keep the nonprofit financially viable; she had the idea to ask women who had been helped by SHA to write their legislators in support of abortion rights and tell their stories and donate time to the movement.

I N 1965, LANA PHELAN was dashing through rain to get to her car after a day at a California medical conference in San Francisco, but she was flagged down briefly by Pat, who handed her a flier. It screamed, "Repeal Abortion Laws!" "I looked at that and said to my husband, 'My God, the only person there with a dab of sense was standing outside in the rain,'" she recalled.

Lana, who became the third in the Army of Three, had also had an illegal abortion. Like Pat, she grew up during the Depression to a family that did not fare well, and she found herself married to a twenty-five-year-old man when she was only fifteen. Her husband worked in a shipyard; she described him as "not a man that made things happen—he was a man that things happened to." She was pregnant within a month of her marriage, and she nearly died in childbirth; she recalled doctors and nurses creeping in and out of her hospital room, asking each other if she was dead yet. She lived, and so did her baby, but her doctor warned her that she would not survive another delivery. Three months later, she was pregnant again.

She was just a teenager, and no one had told her about contraception or sex or her body's reproductive capabilities. Lana had a job working at a Walgreens drug store, and she eventually coaxed information out of a female coworker in the cosmetics department about how to get an abortion. She was directed to a Cuban midwife in the Ybor City neighborhood in Tampa, Florida, whose price was fifty dollars; Lana made seven dollars in a week. She scraped together the money through meager savings, mostly accrued by forgoing meals, sold some of her possessions, and borrowed the rest. The midwife packed her cervix with something—perhaps it was slippery elm, Lana thought later—assured her the pregnancy would pass through her, and sent her on her way, telling her to never come back. But her uterus began to expel its contents during a family dinner, and the abortion was incomplete; she knew something was wrong.

Frightened, she excused herself, feigning a headache, and took a streetcar, then a bus, back to the midwife's house. Initially, the midwife chided Lana for returning, but when she saw the young girl's fear and pain, she let her in quickly and extracted the remaining tissue. After it was over, the midwife put her arms around Lana and gently said, "Did you think it was so easy to be a woman?" She went home, and she did not tell her husband what she had done. Years later, she began corresponding with Pat and Rowena in the Bay Area, operating from the home she shared with her second husband in Southern California.

Lana and Pat would often travel together beyond California teaching four-hour classes on how to self-manage abortions and handing out mimeographed copies of the list in churches and community centers—two tiny, fearless white ladies ready to talk matter-of-factly and in great detail about a medical procedure. Rowena held classes weekly at her home in Palo Alto. The women did not fear arrest; indeed, they welcomed the possibility because it presented an opportunity to challenge local ordinances and state restrictions, the latter being the priority. In 1967, Pat read in a local newspaper that the San Mateo County District Attorney was threatening to arrest the women if they ever taught a class there; this, they thought, was the opportunity they had been waiting for. Pat and Rowena scheduled a class for February 20, 1967, and assembled "abortion kits" with Lysol, Phisohex, an orange stick, an emery board, nail clippers, a hairnet, scissors, a thermometer, and instructions on the "digital method," which involved using sterilized fingers to widen the opening to the uterus, encouraging contractions. They wanted to be sure there was no question of their intent with this class.

Sure enough, Pat Maginnis and Rowena Gurner were arrested in San Mateo for unlawfully advertising abortion through classes and leaflet distribution, which, according to local reporting, meant that they could have faced up to seven years in state prison. Rowena recalled the pair being so overjoyed at the arrest that they nearly burst into song on the way to the station house to be booked. To the *Berkeley Barb*, a weekly underground newspaper that covered such issues as antiwar efforts and the civil rights movement, Gurner said,

"We just want to get this law on trial. . . . We obviously and willingly broke the law. And we did it so that no DA could weasel out because of 'insufficient evidence.'" The women did not go to jail, and six years later, California's Court of Appeals overturned their convictions and ruled that the law prohibiting abortion advertising was too broad, as it "does not distinguish between abortions which are permitted and those which are not," which rendered it unconstitutional.

Later that year, in the fall, Pat and Lana went to Cleveland, Ohio, to talk to people about abortion options. There, they were once again under threat from law enforcement. In a newspaper clipping from the *Cleveland Press*, Lana responded with her classic defiance to a local prosecutor's threat to indict her. "Let them indict away, I'll be here until Friday morning," she said. In a local radio interview about the classes, she continued: "Nobody should pass a law telling women what to do with their bodies. I find it inconceivable and I'll sit in their old jail if need be." Over and over, they did this: Pat would teach, Lana would search for local media opportunities to promote their work and be the unapologetic mouthpiece for abortion rights, and Rowena would strategize and handle logistics and organization, ensuring the books were balanced and that people who wrote seeking help got responses. The list was sent out in exchange for a five-dollar donation.

The classes were carefully disassociated from SHA because such direct action could threaten the group's image and tax status. Instead, they created ARAL to do what Rowena called "all the dirty work." The women were intentional about the language they used, explaining the difference between a pregnant woman and a mother, between a fetus, an embryo, a zygote, and a baby. They intentionally did not presume prior knowledge, discussing female anatomy, menstruation tracking, and an overview of different abortion procedures. It was important not to be condescending—as doctors often were. From there, they discussed practical tips for navigating abortion care outside the United States in countries that were on the list. For abortion care in Japan, they recommended booking the trip through a travel agency (though travelers were advised to not disclose the reason for their travel to the consulate). The instructions for care in Mexico were more detailed. Women were advised to make the initial contact with an abortion provider; a male voice may come across as threatening. If the woman calling did not speak Spanish, which was often the case, they were told to write down the phrase *no hablo español,* and they were advised to plan out the appointment in advance, rather than simply showing up in a foreign country. "The doctors will not try to delay you," assured an outline for one of the classes. Still, if a woman wanted to vet the doctor she had contacted, Pat encouraged her to ask a lot of questions "to see if he knows his business," like whether or not the abortion will be painful or what instruments will be used, since women gained this sort of knowledge in the class. "If you have any doubts about the ability of the doctor, simply walk out." Also, doctors operating in a room that has a dirt floor should be abandoned.

The outline also advised women to avoid using Tijuana doctors for the time being: "situation there critical. Prices high, quacks taking over, doctors moving out" because "Tijuana mayor and Baja governor decide to 'clean up.'" Women seeking abortions in Mexico were also told to have makeup on when exiting the country—"look healthy"—and carry sanitary pads for bleeding after the procedure. After the patient returned home, they were asked to send the Army of Three a letter detailing their experience, including the name and address of the doctor and the price of their abortion, so that the list could be kept up to date. The classes also covered how to handle police questioning, contraceptive methods, abortion law, and, at the very end, self-managed abortion methods.

Letters written among the three women express their comfortable, determined camaraderie. The women are hell-bent on their mission, but it's also clear they have a lot of affection for one another. Lana often sent missives to Pat and Rowena in San Francisco, detailing her media appearances and education events in Southern California, sometimes offering glimpses into her harried life: "Pat, did you get home with my white slip, or did I leave it in some strange place where I must have undressed . . . you know how it is with us abortion ladies." In the same letter, she describes a recipe she has come across for something called "the Humphries Eleven," an approach to abortion that involves black cohosh and wind flower, hot baths and exercise. "This sounds like witch doctor stuff to me, but will pass it along for general information just in case," she writes. "God, what women have to go through because of the stupidity of men!"

The Society for Humane Abortion's strategy was simple: center women in the abortion debate instead of physicians and lawmakers, and until the system could be overthrown, put care directly into women's hands. "The termination of pregnancy is a decision which the person or family involved should be free to make as their own religious beliefs, values, emotions, and circumstances may dictate," the founders stated in the organization's first newsletter. The society recognized the rise of "professionalized" medicine as a paternalistic threat to women's agency and often poked fun at the men who were somehow more equipped to understand women's bodies than women themselves.

Pat and Lana also felt that ridiculous restrictions ought to be met with absurdity of their own kind. In one of their more broadly distributed writings, *The Abortion Handbook for Responsible Women*, they advised those who were seeking to get approval for abortion care on the grounds of "preservation of mental health" like so: "Tell the psychiatrist you want your pregnancy terminated, aborted, whatever euphemism you choose. He will proceed to reiterate the statements of your OB-GYN, i.e., 'You'll just love it when it's born.' Women call this 'the big lie.' He knows better, you know better, but don't argue the point right now. If you feel sufficiently nauseated, be sick on his nice rug. Tell him you often get sick like this; you did the other day, when you flushed the new kittens down the toilet. This is a good opener, and will shake him up regarding your maternal qualifications." In a similar tone, a SHA cartoon depicted a woman asking her psychiatrist how much a diagnosis of psychosis costs for a legal abortion—a commentary on the absurd lengths women had to go to convince a psychiatrist they were "hysterical" enough to get a legal abortion. Pat found her power in humor and relatability and directness. That she was plainspoken, often graphic, was refreshing in an era when women were not expected to know much of their bodies, let alone speak frankly about how they work.

While it is possible to quantify the work that ARAL did as an underground abortion referral service—at least twelve thousand women were referred out, and their system essentially imposed regulations on a previously unregulated network by creating standards for their list—it's harder to place a concrete value on the educational work done by the trio. More underground abortion services formed behind them as the back-alley abortion crisis continued to swell, and those who attended classes walked away with greater knowledge of their bodies and of the resources available should they or others need help.

In 1969, ARAL's principles guided the founding of a new organization called NARAL, the National Association for the Repeal of Abortion Laws, which has gone on to become NARAL Pro-Choice America, a powerhouse national nonprofit with 2.5 million members that organizes around abortion access and lobbies for progressive abortion legislation.

On August 30, 2021, Pat, the last surviving member of the Army of Three, died in Oakland, California, at the age of ninety-three.

CHAPTER 4

In Her Own Hands

HEATHER BOOTH WAS having a very normal, university student sort of day in 1964. She had attended class at the University of Chicago, she had plans to study later, and as she walked through campus on her way to find some lunch, she pulled her jacket tighter around her to discourage the sharpening chill of late autumn. She spotted a friend a few yards away, and she waved, grinning. But her smile faltered when she caught sight of his face. He walked over. "Hey," she greeted him, frowning a bit. "You look like hell. What's going on?"

He stared at her blankly for a moment and then winced. "My sister is pregnant," he said, his voice low.

Heather felt her face freeze. "What can I do?" she asked.

A breath escaped from him, and he shifted his weight from his left foot to his right. "She needs an abortion. I don't know what to do or how to help her, but I know she can't stay pregnant."

A familiar feeling of resolve rose in Heather. She knew his sister, and she admired her deeply. "We're going to figure this out," she told him. "Whatever it takes."

He smiled wearily; the two hugged and parted ways. Conviction pricked at her spine.

Fresh off a summer spent in Mississippi volunteering with the Student Nonviolent Coordinating Committee to register Black voters and set up Freedom Schools, Heather was in possession of that moral clarity that can take root in college when suddenly the injustices of the world are stark and undeniable. It wasn't so much that she hadn't been aware of the need for activism before, but the inequities of the world seemed more vast and more urgent. The Freedom Summer wasn't her first experience with activism—far from it. Heather had also joined the Quakers' efforts in New York to abolish the death penalty, and she had participated in sit-ins organized by the Congress of Racial Equality to protest segregated lunch counters in the South. "I was brought up in a family that believed you should treat others with dignity and respect, and I had been a Girl Scout—you leave the camp site better than you found it," she told me.

Her time in Mississippi helping register Black voters who had been historically excluded from the state's democratic processes had cemented her dedication to a life spent in pursuit of justice. She spent that summer in the Delta town of Shaw, Mississippi, with the Hawkinses, a poor Black family who had endured white supremacist terrorism and ultimately the murder of several of their family members for the high crime of standing up for voting rights, school integration, and fairer wages for sharecroppers. It was the first time in her young life that she was exposed to grief and courage in equal measure. The family risked their own lives to fight for justice, and still, they worked to protect her and the three other volunteers they had taken in. She was awed by them, and the months she spent in Shaw crystallized the ideals that would guide her for the rest of her life.

Back in Chicago, Heather was running out of options trying to find help for her friend's sister. She had been haunting her dormitory telephone, making multiple calls to locate a reputable abortion provider. She spoke in a low voice and chose hours when other students would not be around. Through her civil rights and feminist organizing, she had sent out some careful inquiries, but she kept coming up empty. Finally, she got a call back from someone connected with her civil rights network, telling her to try a clinic on the South Side of Chicago. It was run by Dr. Theodore Roosevelt Mason (T. R. M.) Howard, a Black doctor who had been driven from his home and his job as a surgeon in Mound Bayou, Mississippi, by a series of escalating death threats from the Ku Klux Klan. He had gotten the white supremacists' attention with his vocal support for the Till family after Emmett Till was abducted, tortured, and lynched in Money, Mississippi, a small, unincorporated community in the Delta. Till had been murdered because a white woman told her husband and brother-in-law that Till had whistled at her. He was fourteen years old. A monstrous act of violence against a child.

Dr. Howard agreed to care for Heather's friend's sister. The arrangements were made, the abortion was performed, and Heather and Dr. Howard thought they would go their separate ways. But soon after that, she got another phone call, this time from a Black woman back in Mississippi with whom she'd grown close over the summer. She was frightened; none of the places in Mississippi she had found seemed safe or clean, and she needed abortion care. Heather reached out to Dr. Howard once more. Her phone continued to ring, announcing the troubles of more and more women, and each time it did, she called Dr. Howard. And so her education began. "I knew it wasn't legal, but that's another thing I learned from the civil rights movement—sometimes you have to act against illegitimate authority," she says.

The two never met in person. They spoke by phone, and Dr. Howard patiently answered Heather's questions as they multiplied with her knowledge. *Is it painful? Is there anything you should do in preparation? Can you eat beforehand? Is there medication to dull the sensation?* She began to meet women in person to hear their stories if they needed someone to listen, to explain the procedure to them, and to get the necessary health information from them to make an appointment. After the women had their abortions, Heather would call them to see how they were feeling and to ask how it had gone. If there was a problem the patient raised—the instruments were too cold, the procedure wasn't clearly explained—Heather would pass along the feedback to Dr. Howard and take the opportunity to ask him any questions the conversation had inspired in her as she continued to learn. The obstacle that came up time and time again was cost. Dr. Howard performed abortions for $500, but he also allowed her to book two patients for the price of one abortion, and if a woman came to him with limited resources, he would accept whatever money she was able to give him and that was the end of it.

The need continued to escalate over the next three years, and Heather was realizing she could not handle her one-woman abortion referral service on her own. By then, she was a married, pregnant graduate student with a heavy load of organizing work that she couldn't abandon. It was time to ask for help. She had been getting some assistance from two women's liberation groups she had helped organize, the Westside Group and the Women's Radical Action Project, but people came and went, and she found she needed a stalwart cadre committed enough to the specific cause of abortion access that they wouldn't be frightened by the illegality of the work. To assemble her network, Heather turned to the consciousness-raising groups of the time and feminist workshops, tapping into a wild current of electrified women who were reading books like Betty Friedan's *The Feminine Mystique* and debating how best to achieve a future where the sexes were equal. Heather took care to notice the women who seemed to clearly understand the relationship between abortion rights and female anatomy so that she could quietly recruit them to the cause, funneling them into another participant's living room one autumn day for a meeting. The meetings continued for months as Heather explained what she had been doing, and the women huddled together over coffee and tea and made a plan for expanding the service to include fundraising, counseling, and booking.

From the start, Heather was clear—helping women get abortion care was illegal. Some weren't up for the risk, but others leapt at the chance to take meaningful action. The group came up with a formal name for themselves, the Abortion Counseling Service of Women's Liberation, but they knew they needed something a little more subtle for the women they wanted to help. They settled on Jane. The most powerful entities carry the most innocuous names. Members also referred to it colloquially as "the service," but it is important to note that they all are Jane—not *the Janes*, not *the Jane Collective*. They were women from different circumstances working as one, as Jane, to help provide care to those who needed it. Their individuality, in that context, did not matter, and to hone in on it directly contradicts Jane's mission.

Soon, the service was operating at a consistent rhythm. Chicago women learned of Jane through word of mouth, which spread through the city's women's liberation groups into other communities. Pamphlets were made and passed around announcing the group's mission statement, identifying them as women "whose ultimate goal is the liberation of women in society"; a short paragraph about a loan fund organized by Jane; general information about abortion as a medical procedure, which detailed what to expect before, during, and after the procedure; and a meditation on abortion as a social issue that explains that "society does all it can to make a woman feel guilty and degraded if she has [an abortion]." At the end, there was contact information. Concise ads ran in student newspapers and alternative publications. "Pregnant? Don't want to be? Call Jane," they said, listing a phone number below. Women who needed care would call the number until someone answered (answering machines were not common when the service began, though they did take the risk and employ an answering service as demand grew beyond what a single phone line could handle) and ask for Jane. When the service was able to buy an answering machine, potential clients would leave a message and then receive a phone call from "Callback Jane." The most important part of that initial call that connected patient and Jane was to determine whether the woman on the other end of the line was certain about her choice to get abortion care. The founders of Jane felt it was crucial that they not push abortion on anyone, and when the potential patient showed signs of ambivalence, she was asked to take some more time to think it over. If a woman with financial resources was calling, she was sent to reputable doctors in Mexico or Puerto Rico, where abortion was technically illegal but more loosely policed. Those women were the exception. In 1970, abortion was legalized in New York, and women of means had another option—to make a nearly 800-mile trip and escape legal risk.

"We were dealing with a largely poor, very young, very circumscribed in the sense of what options women had—before there was a battered women's movement, we saw battered women. Before there was a discussion of child sexual abuse, we had kids being brought by their father for abortions," Laura Kaplan, a Jane who wrote the definitive history of the service, says. "In 1970, women with money, women with the psychological, emotional, political ability to get on a plane and fly to New York, did that. So who was left in Chicago for us? Women who'd never left their neighborhood, who in no way could see themselves getting on a plane and flying to New York and getting an abortion."

The next year, Laura, too, had become Jane. A friend of hers found herself unexpectedly pregnant when her intrauterine device failed, and she sought help from the service. "So she went and got her abortion, and afterwards she came to my apartment and was so excited by this experience that she was almost literally bouncing off the wall," she says. It wasn't simply that Laura's friend was no longer pregnant; it was the world of possibility that Jane had opened up for her. She felt she had experienced autonomy in a situation that had previously rendered her helpless. Laura was awestruck. She had to know more; she had been wanting to get involved in the women's liberation movement anyhow. Her friend eagerly ushered her to meet the woman who had counseled her through her abortion, and Laura was told that the next training for abortion counselors would be the following week. "This was the door that opened, and I walked through it," she says.

As a precaution, Jane operated out of several spaces. Administrative meetings were held at the homes of the founders. There was the Front, where a woman seeking abortion care went for her appointment, often with a husband or boyfriend or friend, perhaps with her children, who were left to wait there with snacks and beverages while she was taken to the Place, where the abortion itself happened. The locations varied over the years as a protective measure: at one point, a dorm room at the University of Chicago served as the Front.

Eventually, Jane rented an apartment in Hyde Park to be the service's Place. One Jane would shuttle patients back and forth between the Front and the Place.

––––––

I N 1971, MARY DRISCOLL was working as a nurse in a health clinic run by Rising Up Angry, a radical antiracist social justice group that worked with a rainbow coalition of organizations, like the Black Panthers and the Young Patriots, to organize white working-class youth to advocate for left-wing causes. The clinic referred women who needed abortion care to Jane, eventually striking a deal with Jane to handle the counseling services themselves to keep costs low for their clients, who were often unable to pay much, if anything, for the procedure. "Women would come to us terrified because they didn't know where to go, and they had heard horrible stories of back-alley-type abortions where women were injured, and some of them have had, in the past, that type of abortion," Mary remembers. She was twenty-six years old, married, and her daughter was approaching her first birthday. Her marriage was beginning to disintegrate under the pressure of never-enough-money and never-enough-time, and she could feel the end coming when she realized she was pregnant. Together, they decided not to have another child.

She told a colleague who was the counselor that worked with Jane, and they set up the appointment. Mary arrived at the Front, and it wasn't long before she was ushered, blindfolded, to protect the location of the makeshift clinic and the identities of those providing her with care illegally, to the Place. Time has naturally muddied her memory, but two things remain clear: the genuine care she was shown that day, and the agency she was given during the procedure. Jane was patient, waiting for the numbing agent to fully take effect before beginning her work. "Maybe ten years later, I had to have another abortion. It was legal by this time, and I went to an abortion provider," she says. "And I'm not saying that they did a bad job because they didn't, but it was not the kind of comforting care that I received, having an abortion through Jane."

The service was a group of largely white women who were drawn to abortion work through their experiences in political organizing, particularly in the civil rights and antiwar movements, and their clients mostly came from immigrant communities, low-income communities, and communities of color. "In the women's movement, there was a perspective from privileged white women whose political consciousness about the nature of power and the nature of oppression was limited by their own experience," Laura reflects. Jane was not of that sect, she adds. The focus was on the work.

There were a few women of color who were Janes throughout the service's tenure, but Laura says that when people talk about the disproportionate whiteness of Jane compared to the community that needed the service the most, "it's a fair criticism." Additionally, the risk of the mission weighed more heavily on nonwhite Janes. Once, a Black woman decided she would become a Jane after her abortion, but when she told her Black friends, they encouraged her to think more critically about what that would mean for her own safety, as well as that of her family. "If you wind up getting arrested with these white women, they'll get out, and you'll lose your kids," they told her. "That's real," Laura says. Many Janes who were not white were unwilling to take that risk. In a country where people of color are consistently prosecuted much more harshly than their white counterparts, their hesitancy seems quite reasonable.

As the years passed, the women—those who were in charge, as well as those seeking care—grew frustrated with the lack of control over the care provided in the abortion itself, which was handled by independent doctors who had agreed to work with the organization. Though Jane took great care to keep records of its clients' experiences as a means of quality control against shoddy medical practices, the abortion providers insisted on a certain level of secrecy even with Jane in an attempt to protect themselves from prosecution. When it came to inflated prices, Jane's blindfolded and unnerved clients, and the condition of the motel room where the abortion would be provided, there wasn't much Jane could do directly beyond advocating for the women the organization served as best it could. It wasn't enough. Jane pledged to do whatever it took to change that—even if it meant providing abortions themselves.

The first time Jody Howard, a founding Jane, went to meet Mike, a doctor, it was all very cloak and dagger. Jody was determined to make a deal that gave Jane more say in the abortion itself. Ruth Surgal went with her, but Mike refused to meet with both of them at once, citing the old adage that three makes a conspiracy. "So first I went to talk to him, and I . . . whatever we talked about, and then Jody went to talk to him and got him to come down in money, and she was much tougher than I was," Ruth said in 1999. "But they got to be really, really close friends, and they were friends for years afterwards."

Their friendship became an elemental force in the trajectory of Jane. One day, a patient was panicking as a nurse tried to put a blindfold on her to protect Mike's identity. Exasperated, they called Jody to come and keep the woman calm, holding a pillow in front of her face to obstruct the view of the abortionist. That day provided the opening Jody had been waiting for: she asked to observe future abortions in order to learn the practice, and eventually, he relented. After a while, Ruth began to join in on procedures as well, and slowly, more and more women began to learn how to perform an abortion. Mike left, and the service was truly in Jane's hands. Not only was Jane operating a service to connect women with abortion care; the members of Jane were also performing abortions themselves.

Jane was eventually, inevitably, raided by the police. On May 3, 1972, a group of men, clad in trench coats, surprised a worker and a patient who were entering the elevator at the Place on South Shore Drive. The worker later recalled to Laura that the men "looked so much like cops that they could have been from *Dragnet*." They demanded to know which apartment the women had exited. "Who are you?" the worker asked, adopting a steely tone. The men identified themselves as detectives from the Chicago Police Department's homicide squad, flashing their badges. The patient, who was nauseous from her procedure and frightened by the men, whimpered and began to sob when the men rumbled that they knew what the women had been doing. Sensing weakness, a few officers ushered the patient down the hall to interrogate her. The worker called to her, saying that she didn't have to tell the men anything, but fear won out, and the apartment number spilled from her lips.

"Don't open the door, don't open the door!" the worker yelled, but she was too far down the hall for anyone inside the Place to hear her, and the two were hustled into the elevator, which took them to the lobby, where the officers told them to wait on a bench. When the women inside heard the apartment doorbell ring, they didn't suspect anything was amiss—one thought it was the janitor, come early to clean. When another worker opened the door, only cracking it as a precaution, there were the towering officers. She pushed against the door to shut it, but they pushed harder. When they entered, all hell broke loose. One woman stepped in front of them, ordering them to stop because they had no search warrant. Another raced through the clinic, letting everyone know that they were under no obligation to talk to anyone and assuring them that they had not broken any laws. Meanwhile, the men shouted, demanding to see the doctor. "Where is he?" When they couldn't find him, they settled for arresting six women.

Two groups of three Janes were divvied up among police vans; in the first, one of the women had been the driver that day, chauffeuring women from the Front to the Place, which meant she had crumpled bills collected from clients in her pockets. To decentralize the cash, the three split it among them and searched their own pockets to make sure no evidence remained. Another had a sheet of paper listing the patient roster for the day, alongside the counselors that had been assigned to each. The women ripped it up into tiny shards, paper confetti littering the floor of the vehicle. The other group of three, who were daisy chained together, had notecards with the names and contact information for people who had called Jane. As they hurtled through the cloudy Chicago afternoon to the police station, they tore off the corners of the cards that carried names, addresses, and phone numbers. They stuck the offending bits of thick paper in their mouths, letting their saliva soften them until they could frantically chew and swallow, protecting their clients' privacy with their guts.

Meanwhile, Ruth Surgal couldn't shake the rattle of anxiety. She called the Place, and the phone rang and rang—no answer. But when she got to the Front, all seemed to be in order, and a worker named Jeanne Galatzer assured her that everything was fine; in fact, a group of women had been picked up and taken to the Place not so long ago. The update soothed her jangling nerves. She put away the snacks she had brought over and left, passing two men in the hallway on her way out. Some sense pulled at her, sparking her attention in their direction, but she waved it off and continued on her way. Soon after, there was a knock at the door of the Front; assuming it was Ruth, Jeanne opened the door without caution. When she saw the suits, she knew what was happening. They may have identified themselves, she could not recall in a later interview, but she did turn on her heel to address everyone in the room: "These are the police. You don't have to tell them anything." For that, she was arrested first. "I wasn't handcuffed, I don't think. I was treated very nicely, except I was in a state of perfect terror," she said in an oral history. At least forty men, women, and children were taken from the Front and Place to the police station. All were released eventually except for Jeanne and the six other Janes who were at the Place.

The seven were taken that night from the police station to the women's lockup at Eleventh and State, where conditions were much worse, though they were finally rid of the group of men who had been interrogating them for hours. Judith Arcana, a new mother, was separated from the rest and put in a holding cell alongside two adolescent white girls, whose drunk escapades that night had included stealing a television. One was pregnant and spoke in a thick Southern accent. Judith had given birth recently enough to still be breastfeeding and had to expel her breast milk into a sink while she was held; she was released on bail so she could be with her baby, but leaving her friends in that place was agony. She agreed to go only after they insisted, telling her that she must figure out how to get the rest of them out as soon as possible.

Meanwhile, Ruth and the other members of the network set to spreading the news of the raid and collecting money for their collaborators who had been arrested. The Callback Janes were instructed to tell anyone who could to make plans to go to New York for care instead. The next day, Ruth brought all the money she had collected with her to the courthouse, where, after some debate, the six remaining Janes were allowed out on bail. It cost them $2,500 each.

The service continued without the Abortion Seven, as they were known in the media, though it seemed like tempting fate to pretend nothing had happened. The remaining members, worried they were being watched, established multiple and varied locations of the Fronts and took extra care with their routes from home to the service's locations. For months, the Abortion Seven met with lawyers and discussed legal strategy to fight the charges, which threatened to lock them away for at least a decade and up to 110 years. But before a judge could rule on the case, a higher court made a decision that annulled their legal woes. *Roe v. Wade* rendered abortion legal in the United States in 1973.

All in all, Jane provided an estimated eleven thousand abortions. After abortion was legalized, it seemed their mission was complete, and the service shuttered. But of course, the legalization of abortion was still a far cry from creating equal access to care. The work was not over.

CHAPTER 5

She Will Find a Way

LUCY DIDN'T THINK much of it when her period didn't come. She was starting college, which would be disorienting enough, except she hadn't wanted to go. Her older brother, her best friend, had died of a heroin overdose that August. He had been only twenty-one, and Lucy was mired in a stubborn haze of grief and fury. It must be the stress of her studies and her loss, she thought, when the weeks continued to slip by. It didn't occur to her that she might be pregnant, but it was becoming clear that it was time to see a doctor and make sure all was well. Still, she wasn't concerned. Why would she be? The worst thing she could imagine happening already had.

Her father was a doctor, a man of status in their small town in Ohio, and she was closer to him than she had ever been to her mother. She called him from her dorm at Kent State and asked if he could get her an appointment with a local gynecologist so she could inquire about some "female issues" she was having. She would come home this weekend, just like every weekend before that one because she could not bear to remain on campus. Her father's standing afforded her basically any medical appointment she needed, when she needed it, and this was no different.

In the unnatural light of the gynecologist's office, the physician asked how Lucy was feeling. "I don't know," she responded numbly. "It's just my periods—I don't know, they aren't really regular." During their conversation, she remembers a faint prickle of awareness that the gynecologist wasn't being straight with her—he seemed uncomfortable, like he was talking around something. "You'll want to . . . pursue it further if you don't have a period pretty soon," he stammered. "What does that *mean*?" she asked, exasperated. "Well . . . you're two months pregnant." She stared at him, stunned. He got up and left the room, and a nurse settled into the stool he had been perched on seconds before. Another nurse followed the first, opting to stand. "Oh my God, I don't know what I'm gonna do," Lucy told the nurse. "My parents will kill me." Her voice cracked, and her eyes stung with tears. Once she began to cry, she found she could not stop. One of the nurses handed her a card with a phone number. "If you decide not to go through with this, call this number," she said. "They will help you. They know who we are, and it's safe." Lucy was rigid with shock. It wasn't until she returned to campus that it dawned on her that the nurse had been suggesting a way to end her pregnancy. No one ever said the word *abortion*. It was 1971.

She called her ex-boyfriend. The breakup was recent—her departure for college and his for the Marines had served as a natural way to end the relationship. She couldn't see a future with him because his family didn't seem to like her, but they had been high school sweethearts, and they still cared for each other. When he answered the phone, warm recognition washed over her, and she said it out loud for the first time. "I might, you know, have an abortion," she said into the receiver. She held her breath. It didn't take long for him to answer: "You should do what you want to do." She exhaled. On the one hand, she was on her own, and she felt a piece of herself that had hoped he might care shrivel. On the other, at least she wouldn't have to defend her decision, whatever it would be. A few days later, a check came for her in the mail. It was the last contact she ever had with him.

For the next week, she considered her choice. She made a list of pros and cons, and looking at it all in black and white, she could not see a way to have a baby and raise a child. There was not enough money, not enough resources, not enough space in her suffocating grief. "At that age, I really didn't think, 'Oh my gosh, I'm killing a living thing inside of me,'" she recalls. For a week, she marinated in her anxiety, until she began to feel like she was ensnared in an itchy wool sweater that was two sizes too small. She waited until the phone in her dormitory was free and no one else was around. Then she pulled the card from her pocket and dialed.

From that point, her memory starts to blur; she says she was on "autopilot." The voice at the other end of the line told her they would take care of everything for a flat fee—transportation to and from the airport, plane tickets, a car to the clinic in Dobbs Ferry, New York, where abortion had just been legalized, and they would pay her way home. A driver came and picked her up at her doorstep to take her to the airport, and she noticed another girl sitting in the car. She silently climbed inside. Her fellow passenger avoided eye contact, and Lucy took the hint. The afternoon sun paled as they drove into the early evening. The driver pulled into departures and handed tickets to both girls. When they arrived in New York, a man was waiting at LaGuardia Airport to shepherd them and several other girls, all of whom, including Lucy, were white, into three vans. Lucy's stomach snarled and lurched; her mouth tasted like cardboard. She had been told that she could not eat or drink before the procedure. As she prepared for her travels, that had seemed easy enough because her nerves had overridden any biological need for sustenance. Now, she felt ill from the unsteady rhythm of the plane. She tried not to think about what a helpless position she found herself in now, miles from home, surrounded by strangers, at the mercy of men she did not know. Anything could happen. She breathed deeply through her nose and gripped the army-green knapsack she had brought, hoping to get some stability without revealing the edge of her panic.

At the clinic, they were met by a nurse with a perfunctory manner who informed the cohort that there was some paperwork for them to fill out while they waited. They would go back and change out of their clothes when their names were called, they would have their abortions, and then they would get dressed, go home, and live out their lives. Lucy tried to ignore the tremble in her handwriting as she reviewed her forms. She knew she was doing the right thing for herself and her family, but all the headlines she had seen about women who had died at the hands of unqualified abortionists kept flitting to the front of her mind. The place certainly seemed legitimate, but how could she be certain?

They called her back initially for a sonogram; she was surprised when the technician asked if she wanted to see it. "No, I don't," she said. She was handed another form to sign—"Well, you'd sign here if this is what you want, now's the time to decide"—and Lucy took it. She began to sign, and the tech asked her once more if she was certain she didn't want to see the sonogram. "I am very sure," Lucy replied wearily. She just wanted to get it over with and go home. She was shown a maze of curtains where she could change into a hospital gown, and she slipped behind one, trying to ignore the sounds of girls changing around her. It felt intrusive somehow, even though she knew they were all there for the same reason. She carried her neatly folded tie-dyed T-shirt and denim overalls in her arms, holding the bundle tight against her chest, as she unsteadily walked into the room where she would have her abortion. From there, she only knows she was given anesthesia, and she drifted off into a protected dreamlessness.

When she woke up, she was lying on a bed in a room she didn't recognize. She blinked hard to force her surroundings into focus. She tried to swallow, but her throat was papery. She wasn't sore. There were some fifteen others on beds around her. Some were awake, some were asleep, some were talking, others were quietly crying. A nurse looked up and saw that Lucy was beginning to surface into consciousness. She walked over, and Lucy rasped, "Is it over?" The nurse patted her arm and said, "Yes, it's over. Can I get you something to drink?" Water had never tasted so good. Soon after, the girls were roused and told to get dressed, and they wobbled together back to the vans. Lucy remembers the plane ride because of the overpowering nausea. She spat bile into the bag provided for air sickness and

silently thanked whatever higher power might be attuned to her distress that the plane was small, with only two seats on each side of the
aisle, and that she had the row to herself.

Once she had made it back to her dorm room, she says, "all hell
broke loose." She noticed, for the first time, that she was wearing a
sanitary napkin, and it was soaked through. It was late, and the halls
of the dorm were deserted, so she stumbled into the bathroom to
change clothes and put on a clean pad. Her skin was clammy and her
thoughts were fragmented, but she did register that she was bleeding
so much that getting into her bed might ruin the mattress, and she
could not afford to replace it. Instead, she made a nest of towels and
old sheets on the floor, and fell asleep. When she woke, she knew
she had a fever, and she was still bleeding. She dug out a piece of
paper that someone had given her on the way out of the clinic. She
read it and was somewhat reassured that her body's reaction was
normal, but there was no number to call if she got worse. Friends
came by to check on her: she told them through the door that she
was sick and asked if they would bring her a ginger ale from the
cafeteria. But alone in her room, she began to panic. What if this
wasn't normal, what if she died? She couldn't call the student health
center because they might call her parents. She was fairly certain
they didn't know about her situation; the gynecologist had seemed
so out of sorts talking to her about the pregnancy that it was hard to
imagine him having that conversation with her father. Lucy thought
of her brother and flashed back to his funeral. There had been a boy
there, a friend of her brother's, who gave her his card and told her
to call if she ever needed anything. He had a goodness to him that
had struck her with its purity, and he smiled down at her and said
that her brother had talked about her often and with love. He was a
priest, but when he arrived at her dorm, she felt no judgment from
him, and he sat with her through the next several days, until she
began to stabilize. After that, they were lifelong friends.

Lucy didn't know it, but the clinic in Dobbs Ferry belonged to a
network of vetted facilities that was trusted by the Clergy Consultation Service on Abortion and Problem Pregnancies (CCS), a group
of faith leaders who primarily belonged to Christianity and Judaism

that connected women who needed abortion care with capable providers in the years before *Roe v. Wade*, driven by their God-given commandment to help those in need. Though CCS began in New York City, their mission spread, and it wasn't long before there were chapters scattered across the nation. Rev. William Kirby, a leader in the Missouri chapter and then a chaplain at Stephens College, a private women's school in Columbia, Missouri, described transporting students from the campus to Dobbs Ferry for abortion care. The young women would be picked up from their dormitories as soon as they opened at 5:30 A.M. They were then shuttled to the St. Louis airport, where they would catch an American Airlines flight to LaGuardia; from there, a car would take them to the clinic. The service used a specific American Airlines flight because a nurse that worked with them had trained the flight attendants so that they knew what to do if a woman began to hemorrhage on her journey home.

The service's beginnings are obscured in a tangle of memories compromised by time and ego. CCS was radical, to be sure. It was also overwhelmingly made up of white men who were middle aged and belonged to the upper-middle class. In one version of its conception, according to the recollection of Rev. Finley Schaef, he approached Rev. Howard Moody of Judson Memorial Church in New York City to begin a conversation about a clergy-led abortion referral group in the mid-1960s, troubled by the plight of a woman who came to him while he was ministering in Queens. She was frantically searching for help finding abortion care for her teenage daughter, who had been raped by the woman's husband, and when she explained the situation to Rev. Schaef, he found himself at a loss. The woman left his office, and he never saw her again; he's not sure what she did, but her plight changed him. Rev. Moody, for his part, recalls the idea coming up during a standing meeting among local clergy during which they would discuss "theology and social issues and that sort of thing, and one of the social issues was abortion." There are several competing versions of how the Clergy Consultation Service was founded, but regardless, the service became an important funnel for women who sought safe abortion care, and it helped destigmatize abortion using a religious framework.

Forty ministers and rabbis were invited to the first official meeting to hash out the details of the service, and somewhere between twenty and twenty-five actually showed up at Judson Memorial Church, which would operate as the service's home base. A sense of bafflement among the men who had gathered in response to Rev. Moody's invitation became clear. "Why was abortion such a priority?" they asked. "The reaction of this group of clergy to the abortion issue stemmed from a poor understanding and limited knowledge of the problem as well as a failure to realize that if they were to make themselves available to women experiencing this problem, they would discover needs they never knew existed," Moody and Arlene Carmen, a Judson administrator who helped run the operation, wrote in their book chronicling their work, *Abortion Counseling and Social Change*. Judson Memorial was the perfect home for the service. Though it was technically a Baptist church, the congregation comprised a diverse set of religious backgrounds across denominations. Some, like Arlene, weren't Christian at all. Arlene noted that the church had a particular knack for drawing preachers' kids, who had been repelled by their fathers' strict interpretations of the Christian faith but were drawn to Judson Memorial's justice-driven mission. Outcasts were welcome at the church.

The original consultation group was comprised of nineteen ministers and two rabbis—no Catholic priests were approached, according to Rev. Moody. They announced their presence to the world via a carefully crafted message delivered by Rev. Moody, who served as the spokesman of the service, to the *New York Times*. The announcement, published May 22, 1967, and featured on the newspaper's front page, heavily emphasized the group's moral responsibility to women who were seeking abortion care amid an unpredictable landscape, balancing a desperate need for medical care with fear of legal consequences or of winding up on the table of a con artist or predator. Moody told the *Times* that their mission was not "to encourage abortions, but to offer compassion and to increase the freedom of women with problem pregnancies." The group had legal support from the New York Civil Liberties Union. Though they had carefully talked through the risk they were taking, Moody and Carmen brushed off anyone who counseled caution, which could substantially delay their mission. They had been called by God. It was time for action. Over time, members have cited a variety of Scripture to support their work. There's Leviticus 19:16, which implores believers in Hebrew to "not stand idly by the blood of your neighbor." James 1:27 instructs that pure religion is found in the care of widows and orphans, in serving their afflictions. "Unwanted, unintended pregnancy is an affliction," Rev. Robert Hare said firmly.

The phone rang and rang, insistent and unceasing. People inquiring about abortion care would dial the number that appeared in the *Times*, which connected them to an answering machine at Judson Memorial Church. The message changed weekly. Clergy members served two at a time, minimum, rotating shifts to avoid burnout. In the beginning, the answering machine would explain how to contact the two clergy on call for an in-person appointment. Callers could choose their counselor based on that message, which provided broad information on the denomination and the borough of those who were available. It was a starting point for women who otherwise would have had to feel their way through the dark, hoping to find a reputable doctor through a shaky whisper network.

Arlene Carmen, a no-nonsense Jewish woman who often wore her hair swept up in a tight bun, was firmly at the center of the service. "I'm probably the only Jewish administrator of a Baptist church in the United States of America," she told an interviewer in 1976. She didn't officially start her position at Judson Memorial Church until November, about six months after the Clergy Consultation Service began operations, but she was offering organizational input from the beginning. She had met Howard Moody, whose military-style crew cut belied his politics, through the Village Independent Democrats in 1965, where she discovered a passion for social justice. Though she never had firsthand experience with abortion, it was her matter-of-fact voice that informed callers of the steps necessary to get a referral through the service. Her deep-set eyes observed the world around her precisely as it was. Arlene didn't miss much; she was exacting in all her work. As a direct witness to the women who came to CCS for help, she felt the stakes acutely. She communicated with the physicians the service referred patients to, and she masqueraded as a patient to check out clinics, making sure the facilities were clean and the staff was respectful. The doctors used by the service were required to have a medical license (though not necessarily as a gynecologist), and there was a strong preference for a medical setting over a motel room. If the place and the people initially passed muster, she would continue the charade, though she recalls that often it did not get that far because so many places she visited were clearly unsafe and unsanitary. Feet in the stirrups, lying back on an exam table, she would interrupt the doctor and tell him who she really was—not pregnant, actually—and explain the Clergy Consultation Service's mission, handing over a letter that described the organization in more detail. Even after a doctor had been approved by Arlene or a staff member who had taken a similar tack, referrals to that practice were made on a trial basis. Only one clergy counselor would be authorized to refer to that doctor, and they would urge the patient to report back postprocedure about her experience. If three or four weeks passed without incident, and the reports were all positive, the doctor's information would be distributed to the rest of the CCS. Still, even after a provider was approved, the responses of the patients were monitored and kept as the most important evaluation.

Alongside Rev. Moody, Arlene set the parameters of the service, and she was clear about the consequences of violating those rules: she would not hesitate to kick a rogue clergyman out of the service. "Arlene was the enforcer," Moody recalled in an interview. "And she was wonderful. She didn't mind saying, 'Those clergy are a bunch of shitheads! They don't know from nothin'.' And she would bring 'em around. I mean, they learned that if they didn't follow the rules of our thing, they were in trouble—with her." Clergy would counsel the women who came to them in person, never by the phone. "Fear cannot always be detected over the phone, but it is hard to miss in the eyes of a frightened young woman," Rev. Moody and Arlene explained in their book. "Long-distance phone calls might mitigate against an extended conversation about the guilt associated with seeking an abortion, but conversation in the relaxed atmosphere of a counselor's office provided the women an opportunity to articulate their feelings. Most of the physical or even emotional problems that could be spotted in a moment if the woman is sitting across from you are impossible to detect over the phone."

After a face-to-face discussion with the patient who was seeking care, clergy would make referrals when it was clear that the potential patient had her mind made up about what she needed, but clergy would never communicate directly with a doctor or clinic staff. Only Arlene would take care of those details, and she would do no counseling: there was a clear demarcation of duties upon the advice of the attorney who volunteered for the CCS. "So there was no way in which a conspiracy among clergy, abortionist, and the woman client could be proven," explains Arlene. The only acceptable method was a D&C (dilation and curettage), and patients must arrive at their counseling appointment with a dated note from a physician that included how many weeks into the pregnancy they were and confirmed that they had undergone both a pelvic exam and a pregnancy test. Women had to be referred to out-of-state practitioners to complicate jurisdiction in case the law got involved. Most physicians the CCS referred patients to would only perform abortions up to twelve weeks, especially in the early days of the service, before they had established connections to doctors abroad who were more comfortable with procedures past that benchmark. Still, traveling out of the country, particularly to places like England or Japan, where abortion was perfectly legal, was prohibitively expensive, costing some patients up to $1,100.

Some of these precautions implemented by the service were too burdensome for those who needed help the most. In a *New York* magazine article from August 1969, journalist Susan Brownmiller describes a scene in which a woman calls Rev. Moody to ask about abortion care. The pastor, nervous that the line could be tapped by the government, tells her that she has reached Judson Memorial Church, where they do abortion *counseling*. He had good reason to be cautious: not long after the CCS launched, the service received a tip from a police department that officers had tapped the phone line at Judson Memorial Church, though this was not the same line to the answering machine. Moody begins to invite her to come in, but she's not having it. "I don't need a sermon on the mount, Reverend. I need an abortion," she tells him, before hanging up. Patients with limited resources were especially frustrated with the travel requirements, both for the initial counseling session and for abortion care. This likely contributed to the racial demographics of the patients who were helped by the CCS—the vast majority were white women. The group was, however, aware and concerned with the disparities in abortion care. In their initial mission statement, they wrote: "The present abortion law in New York is most oppressive of the poor and minority groups. A 1965 report shows that 94 percent of abortion deaths in New York City occurred among Negroes and Puerto Ricans." Still, in one sample of 6,455 patients who were helped by the New York CCS chapter, more than 80 percent were white. Another sample from the Chicago chapter of 4,000 cases in 1970 documented a nearly 90 percent majority of the patients at that time as white. "When the New York CCS examined its statistics after the first year and realized that virtually no Black or Puerto Rican women were seeking our help, we concluded that we were doing something wrong—allowing the cost of an illegal abortion to remain prohibitively high," wrote Rev. Moody and Arlene.

Henceforth, they worked to negotiate lower rates with the practitioners involved in their referral network. "It was a very important factor in what we did here at Judson that we had no stake in the issue," says Arlene. "The change that came about was not going to profit or benefit us at all. We didn't have a vested interest." They did have power over the doctors they included in their network. The volume of patients they provided was substantial and abortion providers did not want to violate the standards of the CCS and lose the income that came with the referrals. The service's screening process for patients also alleviated a burden for doctors, who could provide better care with more information and who found CCS patients to be more relaxed because they knew more about the procedure going into it.

Not everyone was a fan of the service. In a letter sent from Elizabeth Canfield, cofounder of the Clergy Counseling Service for Problem Pregnancies in Los Angeles, to Pat Maginnis and Rowena Gurner of the Association to Repeal Abortion Laws, Canfield acknowledges that "Rowena's telephone conversation with me made it clear that you are awfully tired of all of us who are pussyfooting around. I don't blame you one bit," she writes, before assuring the women that "new vociferous converts are being created daily." Pat, for her part, didn't appear to be impressed with the clergy's efforts. In a cartoon she labeled "Hominy Dominy Counselling Service," she depicted a balding man in black, head in hands, seated on a bench. Above his head were the words, in her familiar bold script, "Women's Counselling for Problem Clergymen." For Pat, it was just another group of men influencing what should have been strictly women's business, and her past experience with religious patriarchy did not make her inclined to trust them. Plus, women didn't need counseling, she thought. They needed abortion care, without all the religious mumbo jumbo. Even so, she sent Canfield information about how to get abortion care safely in Mexico, which the Los Angeles CCS used.

In 1968, the service began to expand beyond New York, opening chapters in states across the country, from California to Massachusetts. Among the largest was the Chicago chapter, which was led by Rev. Spencer Parsons, then dean of the Rockefeller Memorial Chapel at the University of Chicago. Parsons was charismatic and known to skirt the rules when he felt it truly necessary to help someone. He developed a relationship with Jane three years prior to the opening of the CCS Chicago chapter and referred patients there often before his chapter opened. Even after Chicago's chapter began officially, he would, in extreme circumstances, refer women to Jane. "Jane was able to help more lower income women than the Clergy Service was because ours often involved travel, and I think that was the great strength of Jane, that low-income women by and large were able to get more help," Parsons said.

The openness of the operation was the point. In the *Wall Street Journal,* Rev. Farley Wheelwright, who served in the Cleveland CCS, put it this way: "There is no abortion underground. . . . We're helping to bring abortion above ground, to make it open, respectable, and eventually legal for any woman to end her pregnancy whenever she and her doctor feel it's the best course." Ensuring women were operating with their full autonomy was a priority for the service. In the late 1960s, the New York district attorney approached Howard Moody about a potential law legalizing abortion—with some restrictions. "One of the things that he said to me was, 'What we wanna do is to write into the law a prerequisite that a woman has to go to clergy for counseling before they can have an abortion.'" Moody recalls in an interview, sitting back and taking a breath. He rubs his hands against his thighs. "Clergy or social worker or combination thereof, and so forth. And I said, no way, Mr. District Attorney, are you gonna get clergy to do that. You're not gonna get this clergy to do it, I'll tell ya now. A woman doesn't need to come to clergy. If a woman wants to come to clergy because she has a moral or theological problem, she can do that—it's always open. But to force her to come to it is to somehow impute to that woman that she doesn't have the—either she's doing something immoral, she doesn't have the ability to make her own decision, or whatever, and that would be wrong."

After a few years in operation, Moody and Carmen decided it was time to expand their mission and open a clinic. They began plotting to do so in 1969 "to demonstrate the feasibility and safety of performing abortions prior to ten weeks of gestation as an outpatient, ambulatory office procedure" and "to expose the hypocrisy of a law which allowed 'therapeutic' abortions for the rich but denied them to the poor." So-called therapeutic abortions were legal; by definition, they were performed to preserve the life of the pregnant person. As of that year, the only way to get a legal abortion in New York was to qualify for a therapeutic procedure, which meant getting two letters from different psychiatrists declaring that the patient was at serious risk of suicide, in addition to cementing approval from an internal committee at the hospital where the procedure would be performed. The way the CCS clinic planned to get around this was to track down two psychiatrists who believed that any woman who was pregnant and did not wish to be a mother was in serious peril because she was considering an illegal abortion, which posed an inherent risk to her life. Above all, by running their own clinic, the CCS felt they would be able to curb costs and offer affordable abortion care to low-income women.

The group was still trying to work through the details of their practice when in April 1970, New York unexpectedly legalized abortion, upending their plans but ultimately making their goal more attainable. The clinic opened the following July, when the new law went into effect, and it served seven hundred women in its first month, most of whom were referred from CCS chapters in other states. It operated sixteen hours a day, from 7 A.M. to 11 P.M., seven days a week. On the recommendation of Dr. Hale Harvey, the clinic's head physician, the facility was decorated to look more like a cross between a daycare and someone's home than a doctor's office. "Harvey's conviction was that even a healthy patient would feel sick in the face of a cold, sterile hospital environment," wrote Arlene and Rev. Moody. "Since abortion was not a sickness, the atmosphere associated with hospitals needed to be avoided." Counselors were able to adjust the rate of the procedure depending on the needs of the patient, and the standard rate was set at $200 for a first-trimester abortion, $100 less than what comparable clinics were charging. By November 1971, they had lowered the cost even further, to $125. More CCS chapters opened more clinics, not always legally, providing care directly to women. The service gradually expanded beyond New York, taking root in thirty-eight states with an estimated three thousand counselors over five years. They grew into the largest pre-*Roe* referral service. Gillian Frank, a historian of sexuality, gender, religion, and race, estimates that the group helped at least a quarter of a million women. But when abortion was legalized nationally in 1973, the service disbanded, feeling that it was no longer needed.

Not long after, the Religious Right began to take shape, making abortion one of the pet political issues of the evangelical church and creating a dynamic that led Americans to largely equate people of faith with antiabortion values.

CHAPTER 6

Disparity

WHEN DONNA MCNEIL was a child, she had wanted badly to be a nun. She was captivated by the Catholic faith she was raised in. She asked her mother if she could dress up as a nun for Halloween, and when her mother replied that doing so would be sacrilegious, she was confused. How could being a nun, in any form, be anything other than good? "I think all my social service stuff comes from that grounding that I had in good parts of Catholicism, and I loved the theater and I loved the stories and I used to collect saint cards and all that," she says. "But I never felt one instant that abortion was wrong." At seventeen, she met a boy who was working as a lifeguard during her family's summer vacation. They had sex on the beach, and when it was over, she knew immediately that she was pregnant. Six weeks passed, and she didn't get her period.

She approached her mother, cautiously at first, but she had never been one to stay reserved for long. "I think I'm pregnant," she said, raising her eyes to meet her mother's. Expressionless, her mother took her daughter by the hand and led her up to the bedroom that she shared with Donna's father. There, Donna's mother pulled her down before a religious print that depicted a soldier, the Virgin Mary behind him, her holy hand on his shoulder. On their knees, her mother began to pray. Donna let it go on for as long as her teenage impatience could bear. "Mom, you can pray, but I don't think it's gonna make me unpregnant," she told her. Somehow, that snapped her mother into focus. A registered nurse, she ushered Donna into the bathroom and gave her a warm vaginal enema "intended to bring on a late period." They waited. Nothing happened. Donna's mother called a doctor, and off they went, to seek certainty. The doctor confirmed the pregnancy, so the next stop was their Catholic Church, where Donna's mother instructed her to go into confession. Resigned, she trudged into the booth and knelt in the darkness. The small window clicked open, and again, she did not mince words. "Father, forgive me. I had sex before I was married. And I'm pregnant." The priest did not react—one supposes that the "sin" itself is not so extraordinary—and, by rote, he assigned her five "Our Fathers" and ten "Hail Marys." She said her penance, but she felt no shame. After it was done, she climbed back into the car, and her mother said the one thing that brought forth a sliver of fear in Donna. "You're telling your father."

She lingered in the corners of the house that evening, waiting for him to finish his dinner, then to properly ingest some of his evening Scotch before settling down onto the couch beside him. She could not look at his face when she told him she needed to talk to him. "What is it?" he asked, turning his gaze on her. She could only find one way to say it. "I'm pregnant."

"How can I help you?" Donna recalled her father asking. Her voice thickened at the memory of her father's gentleness on a day she needed it desperately. "Those have to be the kindest words that anyone can say to you when you're in trouble." She told her father she wanted an abortion, and upon hearing the words in the air, she realized that she had just asked this stalwart Air Force officer who had never even been late with his credit card bill to help her do something that was unquestionably illegal. He told her that he would arrange it, and there was another weighted pause, and he made another declaration: they would, as a family, phone the boy who was involved in the pregnancy. Her mother, who had been hovering in the doorway, joined them as they went back to Donna's parents' bedroom. The telephone was waiting for them on a night table between two twin beds; Donna settled onto one, her parents perched upon the other. She dialed. The boy answered, and Donna's father instructed him to also put his parents on the line. Donna informed them that she was pregnant and would be having an abortion; the boy replied, "OK," and he spent months after that call discreetly sending money to her mother each month until he had paid for half of her procedure. Donna never saw or spoke to him again.

The following week, the trio drove from their home to Baltimore, Maryland, to see an abortion provider that her father's boss, a general, recommended: he had done the same thing for his daughter. Her parents were silent in the front of the car. Her father gripped the steering wheel tightly, and her mother's shoulders kept creeping toward her ears before she would sigh and force them back down again. They were frightened, but Donna trusted her parents to keep her safe. They pulled into the parking lot of a Howard Johnson hotel where they were told they would meet a car that would take her to get her abortion. Donna's father handed $250 to cover half the cost of the procedure to the driver, who was accompanied by another man and an older woman, whose presence was a comfort to Donna. It was another hour's drive that took her, blindfolded, out of the city and into the country, to an old farmhouse.

When she entered the room that would typically serve as the living room, she saw only a table with stirrups in the center of the room, a bright lamp tilted overhead. Her footsteps echoed in the emptiness as she approached. During the procedure, which was performed by a man, a woman Donna had not seen before held her hand and made meaningless but pleasant conversation to distract her from the discomfort. When it was over, she was offered a clean pair of pajamas to wear and sent to a bedroom to rest while another woman was cared for. They returned to the hotel, her father paid the second half of the money that was due, and the family returned home. "The next week, I was on my way to freshman orientation at Syracuse University—no hemorrhaging, no infection, no cramps, no blood, nothing—like it never happened," she says. "I am so grateful to those strangers who helped me that day, who risked their reputations and their freedom to give me choice, and I am grateful to the people that work every day for safe and legal and stigma-free abortions."

She tells me that she's lived a charmed life—she was a college beauty queen, she's had a brilliant career as an artist and an art curator, and she's been able to create a path for herself completely on her own terms. "I mentor young women, particularly in the arts, and I'm really gratified by that work," she says. "I choose my children." Still, watching the Supreme Court ruling that legalized abortion and brought relief to her and others like her dissolve within her lifetime has affected her deeply, "especially at a time where women's self-determinism is growing stronger, and their visibility, politically and culturally, is growing so strong—to have the fundamental right over the ownership of their own bodies taken away from them is a step into the dark ages, and it would never happen to a man." Donna's privilege ultimately helped her to get a pre-*Roe* abortion—as an upper-middle-class white woman, she had the resources to figure out where to go and the money to pay for the procedure. For so many people before abortion was legalized, that was not the case.

When she was growing up, Loretta Ross's family did not talk about sex. Now, she talks about sex all the time—as a founder and godmother of the reproductive justice movement, which was formed by Black women in the summer of 1994 and advocates for the human right to choose whether or not to bear children and to raise children in a healthy, safe environment; it's part of her life's work. After all, she is sharply aware of the worst-case consequences of shrouding sex in secrecy. At eleven years old, Loretta ventured out with her Girl Scout troop to an amusement park in San Antonio. She had dressed smartly for the occasion, donning white jeans and tennis shoes, her short hair neatly pressed. Excitement overwhelmed the girls when they entered the park, and they scattered. Loretta was lost in the crowd. Sure she would reunite with her troop eventually, she wandered the park for a couple hours before she gave up and left, trudging in a direction that seemed like it might lead her home. After a while, a man pulled up alongside her. She had no reason to sense menace or to distrust him; he seemed friendly, and when he asked where she was going, she thought she heard a warm concern in his voice. "I'm trying to get home and I'm lost," she admitted. "Well, jump in, I'll give you a ride home," he told her.

Instead, he took Loretta, a child, into the woods, where he beat her and raped her. She fought until she couldn't any longer. After it was over, he asked her for her address, and through tears and mucus and blood, she told him. He dropped her off at the corner of her street. Blood had soaked into the legs of her previously pristine white jeans. She walked to her house, and entered through the garage, where her sister was doing laundry. Upon spotting her, she made a sympathetic sound. "Oh, baby, you started your period!" Contradicting her sister's assumption with the horrifying truth was impossible, and she was afraid of getting in trouble for straying from the group of girls. She nodded, and told her sister that she would be back with the soiled garments, she just needed to go in the house to her bedroom and put on clean clothes. After she changed, the little girl stumbled back to the garage, handed her laundry over to her sister, and grasped for a facade of normalcy. "I was totally repressed about it, didn't feel that there was anybody I could talk to about it," Loretta says. Today, still, her memory is blacked out from that moment until she was fourteen.

At fourteen, Loretta went to Los Angeles, California, to stay with her great-aunt and great-uncle for the summer. There, her married male cousin, thirteen years her senior, began to sexually abuse her. "I defined it as sexual abuse at the time, but I can honestly say I was a willing participant because he made a quid pro quo," she said in a 2004 interview. "You give me sex and I'll take you out, kind of thing. And so I spent that summer going to nightclubs, pretending I was over twenty-one, and hanging out with this apparently romantic, much older guy." Still, he was grown. He was a man. Loretta was a minor; her cousin was not. Of course, this was her adolescent understanding of what was happening. At the end of the summer, she realized her periods had ceased.

When she returned home, Loretta says she was in denial. Months passed, and she hoped it would just go away, that she was wrong, that this wasn't happening to her. One morning, as she was getting ready for another day of the eleventh grade, pain tore through her abdomen. She was sure she was going into premature labor, and she was forced to tell her mother what was happening.

Her mother trembled with anger; her daughter was in her sixth month of pregnancy. The contractions eventually stilled. Loretta thinks her mother and father discussed abortion, which would have involved a trip to Mexico, but they knew of women who had made that journey and never returned. Plus, they were a lower-middle-class family, and the expense would be formidable. Instead, Loretta was sent to a Salvation Army home for unwed mothers, where she was to wait out the remaining months of her pregnancy, give birth, surrender the baby to be adopted by a stranger, and then return to her life. She had been accepted early on a substantial scholarship to study at Radcliffe College, the women's liberal arts school in Cambridge, Massachusetts, that functioned alongside the all-male Harvard University.

When she arrived at the home, she realized she was the only Black teenager there out of twenty girls. The days were grueling, and she felt isolated. No one spoke. There was no camaraderie, no bonding over their shared situation. The girls slept on cots at night, rose before the sun to pray, and the rest of their hours were filled with cooking and cleaning and laundry. A tutor came on weekdays, but the education they needed the most was never discussed. There was no talk of sex, how pregnancy and the reproductive systems worked, what childbirth would be like.

Instead, there was terror. For three months, she worked inside the compound that claimed to be a safehouse for women to hide their shame—the place was more akin to a prison, with high barbed-wire fences that set the tone. On an April afternoon, Loretta went into labor, and she was rushed to the hospital, where her sister, Carol, met her. Loretta didn't know what to expect from labor; she was still a child herself, and she had never felt pain this intense. It seared through her, hot, splitting; she screamed and thrashed. The doctor hollered above her screams, "Why don't y'all knock this girl out so I can get this baby out of her?" At around four that morning, he did just that. She was unconscious when he pulled her son from her, and when she came to, a nurse was pressing down on her stomach to expel the afterbirth.

Loretta had signed adoption papers while she was in labor. But a few hours deeper into morning, a nurse brought the baby in for her to breastfeed. Maybe it was an accident, maybe it wasn't—the hospital was Catholic, and Black baby boys don't fare well in the adoption system. But she was awed by him. "My son is like I spit him out," she says. "He's got my face." She could not give him up. When she returned home, a mother, everything changed. Her high school refused to reenroll her, never mind that she was an honors student. After a prolonged fight, they allowed her to remain as a student, but she was barred from extracurricular activities that would have put her in a position to represent the school at any sort of event. "I was in a predominantly white high school, and I was in the honors class," she says. "After spending years of holding me up as an example to all the Black kids, now I'm the fallen angel for the Black kids." Radcliffe, too, withdrew Loretta's scholarship, rendering her unable to attend. After she graduated high school, she attended Howard University instead.

Her story, of course, doesn't end there. Trauma isn't static, and it is not a chapter that can be closed with a choice. Loretta loves her son fiercely, but she struggled with the enduring pain of her youth, especially as he grew older and began to resemble the man who had abused and raped her. "I've often said how complicated it is to love your child and hate his circumstances," she reflects. "My son, particularly as he got older and we were able to talk about it, certainly felt like he never got unalloyed, uncompromised love from me."

CHAPTER 7

Roe

ACROSS THE COUNTRY, one year after Loretta became a mother, a young woman in Texas with little income and no knowledge of how to get abortion care became pregnant. Norma McCorvey was small, with barely there eyebrows that were tattooed into expressive, blue-green arches (she shaved her natural brows off), eyes that were perpetually rimmed with liner, and a cloud of curly hair that changed colors when the mood for a new look struck her, which was often. But her signature attribute was her salty, say-anything humor. "I learnt straight on that if you're nice and quiet and polite, nobody pays any attention to you, and I like attention," she said in a nasal Texas twang in one of her last interviews with Nick Sweeney for his documentary, *AKA Jane Roe*. She chuckled.

She had a ninth-grade education, and her mother struggled with alcoholism, a trait that Norma also became prone to, along with a general tendency toward substance abuse. Primarily, even as a girl, Norma was attracted to women, a sin for which, in addition to a growing fondness for beer and cigarettes, she suffered greatly. "I beat the fuck out of her," her mother said in an interview with journalist

Joshua Prager, author of *The Family Roe*. She was married at sixteen years old to a man five years her senior named Elwood "Woody" Mc-Corvey, and she gave birth to their daughter, Melissa, the following year. By that time, the couple had split.

Both of her first pregnancies had been unintended. "Women make mistakes," she said. "And they make mistakes with men. And things happen. It's just Mother Nature at work, you know?" Melissa eventually went to live in Louisiana with Norma's mother, and in 1967, at nineteen years old, Norma discovered her second pregnancy a month after a fling with a Baylor nurse named Pete had ended. This time, when she went for an obstetrical appointment, she asked a nurse about abortion, and the nurse replied that the procedure was illegal in Texas. When Norma brought it up with her doctor, Richard Lane, he steered her toward adoption and recommended a lawyer he had worked with before named Henry McCluskey. The doctor and the lawyer worked together and placed Norma's second daughter with a married couple in Dallas—the husband was an anesthesiologist and one of Lane's colleagues.

The matriarchal line that ran through her family was bent by unintended pregnancy; both Norma's mother and grandmother bore children who were conceived out of wedlock, altering their fates irrevocably. When, in the fall of 1969, the month she turned twenty-two, Norma felt her stomach lurch with morning sickness and her breasts became heavy and sore, she knew she was pregnant again, and she did not want to be. There had been a man named Bill Wheaton who caught her eye playing pool, badly, at a little spot in Dallas called the White Carriage where she tended bar. It wasn't a forever relationship. He, too, left. She wanted an abortion, but she didn't know where to go. Her doctor, the same one who had handled her second pregnancy, told her that he still felt bound by the law and would not perform the procedure.

She approached the lawyer who had handled the adoption of her second daughter to see if he could help. A gay man living in Texas, Henry McCluskey had experienced the cultural stigma of sex, informed by religion and advanced by the law. He told her he would see what he could do, and he called his friend, Linda Coffee, a talented young attorney who was searching for a plaintiff to kick off an abortion rights' reckoning in the state. Norma wasn't chasing the opportunity to become a face of the cause—she simply wanted an abortion. But Linda, along with her cocounsel, Sarah Weddington, needed a plaintiff, and Norma checked their boxes. Norma eventually agreed to sign onto the case as a plaintiff, in part because of her magnetic attraction to Sarah, a curvaceous redhead in her midtwenties whose wit could match Norma's in kind. Over pizza, Sarah asked her where she stood on the legalization of abortion. "I know how I felt when I found out that I was pregnant," Norma reflected in the documentary exploring her life and legacy, *AKA Jane Roe*. "And I wasn't going to let another woman feel that way—not cheap, dirty, and no good." The lawyers told their client that she was likely too far along to get an abortion, but she *could* make history. Norma remained adamant that she wanted an abortion; she just didn't know how to go about getting one.

The lawyers likely could have tried to help her terminate her pregnancy. Linda Coffee has said she recalls telling it to Norma straight: "I thought she was probably too far along to have an abortion under the protection of the federal court." Sarah, for her part, certainly knew of resources south of the border. In her final year of law school, she traveled to Mexico for an abortion and then worked with an Austin referral network. She also knew of an American Airlines flight that left from Texas every Friday for California with a group of women on board who were traveling to seek abortion care. But their client, for all intents and purposes, was not their main concern; she was filling a crucial role. For their suit to generate the legal force necessary, the plaintiff had to be poor, rendering her unable to travel to California or Oregon, the two states where abortion was legal. (Alaska, Hawaii, New York, and Washington legalized abortion later that year.) The lawsuit itself was their priority, and the weight of Norma's interests were limited. In fact, her involvement in the suit practically ended after she agreed to sign on as plaintiff. "I'm not saying I misunderstood," Norma said. "But I thought we were all real clear on what I really wanted." The lawsuit was filed three months before her due date. Her pregnancy dragged on, and her belly continued to swell as her case began its journey through the courts. In March 1970, Norma signed her name to the affidavit that established her as the plaintiff in the case that became *Roe v. Wade*. On June 2, she gave birth to a daughter. Oral arguments in the Supreme Court case didn't take place for another eighteen months, on December 13, 1971, and thirty-two months passed before the federal ruling that would have allowed her to legally seek an abortion.

Sexism doesn't pause at the threshold of any hallowed hall, which, in modern America, is traditionally ruled by men. Jay Floyd, assistant attorney general of Texas, opened his arguments with this: "Mr. Chief Justice, may it please the Court, it's an old joke, but when a man argues against two beautiful ladies like this, they're going to have the last word." It has been called "the worst joke in legal history" and with good reason. Later, when asked by Justice Potter Stewart through what judicial consideration a woman might be allowed abortion care, Floyd said bluntly that it was impossible. "I think she makes her choice prior to the time she becomes pregnant; that is the time of the choice. But once the child is born, the woman no longer has a choice, and I think pregnancy may terminate that choice." During her arguments, Sarah Weddington acknowledged Norma's plight and the outcome of her pregnancy, using the pseudonym assigned to Norma by the courts. "A progressing pregnancy does not suspend itself in order to give the courts time to act," she declared. "Certainly Jane Roe brought her suit as soon as she knew she was pregnant. As soon as she had sought an abortion, and been denied, she came to Federal court."

For the most part, Norma and her story were largely missing from the discussion at the Supreme Court. The judicial process takes as long as it takes, and Norma paid the price for what she could not possibly control. On the day the Court's 7–2 ruling that abortion was legal through the first trimester was announced, Norma glanced at the newspaper and saw the headline (some accounts say she heard it on the radio—Norma wasn't one for details, and she had a penchant for the sort of storytelling that doesn't let bits of truth weigh it down). Standing in the kitchen she shared with her partner, Connie Gonzales, she turned back to her task of wallpapering. Norma told

Connie that abortion had just been legalized in the United States and that she was the Jane Roe from the court case dominating the news. Her phone rang; it was Sarah Weddington, calling to tell her that they had won. "No, Sarah," she said to the attorney. "*You* won."

The ruling grounded the right to abortion in the right to privacy, as established in the due process clause in the Fourteenth Amendment of the Constitution. The decision also rested on precedent established in *Griswold v. Connecticut*, which ruled that the Constitution protects marital privacy, therefore the state cannot interfere in a married couple's right to information and use of contraceptives. In 1972, in *Eisenstadt v. Baird*, the Supreme Court had clarified that states could not deny unmarried people access to birth control. Justice Harry Blackmun, who authored the *Roe v. Wade* opinion, previously worked as legal counsel for the Mayo Clinic and had harbored ambitions of becoming a doctor when he was young. Those personal influences are clear in the opinion, which suggested that abortion rights belonged to doctors rather than to women seeking abortions. The emphasis was on a doctor's duty to do what was best for their patient without government interference rather than on a woman's right to control her reproductive life. The Court also struck a compromise to give states a foothold to preserve their legal interest in regulating pregnancy by using the trimester framework. The justices wrote that throughout her first trimester, a woman had a right to an abortion, but in the second trimester, the state could intervene if the regulations it proposes are reasonably in line with preserving the health of the pregnant person. The state's interest in protecting fetal life in the third trimester, according to the ruling, became "compelling" when a fetus entered viability. Overall, the ruling avoids the philosophical question of when life begins, suggesting that since there was deep disagreement on the question, Texas could not impose its views on everyone else.

The medical profession as a whole didn't do much to advance abortion rights. When *Roe v. Wade* passed, the landmark ruling was ignored by the nation's leading medical organizations, and so no guidance was issued on abortion provision and incorporating abortion care into medical practices. Instead, abortion remained shoved off to the side, a procedure to be done in clinics separate from doctor's offices, which added to the impression that abortion was somewhere outside normal medical care. In addition, there were economic reasons for the clinic approach, in that it made medical sense for abortion to be an outpatient procedure, and designated clinics could provide them more cheaply. But stigma and ideology undergirded everything. Jeannie Rosoff, president of the Alan Guttmacher Institute at the time of the ruling, told authors James Risen and Judy L. Thomas that many obstetrician-gynecologists were uneasy with the idea of women recovering from abortion procedures and from childbirth resting in the same place, worrying that it was too "emotionally wrenching."

After the ruling, abortion access exploded. Estimates of how many illegal abortions were performed pre-*Roe* have varied, but experts (somewhat famously) reported that in 1955 the number was somewhere between 200,000 and 1.2 million. A 1967 estimate put the number at around 800,000 annually. After *Roe*, abortion was not only much more accessible, it was also easier to collect data on. In 1980, nearly 1.6 million abortions were performed nationally, and over the next decade, the number hovered around there, slowly decreasing as contraception became more effective and more widely available. (That is not to say that contraception is a substitute for abortion care.) The Guttmacher Institute found that over six years—three before the *Roe* ruling and three after—deaths from abortions fell 80 percent.

Norma stayed out of the spotlight while the case was ongoing. Still, when Linda Coffee called her in late January with the number of a reporter named Robert O'Brien from the Baptist Press who wished to interview her, she could not resist. Her identity was revealed to the nation on January 27, 1973, when the Associated Press picked up the piece, giving the story a wider reach. Sarah Weddington was quoted in one piece positioning Norma as a hero, saying the plaintiff had given birth "to avert the possibility that the Supreme Court would declare her case moot" because getting an illegal abortion may have done just that, no matter that Norma had always been clear that she wanted bodily autonomy more than to be a sacrifice to a cause. The media interest in her initially was mild, but Norma is the sort of complicated, compelling character that journalists love to write about. As she began to tell her story to reporters, it started to take on a life and movement of its own.

Somewhere during her search for an abortion—it's unclear whether she said this to her doctor or the lawyers or both—she asserted that her bodily state was a product of gang rape at the hands of Black men. Norma was desperate to terminate her pregnancy, and that she couldn't find a path to take control of what was happening to her body surely amplified her anxiety to an unbearable tenor. Still, Norma wielded a weapon that was familiar to her, as a white Southern woman. She used the myths of pure, vulnerable white womanhood and of lecherous, predatory Black masculinity to make her story seem more pitiable to the white men and women who might be inclined to help her. Though she did not target any specific human being with her tale, the parallel to Carolyn Bryant's claim about Emmett Till should not be ignored. As her story gained more attention from reporters, though her story of rape never appeared before the Supreme Court, she told it a few different ways to the strangers who approached her, eagerly listening.

Norma admitted her fabrication in an interview conducted by Carl T. Rowan, a renowned Black journalist who was working on a 1987 documentary called *Searching for Justice: Three American Stories* to offer "an unsentimental view of the Constitution." In the video, Norma and Rowan sit across from each other at a plain wooden table in her Dallas home, shelves burdened with glass bottles and trinkets behind her. "I went to my doctor," she explains tearfully. "He confirmed that I was pregnant, and I told him I wanted an abortion." Rowan gently interjects: "You were raped?"

She looks down guiltily, her thin lips disappear into her mouth. Her entire face seems to stretch, from her high forehead down to her chin, with the effort of considering her answer. She seems to reanimate in a half second and replies clearly, eyes wide and determined. "No, I wasn't."

"You were not?"

"No, I wasn't."

"Oh. So all those stories are not true?" he asks. She nods, affirming that he is correct.

Though Norma's yarn had no effect on the *Roe v. Wade* ruling itself—the alleged rape was not mentioned in the decision—a media maelstrom followed, and antiabortion groups spread misinformation that this revelation meant that the fourteen-year-old right to abortion was rendered meaningless. Norma had also spent the years after the *Roe* ruling easing into the spotlight, trying to find more meaning in her experience of forced birth. But she felt out of place among the polished, educated women of the pro-choice movement, and they similarly felt uneasy with her. She had done what was necessary to secure the win, they thought; many of them wished she would just accept her role and be a silent figurehead or disappear altogether. Let the more poised women take the lead; they were more palatable politically. But if there's one thing that Norma McCorvey was not, it was quiet. Nor was she malleable. In the aftermath, many of these women defended Norma, saying that she had been desperate. In 1969 Texas, what else was she supposed to do? But internally, she was shunned and pushed back even further from the microphone than she had previously been by women who could never truly understand what it was like to be born into circumstances like hers. Still, she worked devotedly at a clinic in Dallas, going toe-to-toe with antiabortion demonstrators with all her vinegary might.

That is, until one day, when she began to be charmed by a pastor and antiabortion activist named Flip Benham from Operation Rescue. Their friendship grew, and Norma felt wanted and validated by the people she had spent years opposing. She converted to Catholicism and made headlines once more as a reborn version of herself. However, at the end of her life, she made a self-described "deathbed confession" that she had always believed in the right to an abortion. She only converted and worked for the antiabortion movement because they paid her well, and as a woman who had wrestled with poverty her entire life, the promise of money comes with an undeniable pull. "If a young woman wants to have an abortion—fine; that's no skin off my ass," quips a gasping Norma from the nursing home in Katy, Texas, where she spent her final days. Plus, the feeling of being valued was a balm, especially after all the years she had spent being criticized as not enough—not educated enough, poised enough, prim enough—or too much—too loud, too crass, too gay. She died from heart failure in 2017.

In the decades since the *Roe v. Wade* ruling, the issue of abortion has come before the Supreme Court dozens of times. Americans have a habit of perceiving the Court as the be-all, end-all of what abortion looks like in this country, particularly when it comes to the original 1973 ruling, but that's a mistake. As legal scholar Mary Ziegler has noted, the focus on the singular *Roe v. Wade* ruling from the Supreme Court is a hindrance to seeing the larger picture. By focusing on this one case, "we have missed many of the tactical decisions, ideological changes, and larger political transformations that helped to create the world of contemporary abortion politics."

The creeping decline of abortion rights cannot be explained simply or attributed to a single person or group. Indeed, the rise of the new right and the religious right, which centered abortion as a Republican red-meat issue, as well as deeply effective, careful organizing among the pro-life movement over time, all contributed pressure that added cracks to what so many assumed was established law. The pro-choice side also made significant missteps. White feminists prioritized their ideology over the needs of poor women and women of color, forming what is known as the reproductive rights movement, which focuses on the right to abortion, overlooking other types of reproductive care. This narrow framing, largely propelled forward by upper-middle-class white women, is what made the reproductive justice movement that formed in the 1990s necessary. Though the *Roe* decision did not create antiabortion activism in the United States, much less the culture wars, it did help the right mobilize around a "pro-life" cause and to clarify strategies to that end.

Ruth Bader Ginsburg, for one, spoke of the weakness of the *Roe v. Wade* ruling long before she became a Supreme Court Justice. Two decades after the decision, she said that perhaps Justice Harry Blackmun went too far in his opinion. The country was not ready. "Doctrinal limbs too swiftly shaped, experience teaches, may prove unstable," she said in a lecture she delivered at the New York University School of Law.

"Suppose the Court . . . had not gone on, as it did in *Roe*, to fashion a regime blanketing the subject, a set of rules that displaced virtually every state law then in force," she continued. "Would there have been this virtually twenty-year controversy we have witnessed? . . . A less encompassing *Roe*, one that merely struck down the extreme Texas law and went no further on that day, I believe . . . might have served to reduce rather than fuel controversy." She went on to say that the decision shut down any potential or ongoing conversation with state lawmakers, fostering resentment and fury. "Around the extraordinary decision, a well-organized and vocal right-to-life movement rallied."

In 1976, three short years after the *Roe* ruling, the antiabortion movement won a significant victory that has shaped abortion access in the United States ever since. Antiabortion congressman Henry Hyde proposed an amendment to the House Appropriations Bill that would bar the use of federal funds for abortion care. The amendment specifically targeted poor women who rely on Medicaid for their health care. At the time, Medicaid helped some three hundred thousand women get abortion care, accounting for about a fifth of abortions in the United States. There was no room for misinterpretation; Hyde made his intentions perfectly clear. "I certainly would like to prevent, if I could legally, anybody having an abortion, a rich woman, a middle-class woman, or a poor woman," he famously said of his amendment in 1977. "Unfortunately, the only vehicle available is the . . . Medicaid bill." This is, of course, the very definition of punching down.

The Hyde Amendment's initial passage and its longevity is due to a very American refusal to acknowledge poverty as anything other than a personal failure. After all, the so-called American Dream is all about pulling oneself up by the bootstraps. Here, the powerful and the privileged like to say, anyone can thrive. Systematic inequality is conveniently ignored and, rather, weaponized against those who face greater hurdles to stability. Starting in the 1960s, welfare fraud started to become a fixation in the media, and though the offenders (who were the exception, not the rule) were mostly male, the idea of a poor person, lazy and unemployed but living high off of government welfare was often gendered female in the popular imagination, culminating in President Ronald Reagan's trope of the "welfare queen" during a presidential campaign in 1976. The myth was primed to thrive in our culture, and it bled into the development and passage of policy like the Hyde Amendment. The idea, the great lie was that welfare queens were living their frivolous lives, getting knocked up, and getting abortions on the government dime. It's another example of powerful men using a threatening narrative to limit the rights of others.

White feminists, lulled into a sense of security by the *Roe* ruling, were not alarmed by the Hyde Amendment's introduction, or the general push by abortion foes to limit abortion funding on a federal level—they trusted the courts to take care of it, even ignoring the warnings of women of color like Faye Wattleton, Planned Parenthood's first Black president, to take the threat seriously. In an ACLU pamphlet from 1975, the organization insisted that "by and large, the courts . . . have unanimously held that Medicaid must pay for elective abortions." The courts did no such thing, ultimately upholding the Hyde Amendment and proclaiming it constitutional. In her book, *Abortion and the Law in America:* Roe v. Wade *to the Present,* Ziegler notes that "abortion rights groups badly misjudged the efficacy of both funding bans and arguments about the costs of abortions." Antiabortion groups had found a crucial victory in going after federal funds, and they also won the support of moderate Democrats at the time, like then senator Joe Biden.

The Hyde Amendment has been permanently in effect since 1980, when the Supreme Court upheld it, though it has existed in various forms. The initial version had no exceptions to it, and though the present version does include exceptions for rape, incest, and life-threatening circumstances, low-income people and abortion clinics rarely have the time and necessary resources to file for coverage. And even if they do, Medicaid reimbursement rates are so low, it's not worth the hassle for most clinics. As of this writing, in addition to low-income Americans on Medicaid, the Hyde Amendment is a barrier for pregnant people in the military to access abortion care, as well as government workers, federal inmates, Peace Corps volunteers, and DC residents.

It took a scant two months for a woman to die as a direct result of the Hyde Amendment. Her name was Rosie Jimenez. She was twenty-seven years old, and she already had a five-year-old daughter, Monique. She, too, was chasing the American Dream; the Mexican American mother was only six months away from earning her bachelor's degree in education from Pan American University in McAllen, Texas. The only money she had that could have covered the procedure was her financial aid check, which was also her shot at a better life for herself and, importantly, her daughter. She had come too far and worked too hard to sacrifice that. She decided to take her chances with a local midwife, who performed the abortion illegally. The next night, Rosie came down with a fever, and her condition worsened as she began to vomit and hemorrhage. She died a week later at the McAllen General Hospital from organ failure, despite efforts to save her that included a tracheotomy to help the young woman breathe and a hysterectomy to remove the source of the infection. Four other women were hospitalized for similar infections in the two months after the amendment took effect. Rosie would likely still be here had she been able to use the Medicaid she relied on for the rest of her health care when she needed an abortion.

But Medicaid bans were just the beginning. Before and after *Roe*, the antiabortion movement argued that abortion violated human and constitutional rights. As Ziegler writes, antiabortion lawyers examined such legal avenues as the Declaration of Independence, the Thirteenth and Fourteenth Amendments, international human rights law, and pre-*Roe* substantive due process cases recognizing rights implicit in the Constitution to potentially provide them the grounding necessary to protect the right to life of a fetus or even an embryo through the courts.

Roe did not change the endgame for the antiabortion movement, even if antiabortion leaders gave up on a constitutional ban on abortion for the short term. Laws like the Hyde Amendment became a step toward overruling *Roe*, and overruling *Roe* became a step toward making abortion a crime across the country, Ziegler says.

It took less than half a century of coordinated efforts for "prolifers" to declare victory and witness the Court overturn the landmark ruling.

PART TWO

The Beginning of the End

CHAPTER 8

Chipped Away

"I WOULD DRINK bleach right now."

Kate shakes her head, and the long, sun-streaked brown hair piled on top of her skull shivers. "That's so bad, and I don't mean it," she quickly adds. But she's exhausted; shadowy crescents hover beneath her preternaturally bright blue-green eyes. It's 2019, and she just graduated from the University of Mississippi a few weeks ago. She's been trying to get an abortion since March, and she was turned away, 221 miles from home, just when she thought it was finally going to be over. Now, she has to return to her apartment in Oxford, where she'll wait out yet another week and return to the clinic in Little Rock for the third time.

Her day began at 3 A.M. with a text from Laurie Bertram Roberts, who heads the Mississippi Reproductive Freedom Fund (MRFF), the nonprofit that was helping Kate pay for her abortion and navigate the logistics of getting care. Around 7:45 A.M., a hulking white medical transport van pulled into the parking lot of her apartment complex, and Kate climbed in to join two of Laurie's daughters, Sarah and Aolani, as well as Laurie's partner at the time, who was driving.

They sped northwest, through Mississippi, Tennessee, and then Arkansas to make her 10:45 A.M. appointment, but a couple of wrecks on the interstate slowed them down. By the time they arrived, they were nearly an hour late.

Tired and dusty from the road—the van's air-conditioning was incapacitated, so the windows stayed rolled down—the foursome exited the vehicle into the warm, weighty Arkansas air. Around fifteen protesters hemmed in the sidewalk to the clinic, and their shouts pelted Kate, overwhelming her. One of them, a woman who was there with an infant nestled in a stroller, shrieked that Kate should carry to term and give the baby to her. A man bellowed that God wouldn't judge her if she would only turn around. It was the image of the baby in the stroller, in the edge-of-June heat, that was seared into Kate's mind for the rest of the day.

Head down, she was ushered into the clinic by the group from MRFF. Kate put her wallet in a dish before going through the metal detector at the entrance, but she couldn't bring herself to take off the vintage necklace with a French inscription—translating to "more than yesterday, less than tomorrow"—and the two rings that never leave her body. She breathed a sigh of relief when they didn't trigger the alarm, reveling in this modicum of control in a situation where she had none. The requirement to leave her cell phone in the van hadn't felt like much of a sacrifice; who would she text? She hadn't told her mother, who was battling breast cancer, about her pregnancy, or her new boyfriend, who lived in a different country. Most of the people who knew what she was going through were in the clinic with her, with the exception of Laurie herself, who had been forced to stay home due to a neck injury.

Kate was called back to an exam room quickly; the rest of the appointment was a blur. There was some complication with the funding for her procedure, and a sharp admonishment from an administrator at the clinic about that and her tardiness brought forth the tears she had been determined to hold back. She was released into the waiting room, where scenes of a baby shower played across a TV screen, and then she was called back again for an ultrasound. She was relieved to see her favorite clinic staffer in the exam room; at a prior appointment, Kate had broken down in heaving sobs because she was frightened and wished for her mother. The staffer held her and assured that they would all serve as her mother throughout the process, if that's what she needed. But today, the energetic, warm woman grew quiet, and Kate felt her body tighten with fear. "What's wrong?" she demanded.

"Oh, things are just going to go a little differently today," the staffer replied, trying to keep her voice light.

"What's wrong?" Kate insisted. She tightened her jaw against the bile that was rising in her throat.

The ultrasound was showing the fetus at twenty weeks, measured by her last menstrual period, but Kate's appointment was for someone who was at eighteen weeks' gestation. (Gestational age is calculated in two ways: postfertilization, which is from the moment of conception, and from the date of a pregnant person's last menstrual period. The latter is used most by medical professionals.) The extra two weeks triggered a forty-eight-hour waiting period and state-mandated counseling about fetal pain. This concept had been disproven more than a decade earlier, with a group of doctors from the University of California, San Francisco, who analyzed hundreds of articles from medical journals and concluded that fetal pain is "unlikely before the third trimester," though the research has not dissuaded antiabortion lawmakers, who based the gestational limit on this idea of fetal pain. This meant that the foursome would have to return to Mississippi and try again for an appointment next week. That appointment would be her final chance to get the procedure in Little Rock; abortions after twenty-two weeks were illegal in Arkansas. As a nurse explained the situation and began her required monologue about fetal pain, Kate's eyes filled with bright white light and she gagged.

I met Kate, then a twenty-five-year-old Texan with hopes of becoming a social worker, for the first time by the pool at a hotel in Little Rock, the evening after she was turned away. Her finger-tips were stained bright orange-red from snacking on Flamin' Hot Cheetos, and she wore the summertime uniform of college girls in the South—oversize T-shirt, athletic shorts, sandals. She greeted me with a warm familiarity and said she hoped I can explain what just happened to her because she was too afraid to google much of anything.

Kate wants a houseful of kids someday, with the right person. The man who impregnated her is not that; when they were intimate, she was intoxicated and unable to consent, to such a degree that she doesn't recall everything that happened. When she told him she was pregnant and she wanted an abortion, he told her it was her choice, and he would support her. He went so far as to drive her to the Little Rock clinic the first time, and he promised to pay for her procedure. Kate didn't want to go to the Jackson clinic because it felt too high profile to her, and she was afraid she could be recognized: the Jackson Women's Health Organization was the last abortion clinic in Mississippi, and it routinely drew a dedicated cadre of protesters. Skirmishes between the clinic escorts and the protesters were often posted to Instagram and TikTok, and while the escorts took care not to let anyone seeking care get caught in the cross fire, the social media buzz could be alienating to potential patients who didn't realize that those interactions happen between set shifts in which patients were escorted in and out of the clinic as a group.

It took her a few weeks to even set up that first appointment. She had to sift through Google results that brought up crisis pregnancy centers that wouldn't actually help her, and then she called a clinic in Memphis, but the receptionist she spoke with sounded overwhelmed, causing her anxiety to swell. Finally, she made an appointment in Little Rock for March 8, and she, along with the man who had impregnated her, made the drive together for the first time. They were in the car by 4 A.M.; Kate wanted an early morning appointment so she could make it back in time for a night class.

He had promised he would do whatever it took to take care of the pregnancy, including help pay for it, so Kate was surprised to get a call later asking for payment upon her next visit. She learned that while she was in the exam room, he had declined to pay. She confronted him, and he asked her to carry the baby to term and give it to him. She refused. The confrontation escalated to the point that, she says, he slashed her tires on the morning of her third appointment, causing her to miss it. That's when she decided she needed help.

Kate spent most of the journey back to Oxford from Little Rock curled up on the floorboard of the van. After lunch, Sarah and Aolani stopped at a Walmart, where they bought a thin foam mattress pad and a tie-dye blanket to make a pallet for her. As the van hurtled down the interstate, the driver chugged energy drinks, slinging expletives out the window every so often at other motorists. Air roared through the open windows, and a vent in the top of the van clattered, making it impossible to talk much, other than the occasional good-natured bickering between Sarah and Aolani. Kate lay there quietly, occasionally picking up her phone only to set it back down. Sweat pasted her two-sizes-too-big T-shirt to her back, and the folds of the blanket left creases on her legs. Sarah passed her phone around every so often to share an amusing Tumblr meme. Kate humored Sarah, but her smile hardened into more of a grimace.

"I can't believe I have to do this all over again in a week," Kate mumbled as we waited to use the restroom in a grimy gas station near the Tennessee state line. She was eager to get home to her dog, who had been her devoted companion through the ordeal, sleeping in the bathtub on the nights that Kate was too sick to move from the toilet. When we pulled into the parking lot of her apartment complex, she quickly got out of the van, though we had to wait for a nosy neighbor to return inside. "Let us know if you need to talk," Sarah called after her. Kate didn't look back.

Less than a week later, on a rainy Thursday morning, they began the process all over again. This time, she got her abortion, just shy of the state's gestational limit. If she had waited even a few days longer, she would have been rendered ineligible for the procedure, which would have meant a journey to Florida or Colorado. What's more, if she had started this arduous process a few weeks later, she might not have been eligible for an abortion in Arkansas at twenty-one weeks. That year, legislators in Arkansas passed a law banning abortions past eighteen weeks, shaving four more weeks off the window for the procedure, but its opponents sued the state and a federal judge temporarily blocked it from going into effect.

"When I got back to my apartment, I just laid down with my dog, and finally, I had a sense of control again," she says.

Kate found herself at the mercy of antiabortion policies in two different states: Mississippi and Arkansas. In Mississippi, only one abortion clinic remained, and it was subjected to annual legislative attacks. The state has a single Planned Parenthood, in Hattiesburg, that distributes birth control but does not provide abortion care, which, according to a spokesperson for Planned Parenthood Southeast, "is because the state of Mississippi intentionally has made it next to impossible to be an abortion provider." A federal judge struck down two attempts by the state to place a gestational limit on abortion: first, a 2018 law that would have banned abortion after fifteen weeks, which was eventually the vehicle used by the Supreme Court to overturn *Roe*, and in 2019, another law that would have banned abortion as early as six weeks. Both measures had sailed easily through the state legislature and were signed by Gov. Phil Bryant, who has famously said his "goal is to end abortion" there. The Jackson clinic's capacity has been slowly whittled down by an unceasing onslaught of legislative attacks. A 2012 law that would have required abortion providers in Mississippi to have admitting privileges at a nearby hospital was passed with the express purpose of closing the state's last remaining clinic but was ultimately deemed unconstitutional. Licensing laws laid out onerous requirements for abortion clinics in the state to meet the standards of an ambulatory surgical center. At one point, the clinic was only offering abortion care three days a week. Patients who did manage to get an appointment at the clinic were required to listen to medically inaccurate state-mandated counseling, a twenty-four-hour waiting period, which meant two separate trips to the clinic, and a required ultrasound. As of 2017, at least half of pregnant people in Mississippi traveled out of state for abortion care, and even then, the surrounding states in the Bible Belt weren't much better off. Tennessee had six clinics in operation when Kate tried to get an abortion, and Alabama and Louisiana had just three each. Arkansas was down to two. These states featured a patchwork of Targeted Regulation of Abortion Providers (TRAP) laws, policies aimed at limiting access to abortion care through seemingly harmless provisions about hallway widths or expensive medical equipment unnecessary to abortion.

In Arkansas, Kate encountered many of the barriers that are aimed to deter pregnant people from receiving abortion care—a burdensome waiting period, misinformation about her own body's processes, a gestational limit. There are, of course, many more: the waiting period, at the time of this writing, is now seventy-two hours, a day more than Kate was subjected to. Telemedicine, in which abortion pills are administered remotely via a drawer that is controlled by a physician, is banned by Mississippi, so patients from areas like the rural Delta must physically travel to the Jackson clinic if they want abortion care from medical staff. The state also requires documented consent from the parent of a minor who seeks abortion care and prohibits abortion on the basis of sex selection (which subjects patients to invasive questioning that forces them to justify their wish to not be pregnant). The state has a trigger law that declared abortion illegal when *Roe v. Wade* was overturned a few short years after Kate's abortion.

For the purposes of this book, before the fall of *Roe,* I identified twenty-six post-*Roe* states where the right to an abortion existed primarily for a privileged few and the majority had to overcome obstacles that are incompatible to their resources and their lives to get the care they needed, often pushing them further into pregnancy. I applied a framework established by the Guttmacher Institute, a reproductive rights think tank, which used six extreme antiabortion bans and limitations as benchmarks. Many states that fall into this category have several of these onerous restrictions on the books, and even if some of them are not in effect, their existence shows the spirit of the lawmakers who enacted them. Post-*Roe* states have passed at least one of the following restrictions through their legislative bodies:

A pre-*Roe* ban on abortion that was not removed after the 1973
   Supreme Court ruling
A law that prohibits abortion after six weeks
A law that prohibits abortion after eight weeks
A trigger ban, which bans abortion in the event that the *Roe v.
   Wade* ruling is overturned

A near-total ban, which is, as defined by Guttmacher, "a law
enacted after *Roe* to prohibit abortion under all or nearly all
circumstances"

A state constitutional amendment that declares nothing within
that document protects the right to an abortion

In its analysis, Guttmacher includes four other states as being
post-*Roe*: Florida, Indiana, Nebraska, and Montana. These states
don't have the bans listed above but have made significant moves
toward outlawing abortion that, Guttmacher states, demonstrate
they are "likely to ban abortion as soon as possible without federal
protections in place." Another state, Wyoming, passed a ban in 2022
before *Roe* officially fell. That post-*Roe* states existed before the federal right to abortion was demolished is eerily familiar; in the years
before abortion was legalized federally, women traveled to states that
had preemptively made abortion safe by declaring the procedure legal. Now, here we are again.

In these states, the work of abortion funds, activists, and clinic
staff has been crucial. For Kate, it meant the difference between getting the care she needed and being forced to carry to term. Thankfully, Laurie and the Mississippi Reproductive Freedom Fund came
through.

In addition to being a dynamic activist, Laurie Bertram Roberts is
a Black woman with seven children. She lives below the poverty line;
her family cobbles together a humble life off food stamps, government assistance, and the odd jobs they do to survive. Laurie spends
much of her time bedridden due to painful fibromyalgia, but her
phone and her laptop are never far from that bed, basically operating as digital appendages. As a founder and excutive director of the
Mississippi Reproductive Freedom Fund, the only abortion fund in
the state, Laurie runs an organization that is not seamless nor neatly
organized, but it is powerful. She and her family help pregnant people get their abortions, and they work to keep them as comfortable
as possible throughout the process, sometimes smuggling clients in
abusive relationships out of their homes for the procedure.

The fund doesn't stop at abortions. Laurie is a true believer in the reproductive justice framework. MRFF helps local women pay for health care, diapers, food, contraception—really, wherever there's a need, the fund will fill it. She delights in showing me several boxes full of Barbies, in every shape, size, and color, that she had purchased for a playroom for her clients' children. "Ask people what's going on, and they're going to spill their story, and through that narrative, you're going to find out what you need to know," she says of her philosophy. "No one comes to us just needing one thing. Needing abortion funding is usually one part of their greater struggle of being a low-income person."

Laurie preaches this belief in social justice to her own family as well; her kids have grown up with it as the center of their universe, in the way that most other kids in Mississippi grow up experiencing evangelical Christianity. Laurie cofounded the fund in 2013 with a friend, Yolanda Walker, and two of her daughters, one of whom, Kayla, now a mother herself, had needed an abortion when she was fifteen. The other was Sarah, who traveled with Kate to Little Rock. Both daughters work for the fund as abortion doulas. It is a full-on family affair that also runs with the help of other dedicated Mississippians with whom Laurie has found community.

But the work, which takes a lot from her to keep it afloat, has extracted a toll. Two years before we met, her mother passed away while Laurie attended a retreat in Atlanta, and she's haunted by what she's missing out on as a result of her never-ending mission. "The last thing my mom had said to me before I left was, 'Do you have to go? I really wish you would just stay home this time,'" she remembers, wiping away tears. "And that will stay with me for the rest of my life."

"I wish I would have spent more time with her and worked a little bit less. I know she was proud of me, and she understood the work I did; she was never mad at me. But you never get that time back. I know my kids sometimes wish that I didn't spend so much time saving the world, as they say. So right now, my challenge is finding balance." She says she doesn't want to end up like Alice Walker, with a daughter who once hated her for never being there (though the mother and daughter have since reconciled). That's the beauty of Laurie's organization being so closely intertwined with her family: she gets to live firmly in both worlds. Still.

"Activism is a sacrifice, right? It is what it is."

When I visit the house in West Jackson that she and her family call "the fund shack" in 2019, it is teeming with activity. It's a modest one-story house, with a front porch framed by lacy white wrought iron, shot through with rust. Bars are clamped protectively over the windows. Some of Laurie's kids are there: Kayla, Sarah, and Aolani all flit through the house. Local activists from youth empowerment and LGBTQIA+ organizations drift in and out. An unexpected donation of several mattresses is delivered. Fund volunteers intermittently pop into the room where Laurie sits in bed, chatting with me, her lower half wrapped in a blue sheet—the worn cotton is the only thing that feels tolerable against her skin when her chronic illness flares. Roofers work in the hot sun to replace the worn-down shingles; Laurie tells me it took her a few tries to find a reliable crew that didn't mind working for a group that funds abortion care in a "Black" part of town. But she seems to have hit it off with these guys. A day or two prior, the subject of condoms came up when she was talking with them, as it tends to around Laurie, and soon enough she was using a wooden penis model to demonstrate how to properly put on a condom. The men left that day with a generous bag of free rubbers. "I'm very plainspoken about sex," she says, shrugging.

Laurie is actually plainspoken about just about everything. She doesn't much care for bullshit, and she'll quickly let you know it. She knows firsthand there are worse things than appearing abrasive: Like being denied an abortion when your back is against a wall. Like nearly dying in a Catholic hospital because the doctor is more interested in saving your fetus than the life of a woman with other children at home. Like being a low-income woman of color in a state with a long record of denying the humanity of those who look like you. All those factors, and all this personal history, contribute to why she's doing this work and why it is messy and chaotic—because such is the life of someone who lives with the odds stacked against them, and such are the lives of those who come to her for help.

"We're all poor women and femmes and people of color, for the most part. We have a couple of low-income queer white folks who are part of our group," she says. "To be part of our leadership, you have to be a low-income or working-class person, period. We're not apologetic about that at all, and we're unapologetically Black as fuck. You can either rock with it or kick rocks; we don't care."

Mississippi raised Laurie. It's where she fled to escape her abusive husband when she was twenty-seven; it's where she went to college, where her kids grew up. It's where she found her identity as a hell-raising activist in her own right, surrounded by other activists, many of whom had a rich history in the civil rights movement. Importantly, it was the first time in her life where she found herself in a majority-Black space, and that, for her, was powerful. "I generally talk about Mississippi being the Broadway of activism," she tells me. "If you can make it here, you can make it anywhere."

It is, of course, undeniable that working in the nation's most poverty-stricken and disease-ridden state comes with a very specific, very demanding set of challenges. Low-income women suffer the most in the state's abortion desert, making Laurie's job all the more crucial. According to 2020 data from the Kaiser Family Foundation, more than one in ten women in Mississippi receive health care coverage through Medicaid and likely can't afford to pay for an abortion or nonemergency contraception on their own. In 2016, the state health department closed nine clinics; the following year, two-thirds of the department's regional offices were shuttered due to a series of budget cuts. According to Laurie, some women she knows who rely on Medicaid have had to wait up to six months to get birth control. "I don't think [the rest of the country] understands that the structural barriers are at every turn of care, that it starts before people even have sex," Laurie says. "So like, if you're a young woman in Mississippi, especially a young woman of color in Mississippi, before you even have a sexual life, you're in a world that is stigmatizing and shaming about sex."

Mississippi operates in extreme conditions, but make no mistake: that situation is the result of decades of gerrymandering and disempowerment of the nonwhite people who call it home. It is the Blackest state in the union, and while people unfamiliar with it see it only in the context of its blood-red legislature, assuming that the conservative lawmakers are a product of the culture writ large, to talk about Mississippi's struggles without talking about the earth-shaking activism and organizing that has been the heartbeat of the state for centuries is misguided at best. Laurie and her team are part of a legacy that has long fought for reproductive justice alongside civil rights and voting rights. While we're staring down the barrel of a post-*Roe* America, Laurie and others like her who are operating in hostile states have been laying the foundation for the future of reproductive health care in this country. As long as people in the South are getting pregnant and need help, the Mississippi Reproductive Freedom Fund will be around, she says.

CHAPTER 9

Trapped

WHILE STATE SENATOR Wendy Davis was preparing to leave her boyfriend's downtown Austin apartment on the morning of June 25, 2013, she decided she had better reconsider her shoes. She had risen early that morning to carefully prepare for the day, cranking up Austin singer-songwriter Bruce Robison's country ode to the steadfast nature of Willie Nelson. The steam rising from the filled bathtub soothed her, as did the familiar rhythm of the song that asks over and over: What would Willie do? She took a deep breath. "So when it's all too much (what would Willie) / When the game gets rough (what would Willie) / When they call your bluff, what would Willie do," Robison sang. Davis exhaled and lifted herself out of the tub.

The sun was beginning to rise when the doctor showed up. There was no real way around it: Davis would need to wear a catheter to get through the day. After all, she was only human. The doctor was friendly, but she had brought a large bag meant for a hospital bed with her instead of a leg bag. It was too late to find an alternative, so the tubing had to be carefully wrapped around her leg, the bag attached precisely so it would be hidden under her dress. When it was over, she carefully applied her makeup and fixed her hair, trying to adjust to the cumbersome new burden. She slipped into a fitted dress, splashed with gray and white and blue flowers, and pulled on a light, gray-striped cream coat to smooth out any bulk and to ward off the chill of the chamber, adding a double-strand pearl necklace and earrings to match. Any sign of weakness could cost her dearly. As a woman, she would be expected to look polished on the floor of the Texas capitol, though she wouldn't be given any leniency in physical endurance or procedural knowledge.

Davis donned a pair of flats, gathered her materials, and headed out the door. As it closed behind her, she paused, considering what she was about to ask her body to do. She pivoted, scurrying back inside and reaching for her dusty but still bright-pink running shoes, which she carried into the Texas heat.

Davis had walked through the statehouse many times, but today, every step felt leaded with intention. Her Republican colleagues had been pushing forth a new antiabortion omnibus bill, and she was planning to filibuster for thirteen hours to run out the clock and thwart a final vote. Senate Bill 5 proposed medically unnecessary regulations that would drive abortion clinics out of business and threatened to drastically reduce access to care in the state.

The legislation would ban abortions after twenty weeks' gestation, a benchmark determined by propaganda about "fetal pain." Safety standards for clinics would be elevated to be on par with those required at ambulatory surgical centers, the cost of which would put most clinic owners out of business. Abortion providers would need to secure admitting privileges at a hospital within thirty miles of where they practice, which, in Texas, is no small feat. In 2016, 11.4 percent of hospitals in Texas were affiliated with the Catholic Church; they would be unlikely to work with abortion providers. As of 2017, there were five regions in Texas where the only community hospital was Catholic owned. Three years later, Catholic health systems were still growing quickly: four of the ten largest health centers in the United States are Catholic, and the number of Catholic-owned or -affiliated short-term acute care hospitals grew by 28.5 percent between 2000 and 2020, as non-Catholic hospitals declined by 13.6 percent, according to Community Catalyst, a nonprofit national health advocacy organization. Even if a hospital is not outwardly religious, in conservative states, there is always a good chance that someone powerful on the board is, or an important voice on the hospital committee that would grant the privileges is staunchly antiabortion. The bill also required physicians to administer medication that expels a pregnancy in person, rather than by telemedicine, which makes it practically impossible for women in rural areas to access medication without having to travel. These measures are known as Targeted Regulation of Abortion Providers, and they go well beyond what is necessary to ensure patient safety.

The law at the center of *Planned Parenthood of Southeastern Pennsylvania v. Casey* is considered to be the original TRAP law. The 1992 Supreme Court decision conceded that the states had jurisdiction to restrict abortion, so long as the restrictions did not amount to an "undue burden" on a person seeking an abortion, an amorphous standard that the court defined as existing when the law's "purpose or effect is to place a substantial obstacle in the path of a woman seeking an abortion before the fetus attains viability." In 1988 and 1989, the Pennsylvania legislature passed a flurry of abortion restrictions: a counseling session with state-mandated materials designed to deter people seeking abortion care; a twenty-four-hour waiting period between a patient's initial visit, during which she would receive the counseling, and her abortion; a minor seeking an abortion had to secure the consent of at least one parent; and a married woman had to notify her husband. The *Casey* decision allowed all the provisions to stand except for the latter one. Over the next couple of decades, the strategy to overwhelm clinics with restrictions gained popularity, and it occurred to the antiabortion movement that if they could engineer these restrictions to come with an economic cost, they could shut down clinics one by one. Senate Bill 5 came out of model legislation put forth by one of the leading antiabortion organizations, Americans United for Life.

Around 8 A.M., when Davis entered her office, it was filled with staffers, some of whom were from other Democratic offices in the legislature. Paper flew around the room as they frantically worked to finish pulling together material for the filibuster: binders were swollen with personal and expert testimonies on the burdensome impacts of such antiabortion restrictions, detailed data breaking down the costs and laying out the absurdity of the requirements, and stacks of legal documents to bolster Davis's argument against the legislation.

They needed to be sure there was enough material to run out the clock on a vote. There were three short hours left to prepare. As the time passed, Davis became increasingly uncomfortable. The tubing on her catheter kept loosening, sliding down her leg and below her hemline. Twenty minutes later, she asked a staff member to reach out to the doctor who had visited earlier that morning; this clearly wasn't working. A nurse arrived around 9:15 A.M., and she swapped out the excessive rig for a simpler leg bag. Now, Davis thought, she could concentrate on the task at hand. But as another hour ticked by, she began to realize that this wasn't working either. Nothing had drained into the bag, and her lower abdomen was growing sore. Her team reached out to the doctor again, but by 10:30 A.M., the situation still was not resolved, and she was due out on the floor to begin at 11:11 A.M. sharp. After that, she would have to remain standing until midnight. Anxiety was starting to take over, and in desperation, she burst into the bathroom of the senate ladies' lounge to try and remove the contraption herself, but she couldn't dislodge it from her body. Davis's chief of staff came in just in time, with the nurse in tow. She had struggled to find a place to park because of the attention the bill and Davis's planned filibuster had drawn, and she had run several blocks to make it just in time. The nurse cleared a blockage that was the cause of the problem, and Davis instantly felt relief. Now, it was time to begin. She smoothed out her dress and strode out onto the floor.

The gallery was bursting with hundreds of people—mostly women. Those who had showed up for Davis wore burnt-orange T-shirts emblazoned with words in white—"Stand With Texas Women"—which had been distributed outside the statehouse by pro-choice groups. Proponents of the antiabortion bill wore light blue, and a tight cluster of them occupied the section of the gallery that hung above her desk. Her heart thudded in her chest, and blood thumped in her ears. She approached her desk, lonesome without its accompanying chair, which had been removed since Davis was required to deliver her filibuster with both feet firmly on the floor through the next thirteen hours. The rays of the Texas sun shone boldly through the tall windows of the senate chamber. The session was called to order by the lieutenant governor, and when Lt. Gov. David Dewhurst asked Davis if she still intended to filibuster, she answered firmly. "I intend to speak for an extended period of time on the bill," she said, keeping her voice steady. "Thank you very much." She launched into her remarks.

Two hours into her filibuster, Davis began to wonder what she had gotten herself into. Her back ached insistently. She tried to shut out her body's complaints and replace it with the energy in the room. She took up a binder filled with personal testimonies from Texans who had been turned away from giving public comment in an earlier hearing of the bill. Throughout her time on the floor, more emails with testimonies poured in, while frantic staffers rushed to print them and deliver them to Davis. There were sixteen thousand stories in all, none of which Davis had gotten to read ahead of time. As she read them, she processed the emotion they invoked in her, and she feared that she might buckle under the weight of that pain. One story rang so familiar that at times she felt as though she were reading her own words. Davis had undergone two abortions; both pregnancies were desired. In 1994, she lost a son, Lucas, when the pregnancy became ectopic, attaching itself to a fallopian tube rather than the uterus. "The only medical option was to have surgery to terminate the pregnancy and remove the affected fallopian tube—which in Texas is technically considered an abortion, and doctors have to report it as such," Davis wrote in her memoir. After her abortion, after she had grieved the loss of a potential life that she very much wanted to foster, she and her husband, Jeff, decided to try to conceive again. When she discovered she was pregnant, the couple was euphoric. When the doctor told them that they would be having a girl, a sister to Davis's two daughters, they decided to name her Tate Elise. She went to what she thought was a routine doctor's appointment in her second trimester without her husband when the doctor told her that this pregnancy, too, would not come to term. Her daughter had a severe brain abnormality. The chances of the child surviving were minuscule, and even if Tate did live outside the womb, she would suffer intensely and likely live in a permanent vegetative state. The doctor's hands shook as he told her the prognosis.

"I couldn't breathe. I literally couldn't catch my breath," Davis wrote. "I don't remember much else about that day other than calling [my husband] Jeff, trying to contain my hysterical crying. The rest of it is a shocked, haze-filled blur." The couple sought other medical opinions, but they were all the same. The pregnancy was terminated, and Davis underwent a cesarean section. "An indescribable blackness followed," she wrote. "It was a deep, dark despair and grief, a heavy wave that crushed me, that made me wonder if I would ever surface." Through Davis's testimony on the floor of the senate, she struggled to push down the flashbacks and stay in the present moment, focusing on the stakes of the day over the searing pain of her past loss.

During Davis's remarks, Republicans in support of the bill conspired to call point of order the requisite three times to shut her down, their only weapon against a filibuster. The evening wore on, and Davis began to speak on the aftereffects of a 2011 budget cut of $77 million to family planning services in Texas meant to dismantle Planned Parenthood clinics and similar services in the state. As a result, more than 155,000 Texans lost access to reproductive health care, including contraceptive services and cancer screenings. The 2011 cut was fueled by abortion stigma, and it shut down one in every four family planning clinics in the state. Low-income families that relied on those clinics for affordable care were affected the most. Davis emphasized the trauma that ensued when great barriers were placed between people and reproductive health care. Meanwhile, the state's Alternatives to Abortion program, which provides funding for crisis pregnancy centers, saw an increase of $300,000 to their $8 million budget.

Sen. Robert Nichols—who perhaps was trying to increase his clout with Texas Right to Life—interrupted Davis with the first point of order, insisting that she had gone off topic and her argument was no longer germane. It should be noted that filibusters in this country have often bordered on the absurd, lending themselves more toward political theater than serious rhetoric. Indeed, during a filibuster led by Sen. Rand Paul to run out the clock on a confirmation vote to the Obama administration in the US Senate just a few months earlier, on March 6, Sen. Ted Cruz supported Paul's efforts with a reading from Shakespeare's *Henry V*, and in protest of the Affordable Care Act, Cruz read Dr. Seuss's *Green Eggs and Ham* while quasi-filibustering. Sen. Strom Thurmond read aloud the voting laws from each state, along with President George Washington's farewell address, in an effort to prevent the passage of the Civil Rights Act of 1957.

Lt. Gov. Dewhurst upheld Senator Nichols's point of order.

The rules of the filibuster forbid leaning on a desk or chair for support, and Davis's back pain had been steadily escalating. It was becoming unbearable. She paced around her desk, rubbing at her lower back, willing her stubborn muscles to release. A messenger skittered onto the floor with a back brace, and Sen. Rodney Ellis stepped forward to intercept it, passing it to Davis. She took it gratefully, but she struggled to put it on while holding the microphone and continuing to speak; he moved to help her. Forty-five minutes later, a point of order was called on the basis that Senator Ellis had "assisted" Davis in filibustering, even though the spirit of the rule is to prevent someone else from taking the floor and relieving the original person delivering the filibuster. The point of order was, once more, upheld. It was only 7:24 P.M., and the sun was beginning its slow, summer descent, casting the senate chamber in amber. Fury rose in her.

As the night deepened, her voice took on a steely edge as she addressed her colleagues. "But you can imagine, or maybe you can't, how a woman feels to be told that her feelings on those issues, that no matter how difficult, no matter the circumstances that she's dealing with, if she can't fit into every one of these little square pegs that she's going to be asked to fit into by this bill, she is not going to be able to exercise her constitutional right," she declared. "And what's so disturbing is that we don't seem to care. And maybe that is because so many of us on this floor have never had to face that and never will face it, because you don't have the equipment." She kept her face expressionless. "And I've got it, and my daughters have it, and other women that I care about have it, and women who I don't know have it." At 9:31 P.M., the third and final point of order was called. As before, Davis had gone into a previous bill passed by the legislature that forced a pregnant person seeking an abortion to listen to the electric pattern produced by tissue that could eventually form a fetus's heart; if they refused, the physician was required to describe aloud what they saw on the ultrasound. The patient also had to undergo a transvaginal sonogram twenty-four hours before being allowed to access abortion care. Again, she was trying to establish that all these regulations add up to become an extreme burden on patients, but still, the lieutenant governor ruled in favor of Sen. Donna Campbell, who had called the point of order to claim that Davis had strayed from her filibuster topic.

The only path forward was for the Democrats to band together and stall, though Davis had to remain standing. And so they did, slowly drawling through procedural motions while Davis remained planted on the floor. At 11:15 P.M., according to Davis's memoir, the microphones of the Democratic senators were shut off. The chair refused to recognize them. The gallery roared. Meanwhile, Sen. Leticia Van de Putte had recently arrived from her father's funeral in San Antonio and was taking in the scene before her. She had lost her dad suddenly, unexpectedly, in a car accident, and she was still reeling from her loss. The appalling conduct in the Texas senate had brought her back, despite her plans to stay with her family that day. She could not ignore what was happening in the chamber; she was enraged. She, too, sought recognition from the chair to speak, and she was resolutely ignored. "Did the president hear me or did the president hear me and refuse to recognize me?" she asked pointedly. There was no response.

Finally, she was recognized by the chair. "At what point must a female senator raise her hand or her voice to be recognized over the male colleagues in the room?" she bellowed. The room vibrated with an affirmative response from the onlookers in the gallery and the noise fell over the lawmakers, making it nearly impossible for them to continue further business. It was about a quarter till midnight. Still, the Republicans tried to carry forth a vote, dashing from their desks to the dais to communicate their yes votes to the secretary of the senate. The presiding officer slammed his gavel onto the podium. "SB5 has now passed." It was 12:03 A.M. An argument broke out between parties over whether the vote was valid and at what time it had officially been declared.

At nearly 3 A.M., Lt. Gov. Dewhurst declared the bill dead, but he blamed the "unruly mob" in the gallery. The crowd had been shooed out of the gallery, but they remained gathered in the rotunda, waiting to hear what would become of the bill. Cecile Richards, daughter of former Texas governor Ann Richards and then president of Planned Parenthood, was among them. She looked down at her phone, reading a text, and smiled broadly. The text was from Davis. "The lieutenant governor has agreed that SB5 is dead," she read into a microphone. Together, they celebrated. Exhaustion melted into exuberance.

The victory was temporary. Gov. Rick Perry called another special session the next day for July 1 so that the bill could be taken up once more. "We will not allow the breakdown of decorum and decency to prevent us from doing what the people of this state hired us to do," he said.

Senate Bill 5 was reintroduced in the Texas House of Representatives as House Bill 2 (HB2), where it passed 96–49, later passing the state senate 19–11. Governor Perry signed the bill into law on July 18, and it went into effect the following October.

Down the street from the capitol, Nikiya Natale watched the proceedings from her worn futon, alone and pregnant, in the sparsely furnished apartment that she inhabited as a law student. Her cat, a fluffy black Maine coon mix named Zaire, meowed loudly from across the room, but Nikiya was transfixed. Bitter rage burned in the back of her throat—that Davis had to do this, that this clearly unconstitutional bill was even being considered, that these men were using so much energy to find a way to make a procedure she needed even harder to access, that they would never know what it was like to be in a body like hers.

She was then twenty-six years old, propelled by dreams of helping immigrants traverse America's gnarled immigration system, but she was burdened by debt made worse by the demands of law school, which required strict focus and left no time or energy for any sort of employment. She had been living off her student loans, and now the date for the bar exam was quickly approaching, which came with expenses of its own. Her credit cards were all maxed out, and like so many other American students, she shouldered the debt and hoped with all her might that it would lead to employment and enable her to pay it down. The only way she was able to afford care was through financial assistance, which was granted through the National Abortion Federation, which covered the expenses—she paid the initial $100 for the ultrasound. Though she comes from a politically liberal family—she refers to her father as "the ultimate feminist," with an affectionate grin—and she knew her friends were of like minds, she found herself unable to tell them that she was pregnant and needed abortion care. Only one other person in her circle (that she knew of) had had an abortion, and she was not close enough to her to confide.

Nikiya is a white, first-generation college student, and she felt pressure to keep rising to the responsibility of that status. Law school had already been tough. She made friends, but she felt ill at ease amid the wealth her classmates inhabited comfortably, and imposter syndrome nagged at her constantly. What if admitting she needed an abortion disappointed her family? What if her friends decided she was trash? What if her accidental pregnancy affirmed that she never belonged in the first place, that she wasn't smart enough or savvy enough to keep up with her peers after all? "I had just graduated," she remembers. "I didn't want to be a parent. I couldn't be a parent. I wanted to start my career."

Her education gave her the knowledge that the newly passed Texas law would not go into effect immediately, but still, she held her breath until the day of her first appointment arrived. She knew that she was one of the lucky ones. As a woman in tune with her body, she knew quickly that she was pregnant, and she was able to act early.

Even so, a sense of dread that she would be turned away, that somehow these men would find a way to interfere, would not lift from her shoulders. When she arrived at the clinic, the froth of protesters sent electric anxiety up her spine that mingled with outrage. She tried to keep her eyes focused on each step she took forward, pressing her lips together to bar the colorful insults she wanted to scream back at the bullies demanding that she turn around. Between their frenetic shouts and the knowledge that she would only be able to get an ultrasound and state-mandated "counseling" that day, weariness took hold of her bones as she stepped into the Austin Women's Health Center. She was surprised to see that the majority of patients in the waiting room were women of color. "Austin is a pretty white town," she says. Everyone there was kind, but she wanted to get her abortion and move on with her life. The counseling session was first, and Nikiya was handed a booklet with blue-and-white lettering on the cover that said *A Woman's Right to Know*. She scoffed at it, bristling at the assumptions made by people she would never meet, who did not know her or her circumstances at all. "I really don't need this," she told the counselor. "I already googled everything."

"I know. The state requires that I give this to you, so look at it and consider all your options," she replied.

The options, according to the booklet, are plentiful, never mind that they're divorced from the reality of low-income people in this country, who comprise the majority of abortion patients in the United States. Nikiya received the 2003 edition of the booklet, which was more moderate than the later 2016 version, most recently in use. The 2003 booklet, while still egregious and stigmatizing, managed to generally avoid the term *baby* and mentioned the myth of fetal pain only in passing, referring to it as a concept that had not been definitively proven.

But in the current 2016 revised booklet, the so-called facts have been stretched to such a degree that they are rendered unrecognizable. Repeatedly, the word *baby* appears in place of *fetus* or *embryo*, and at the top of the second page in slanting red letters, the booklet alludes to the myth of fetal pain, though the wording has been carefully contrived. Anyone who doesn't know the ins and outs of this language would conclude that their abortion would be painful for the fetus inside them, though it does not have a nervous system. "Newborn babies are able to feel pain. We know that babies develop the ability to feel pain while in the womb. In consideration of the potential for fetal pain, Texas law currently limits abortion to under 20 weeks." The phrase "in consideration for the potential" is doing a lot of work to plant a disproven possibility in the minds of people who are simply trying to get medical care.

Several pages are devoted to walking the reader through "your baby's" development, which addresses "you" and "the baby's father" throughout. Deeper in, the booklet describes the risks associated with abortion, though another red-lettered caveat at the top of the page allows: "The risks of having an abortion can vary depending on several factors," which are identified as death, physical risks, mental health risks, future infertility, and breast cancer risk.

The phrasing is precise, and it's clear that the writers are treading carefully with guidance from a legal expert. The intention is clear: to manipulate pregnant people into carrying to term despite whatever their feelings are about the pregnancy. If the mission to dissuade through this booklet succeeds, the options are to keep the baby and fight for child support and enter into the red tape of government assistance, pursue adoption, or surrender the baby at a local fire station or hospital. Nothing is mentioned regarding the potential mental or emotional fallout from those decisions.

Nikiya, for her part, pointedly left the booklet behind when she was ushered to an exam room for her ultrasound. It was done transvaginally, which surprised her, but even so, the provider (or maybe it was a tech, she can't recall) was unable to get a clear look at the embryo. She would have to come back a couple weeks later so they could try again and be sure there was nothing abnormal about the pregnancy. It was during that two-week gap that she watched Davis filibuster, trying to slow her racing mind that kept trying to build some sort of backup plan in case everything came crashing down before she could get abortion care in Texas. Anything felt possible; her body was braced for an unexpected drop at any minute.

The weeks finally passed, and when she went back to the clinic, the staff was able to get a better look and locate what is sometimes referred to as a "heartbeat," though there is no heart at that point in pregnancy: the sound comes from an electrical current where a heart could potentially develop. "Do you want to see it?" the tech asked Nikiya. "No, I'm good," she responded. They sent her to a pharmacy to pick up medication for any pain that her abortion could cause her, and she went home to wait the required twenty-four hours until she could return to the clinic and get her medical abortion. The next day, for the third time, she made her way into the clinic, past the rabid protesters, so she could take a pill and go back home to take the rest of the medication and complete her abortion. At her follow-up appointment two weeks later, the staff confirmed that it was all over. She doesn't remember a lot of the details of her abortion; she says she blocked a lot of it out. "My abortion saved my life," she says. "I just don't know where I would be now if I had a kid when I was twenty-six, and the federal government would eat me alive because I wasn't able to pay my federal student loans. It allowed me to live a life that I want to live, and I'm grateful that I had access because a lot of people don't."

A couple of years later, Nikiya did have to navigate getting an abortion in the post-HB2 landscape. In some ways, this time around was easier. She had passed the bar and was working as a nonprofit lawyer, and she was much more mentally and emotionally stable without the weight of school and the uncertain future. When we speak, this is the woman I see—confident and unapologetic, with a swipe of red lipstick, full, curly black hair, and a steady gaze—and it's hard to imagine the frightened young student she describes trying to get care years earlier. This time, she needed a surgical abortion, but there were fewer clinics to choose from. Fortunately, she lived in Dallas at the time and was able to get appointments there. The first appointment was without significant incident: she went through the counseling process again and had the ultrasound before returning home to wait out the remaining twenty-four hours before she could get the care she needed. Thankfully, there was only one protester outside this time, but when she arrived for her appointment to have an abortion, she was told the clinic could not accept cards at the time because something was wrong with its system.

Though this time she had health insurance, she could not use it to help offset the cost of the procedure, according to Texas law. She and her partner had to drive back to her house to get her debit card, and then drive around the city and find an ATM. Making matters worse, "you're not supposed to eat before a surgical abortion, so I was pregnant and starving," she recalls. Eventually, they were able to get the cash together, and she had her abortion.

The law was challenged through the courts, and so it began its long journey through the legal system until it reached the Supreme Court in the *Whole Woman's Health v. Hellerstedt* case. On June 27, 2016, after nearly three years of the law's onerous requirements on clinics, the Court issued a 5–3 ruling that said the law was unconstitutional because it created "undue burden" for women seeking care. The opinion, written by Justice Stephen Breyer, underscored that the state had failed to prove medical necessity for clinics to adhere to ambulatory surgical center standards. "Nationwide, childbirth is 14 times more likely than abortion to result in death," he wrote, "but Texas law allows a midwife to oversee childbirth in the patient's own home. Colonoscopy, a procedure that typically takes place outside a hospital (or surgical center) setting, has a mortality rate 10 times higher than an abortion." Breyer also noted that the mortality rate for liposuction, which is also an outpatient procedure, is twenty-eight times that of abortion. Regarding the admitting privileges provision, he wrote: "We add that, when directly asked at oral argument whether Texas knew of a single instance in which the new requirement would have helped even one woman obtain better treatment, Texas admitted that there was no evidence in the record of such a case." It was a clear victory for abortion rights, and it helped clarify the intangible definition of undue burden as put forth in the *Planned Parenthood v. Casey* ruling.

Even so, the damage was done. Over two years, the number of abortion clinics in Texas dropped from more than forty to a scant nineteen. (Texas is the second-largest state in the country in both geographical size and in population, which comes in at around twenty-nine million residents.) Only a few clinics have been able to reopen their doors since that ruling; the now-deceased law changed the landscape of abortion access in Texas for the foreseeable future. "You could have a legal win on paper, and even a really strong one, which we did, but that doesn't necessarily mean communities can recover and clinics can reopen," says Amy Hagstrom Miller, a white woman who served as a plaintiff in *Whole Woman's Health v. Hellerstedt.* "The cruelty of a law like this by its design really does have a lasting impact, and it doesn't improve health and safety—in fact, it rolls it backwards in a very devastating way." Hagstrom Miller owns and operates nine abortion clinics in five states under the Whole Woman's Health brand.

The lasting impact that Hagstrom Miller is referring to is felt the deepest by rural people, low-income people, and people of color. Research by the Texas Policy Evaluation Project at the University of Texas at Austin lays out the toll the law took on patients. Those who lived near a clinic that the law shuttered had to travel, on average, four times farther to access care, which also meant an increase in costs—gas, child care, food, a potential hotel stay. The additional burden also meant a 13 percent increase in second-trimester abortions, which are more expensive and more of an ordeal than a simple first-trimester medication abortion, even as the number of abortions overall declined by 18 percent. At least 100,000 pregnant Texans, and potentially up to 240,000, have attempted to perform an abortion on themselves, according to a 2015 study. While self-managing abortion can be perfectly safe with the right support and knowledge, when pregnant people find their options limited and could be relying on misinformation, there is certainly potential for harm, not to mention the legal risk. The researchers have also found that as of 2015, HB2 had disproportionately affected Hispanic people seeking abortion care. The abortion rate decreased 25 percent among Hispanic women in Texas overall in 2015, two years after HB2 was passed, and those living in a county where a clinic closed saw a 41 percent decrease. For Hispanic women who had to travel a hundred miles or more for abortion care, their odds of getting an abortion decreased by an alarming 43 percent.

The Supreme Court ruling did not automatically invalidate other TRAP laws. According to the Guttmacher Institute, twenty-three states still have regulations that are medically unnecessary and designed to burden clinics. The pressure on clinics has only continued to build in the years since.

CHAPTER 10

The Maze

IN TUSCALOOSA, ALABAMA, the West Alabama Women's Center is among a cluster of nondescript businesses that surround a pool of steaming asphalt. The faded brown brick building is set back, tucked away from the main road, between a crisis pregnancy center and an insurance office. The clinic first opened in 1993, and the building gives off a weary air—*I'm still here*. For now, the weathered white poles across the parking lot from the clinic stand ready but alone; there are no protesters pressing against them today, flailing and shouting to catch the attention of patients. The air is sticky with the rain that never fell but still might. A rusted iron bench waits under the awning that shelters the concrete walkway leading up to steel doors. Hazy, fluorescent light leaks out from foggy, reinforced windows.

Inside, past the receptionist's desk, in the last room on the left down a hallway lined with exam rooms, a Black woman who wants a baby sat in a plastic chair, back straight, legs crossed. Tamika has high cheekbones, a glowing complexion, and wide, expressive eyes framed by feathery eyelashes. She's dressed comfortably for her appointment, in a black mask, black leggings, a black V-neck, and stylish burgundy Nikes. The initial shock of her circumstances has faded, but still, it seems like some sort of cruel joke that this woman who wants to be a mother so badly is getting abortion care. It's 2021, in the final shimmery summer days of August. Hurricane Ida bore down on the Gulf Coast, causing flooding and torrential downpour in Alabama, though everyone is aware that it's much worse to the south, closer to the water.

Rumors of too-full hospitals facing evacuation and nurses that manually pump ventilators to keep patients alive through power outages have been drifting up from Louisiana. The pandemic has crescendoed into another wave with the Delta variant, and people are beginning to realize that the vaccines won't mean a total return to normal, in part because the basic premise of inoculation against dangerous viruses has become politicized to such a degree that large swaths of the population have refused them. An air of dread mingles with the humidity. Tamika's employment ended in April 2021, a little over a year after the pandemic began, and she's been without insurance ever since, complicating her ability to access birth control. She wants to be a mother on her own terms, when she feels she can provide a stable life for her child—and this chapter in which her income is sporadic, she's uninsured, and the world is facing a pandemic that seems to be unending isn't it. "It's hard enough to have a baby when you're financially stable and fully insured, but when you don't have that, that's a whole 'nother level of stress," she says. "And not only stress, it's a whole different ball game when you're poor, Black, and pregnant, especially in the South."

A decade of misdiagnosis had passed before an ob-gyn an hour away in Birmingham finally told Tamika that she had fibroids, and the lost time had decimated her egg count. Before the pandemic, she had been seeing a fertility specialist to explore her options. The visit had been expensive on its own, but when the doctor told her how much it would cost to freeze her eggs, her jaw dropped. The number has remained with her: $28,000. "Money is tight for everybody," she says. "I don't know anybody who just has an extra $28,000 lying around, so it was something I just had to put off. I couldn't afford it."

Her insurance coverage from her old job through Blue Cross Blue Shield expired in May, and after that, she tried everything she could think of to get birth control. Even if the chances of getting pregnant seemed slim, she didn't want to take the risk and lose yet another egg. If she could get pregnant, she wanted it to happen when she could carry to term and start the family she'd been dreaming about. She tried to get health care through the Affordable Care Act, but they wanted to evaluate her eligibility based on the previous year's income, which didn't make sense, now that she was no longer employed. She was denied coverage. She looked into paying for it out of pocket, but it would have set her back $185 monthly; without income, that sort of expense wasn't realistic for her budget. Then, she reached out to the Health Department. She called and left voicemails and sent emails, but everything went unanswered, and taking her chances in a state where many were refusing vaccines even after they finally became available made her uneasy. To enter the Health Department felt risky; people were dying and she did not want to join them. She also contacted a local community clinic and was again met with silence. The uncertainty of the pandemic led to staffing shortages, backed-up patient care, and sporadic, unpredictable hours. Next, she tried online outlets—NURX, The Pill Club, that sort of thing—and at first, it seemed like it might work, but when she disclosed that she was on medication to manage hypertension, she was rendered ineligible. "The health care system has failed me," she says.

Tamika has found some measure of reprieve at West Alabama Women's Center, which is owned by the Yellowhammer Fund, a local abortion fund that was able to assist her with the costs. She says the care she's gotten through them has made her feel somewhat human again. "I thank God for this clinic," she says, and she considers herself lucky to live in Alabama, in a city that still has an abortion clinic, rather than a state like Mississippi. Still, she cannot have what she really wants: stability, a life without the crushing fear of a global pandemic, the resources to raise a child in a safe, healthy environment where she feels she can meet all the needs that could possibly arise for herself and her family. "I don't know if I'll be able to get pregnant again." Her words fall, cold and wet with grief.

She is acutely aware that childbirth for Black women in this country is dangerous. The United States has one of the highest maternal mortality rates among developed nations, and Black women are two to three times more likely to die than their white counterparts. Her past experience with the medical system hasn't left her feeling like her life and the lives of those she loves matter much. One close friend had an ectopic pregnancy that was ignored by her male ob-gyn; she complained of pain and he accused her of trying to get drugs from him.

Tamika was worried, so she sent her friend to see her doctor in Birmingham, who confirmed the pregnancy was ectopic and rushed her new patient into surgery, where she had to remove an ovary in addition to the pregnancy that could have killed her. While she was performing the surgery, she discovered that the woman's pancreas was also in danger of rupturing. Another friend nearly died in childbirth when her baby emerged facing the wrong way and got stuck. She says the doctor used forceps to get him out, damaging his arm and causing severe vaginal tears. Her friend was hemorrhaging, and she says the doctor told her that they needed to "hurry this up"—her shift was ending, and it was picture day at her son's school. These stories haunt Tamika: that they all involve Black women and align with her own experiences cannot be coincidental.

For years, Tamika endured painful heavy periods that stretched on for weeks and left her dizzy and weak. In 2008, when she was newly graduated from college and had just become ineligible to remain on her parents' insurance, the bleeding and the cramping became unbearable. Unsure of what else to do, she went to the state health department, where she was told that finding the right kind of birth control would help her body find a regular menstrual cycle again. For years, she cycled through different types of hormonal contraception. Nothing worked, and she increasingly felt as if she were some sort of alien, struggling to convince people of an entirely different civilization that she was in trouble and needed help. "I'm not asking for a miracle. I just don't want you to put a Band-Aid on a bullet wound and send me out of the door," she says.

When she got her own insurance, she thought it could be the golden ticket to finding some relief. At the very least, she could return to a doctor she was familiar with, a man she had seen when she was covered through her parents. He encouraged her to try an IUD (intrauterine device), but the insertion process was painful. Her pain and the bleeding continued until it reached a point where she lost consciousness, and she was sent to the emergency room because her white blood cell count was too low. She was admitted to the hospital and stayed for five days. The doctors there put her on antibiotics and removed the IUD. Even at the hospital, no one thought to check for fibroids, no matter that an estimated twenty-six million women between the ages of fifteen and fifty suffer from them, or that Black women are two to three times more likely to develop them, and those benign tumors appear at younger ages and are greater in number and more severe than in white women. "Fibroids run in my family: it's just something that Black women are more genetically predisposed to," she says. "All five of my first cousins have it. My grandmother had it."

Inside Tamika, a fibroid that she estimates was about the size of an orange had glommed on to her uterine wall. When the IUD was inserted, it irritated and inflamed the fibroid, amplifying the pain, which radiated throughout her body. She told a cousin about what she was going through, and her cousin sent her to the fertility specialist in Birmingham, a Black woman who quickly performed an ultrasound and diagnosed Tamika. Within three months, the fibroids had all been removed. "She saved my life," Tamika tells me. "She gave me a return to normalcy." The specialist who helped her wasn't a magician: she was a Black woman who knew what to look for, because she knew other Black women were suffering and being dismissed as weak by people who could never fully comprehend the cost of living a life shaped by pain.

Women's bodies are palimpsests of sexist medical presuppositions, influenced by and under the influence of abortion stigma. The history of bodies with uteruses being disregarded when they are ailing winds back centuries, explained away as "hysteria" or assumed as weakness by the medical profession, which has been traditionally controlled by men. This attitude—that women's bodies are defined by how men believe they should function—propels abortion stigma forward and complicates what should be a straightforward practice of basing reproductive health care on the needs and experiences of the patient. Instead of the simplicity of providing medical aid and testing in response to a patient's self-reported symptoms, which seems so much more attainable in other arenas of medicine, people with uteruses are met with skepticism and patronizing attitudes. Tamika was forthright about her pain, and she searched for solutions, but her anguish was not taken seriously. That pattern has altered her reproductive life, her ability to have children on her own terms, her future as a parent. Her basic human rights have been violated.

Abortion stigma does not just affect abortion—it leaks into all aspects of reproductive health care and education. It's present in sex education, birth control practices and attitudes, routine gynecological care, prenatal and postnatal care, and sterilization. Katsi Cook, an elder Mohawk midwife, has observed: "Women are the first environment. We are an embodiment of our Mother Earth. From the bodies of women flows the relationship of the generations both to society and the natural world. With our bodies we nourish, sustain and create connected relationships and interdependence. In this way the Earth is our mother, our ancestors said. In this way, we as women are earth." Her words are wise and powerful; if only women were truly seen this way, if only they were treated with such respect when they seek care for their bodies.

Women of color like Tamika are often faced with institutional racism and generational trauma when they approach the medical profession with a problem, and that's in addition to the general suspicion their gender earns them. Those ingredients concoct a potent poison that has resulted in death, for sure, but also in the loss of life in the sense that people whose bodies are biologically coded female have been unable to live their lives to their fullest potential. These paths of activism were paved precisely because women's bodies, pregnant bodies in particular, are treated like there is already something wrong with them by virtue of their reproductive function. In our culture, "we fundamentally believe that pregnant people are worthy of suspicion and therefore control," points out Rafa Kidvai, Legal Defense Fund director at If/When/How, a reproductive justice nonprofit that seeks to fight the criminalization of pregnancy and abortion.

———————

I**T STARTS YOUNG.** Girlhood is laden with reproductive stigma and stereotype. From the time we are children, we are taught to cosplay as mothers. Dolls are shoved into our arms, and our aspirations are molded to grow toward what patriarchal forces would have us believe is our highest calling, to bear children and raise them to continue to uphold the hierarchical structures that keep sexism and racism firmly in place. Some of us learn as children to care for younger siblings with a maternal air, to keep house, to prepare food for our families, in the unspoken service of one day being a wife and a mother in a nuclear family. When the day comes and we bleed, we are informed that we are no longer children and that this is an important step toward motherhood. In parallel, we learn to fear our bodies and their terrible powers. So long as we are unwed, pregnancy is the second-worst possibility. Abortion is the worst.

Perhaps a girl goes through sex education; perhaps it is abstinence based, as mine was. Maybe the graying, male volleyball coach who heads up the health class begins that week with a droll assessment: "Ladies, everything can be avoided if you'll just keep your legs closed." The rest of the week is filled with a series of photos of infected genitals, a smattering of shame-filled, cautionary tales, maybe some half truths about the effectiveness of birth control. Abortion is too loathsome a word for a room full of children, and still, it is somehow present among the long list of just-don't-do-it consequences of sex, the thing too bad to say out loud. The barriers to reproductive health care start, as Bertram Roberts pointed out to me, before people even have sex.

Birth control is waved away as only somewhat effective; I've heard one abstinence educator liken it to jumping off a roof with a large umbrella, as in, the resistance may slow the fall, but bones will still break, and no one can say for sure how bad it will be, except there will be pain. For my part, I thought condoms had tiny holes in them that sperm could swim through, as if sperm could shrink and pass through rubber at a subatomic level to fulfill the desperate mission to get to an egg. If that's true, then why bother with contraception at all? Perhaps, as a teenager, you hear that birth control is an abortifacient. Abortion, it bears repeating, is the termination of an existing pregnancy. By definition, it can only happen after an egg has been fertilized and an embryo is forming in a uterus. Hormonal contraception prevents pregnancy by stopping ovulation and by thickening the cervical mucus to make it difficult for sperm to swim, which means the egg cannot be fertilized in the first place. It does not terminate an existing pregnancy. Fear of abortion has muddied fact. Stigma taints science.

As we age, it continues. Even beyond the barriers to access to affordable reproductive health care in this country, such as who has the knowledge to navigate that and who does not, a woman's body is still disobedient, with all its blood and power and intricate systems. Procreation seems to be the endgame in American medicine, which often fails to see women as full human beings with their own hopes and fears and wants. This is especially true for white women, whose fertility is prized as a means of continuing a tradition of white-held power in this country. Eighteen states allow physicians to refuse to give a patient a wanted tubal ligation or a hysterectomy, no matter if she already has all the children she wants, no matter if she bleeds so much that her world swims before her eyes. There are plenty of physicians, especially in the more conservative parts of the country, who will ask for spousal consent or refuse care on the basis of a patient's potential to continue to bear children, holding a woman's agency and well-being hostage. Such measures run parallel to abortion bans and restrictions in their tone and intent. They reek of control, of know-better paternalism.

FOR WOMEN OF color, there is a specific element of white supremacist control to the policies that regulate their bodies. It's hard to hear a story like Tamika's and think anything more optimistic than that all the doctors who saw her simply didn't care about her. They could not be bothered with her pain, her fertility, her aspirations, her autonomy. She did not have money, nor insurance, nor light skin, nor any advocate beyond herself. Reproductive care is racialized. The politicization of abortion affects all people with uteruses, but we cannot ignore the different degrees and nuances to who gets what sort of care and how. Black women who seek abortion care are also accused of committing genocide against their own people. Predominantly white antiabortion organizations have installed billboards in Black neighborhoods with twisted versions of antiracism slogans: "Black Babies Matter" and the like.

When she was walking into West Alabama Women's Center for her first appointment, Tamika was subjected to the opinions of "two gentlemen," as she generously calls them. They shouted at her about her baby's heartbeat, and she suppressed her rage, but let an eye roll through her composure. "That's fine and dandy. I know that my baby has a heartbeat," she says, sarcasm coating her words. "I have a heartbeat. The Black men that are being slaughtered in the streets have heartbeats, too. And nobody seems to care about that." These issues are related, whether the (most often white) people who stand outside of clinics want to acknowledge it or not. Political activist Angela Davis wrote: "When Black and Latina women resort to abortions in such large numbers, the stories they tell are not so much about their desire to be free of their pregnancy, but rather about the miserable social conditions which dissuade them from bringing new lives into the world."

Latinx pregnant people experience their own barriers to abortion care. I am not, however, here to perpetuate the myth that Latinx folks are somehow more antichoice than everyone else because they are often Catholic. In her book *De Colores Means All of Us: Latina Views for a Multi-Colored Century*, Elizabeth Sutherland Martínez writes that "Latinas' views on reproductive rights are often more radical than Anglo women's views and not 'conservative,' as some people say, because their definition of choice requires more profound social change than just abortion rights or preventing pregnancy." Assumptions to the contrary are rooted in "a racist arrogance," Martínez points out, a white feminist paternalism that uses general knowledge of Catholicism as a "guise of understanding our culture," while shoving off any real responsibility to engage with Latinx rights. Latinx pregnant people in the United States are also subject to a medical system that has long disregarded their needs and historically seen their bodies as more appropriate for medical testing than genuine care. For undocumented folks, medical care poses a threat to their safety, their families, their home: they fear medical staff will expose their status and they will be deported, and of course, having federally subsidized medical insurance is out of the question. If they live in a border state like Texas, perhaps they must pass through immigration checkpoints to get to a place that offers care, risking deportation in a different way. In this country, we care so much less about the humanity of nonwhite people than we do about upholding white supremacy, no matter how "pro-life" we may claim to be.

Abortion stigma infects prenatal care when the life of a fetus—no matter how wanted, that's not part of this conversation—becomes more important to the medical decision makers than that of the mother. In postnatal care, after the baby is born, the shadow of abortion stigma appears in the casual it's-just-the-blues dismissal of postpartum depression and in our culture's saintly, shiny portrayal of new motherhood as a state of heightened being, rather than of someone who needs support—from a partner, from the government, from a medical team. The baby has been born; pro-life mission accomplished. All done.

There are also immediate barriers to abortion care. Before *Roe* was overturned, a young Black woman I met in Huntsville named Jazmin told me that when her gynecologist confirmed her pregnancy the week prior, she claimed that abortion in Alabama was illegal. That was not true, and it's difficult to believe anyone who practices medicine could be honestly mistaken about such a thing. As a reporter who has covered reproductive health for more than six years, I've heard from people of all backgrounds about what has made it difficult or impossible for them to access abortion care when they needed it. Money has consistently been the biggest barrier, especially when travel is necessary. Among the many other obstacles are: inability to get paid time off for the procedure and to accommodate any extra appointments required by the state due to waiting periods; transportation challenges because the patient shares a car with several other members of their family or the bus routes in their city are unreliable or they can't afford gas or they have to travel to another state entirely to get help; and difficulty getting childcare (at least 60 percent of abortion patients already have at least one child). Appointments are frequently cancelled or missed because of unexpected bad weather; cancellation of the fly-in abortion provider's flight, rendering the provider unable to get to the clinic; or a mix-up because the patient accidentally went into the crisis pregnancy center next door to the clinic and was kept there so long that they missed their appointment.

Interior barriers may also exist, and those cannot be discounted: An abusive partner who intentionally impregnated them so they couldn't leave once and for all. PTSD. The crushing weight of what it means to be a person seeking abortion care in a hostile state.

That night after I met Tamika, the clock inched closer to midnight. Time was running out for the Supreme Court to weigh in on a new Texas law, set to go into effect on September 1, that would ban abortion after about six weeks' gestation. The law also encouraged vigilantism among antiabortion citizens by including a clause that promised a $10,000 bounty to any citizen—not necessarily a resident of Texas—who reports an instance of someone "aiding and abetting" abortion past six weeks that checks out and results in prosecution.

That afternoon, I was confident that the Court would intervene. The law was clearly unconstitutional, violating the trimester framework established in *Roe* and the undue burden standard of *Casey*. Besides, they've always intervened in state measures that so blatantly disregarded precedent. Alone in a featureless hotel room in Tuscaloosa, I lay in bed, refreshing Twitter over and over, feeling increasingly anxious. Midnight came and went. The law stood.

CHAPTER 11

The "Abortionist"

IN EVERY ABORTION provider's life, there are two specific, significant moments—one in which they realize that they want to provide abortion care as part of their medical practice, and another wherein they understand what it really means to do that work. For Dr. Aaron Campbell, that first moment came shortly after his father's death.

Campbell originally double-majored in biochemistry and philosophy when he was a student at the University of Tennessee, Knoxville, but he always knew medicine would be the path he would eventually choose when it came to his life's work. (He dressed up as an ob-gyn for Halloween when he was fourteen years old, in 2005, stepping into his father's everyday uniform for the first time.) As a student, he was a regular presence at the only independent abortion clinic in Knoxville, where his father served as medical director. The building was just a block north of campus, and he would routinely swing by in between classes to bring his dad some Boston Kreme doughnuts from a bustling Dunkin' Donuts that was wedged inside the ground floor of one of the residence halls. Father and son would share the treats and catch up.

It was during one such visit where Campbell saw the products of conception for the first time. "I was already pro-choice at that point," he said, "but I think if anyone sees something like that it completes part of an understanding of what really happens." He found that he was fascinated, not repulsed. At the stage in pregnancy when most abortions are performed, at around eight weeks, he added, it's a gestational sac and pregnancy tissue.

Dr. Morris Campbell had been an ob-gyn since long before the birth of his son, whom he delivered himself. Soon after Aaron entered the world, he decided to quit delivering babies and focus on helping the pregnant people who came through his doors who did not want to continue their pregnancy. As time went on, he began to also pitch in beyond his own practice—providing care at the Knoxville Planned Parenthood and occasionally driving a few hours west to Nashville to help out there as well.

Once, when Aaron was a boy, father and son went on a road trip. It was in that in-between of adolescence when the world is starting to come into sharper relief, with all its texture and complexities and gray-toned mystery. He was starting to understand what his dad did when he went to work. As a kid in East Tennessee, he sensed the discomfort around the word *abortion* in his community. It was beginning to dawn on him that his dad's occupation had led to some precautions the family took that he didn't see in his friends' families: living a half hour away from the clinic, remaining unlisted in the phone book, being told to simply say his dad was a doctor if he was asked by someone unfamiliar. He wanted to know why his dad was an abortion provider. Morris probably anticipated these questions from his inquisitive boy, and he told him about what it was like to graduate medical school in 1973, the year the *Roe v. Wade* decision came down from the Supreme Court. He told his son that when he was a student, he saw the damage caused by outlawing abortion—the lives that were ruined, the bodies that were brutalized. He saw women sent away to what he referred to as "Aunt Sally's farm" for the summer, clouded in shame, only to return in the autumn with a baby, as if it had magically appeared, as if there had been no blood or pain or mucus or sex. As if life remained unchanged.

"He didn't like the way that women were treated who had unintended or undesired pregnancy," Aaron recalls. Upon hearing this, respect settled in his slight chest, and as he grew, so did that feeling. Now, he has a coat hanger tattooed at the top of his left forearm, usually hidden by his shirtsleeve, but it serves as a physical symbol of that conversation and of his father's legacy.

In June 2012, between his junior and senior years of college, everything changed. His father had a hemorrhagic stroke. For a few years, Morris had felt his heartbeat quickening, thumping out unpredictable rhythms in his chest, and he had been diagnosed with atrial fibrillation, which was being treated with blood thinners. Aaron reckons that a blood vessel burst and that, combined with his high blood pressure, made it difficult for his body to recover. Aaron's parents were recently divorced by then, and Morris had given Aaron his power of attorney. Morris was not the sort of person to leave much up to chance, and he had discussed his wishes with Aaron consistently from the time Aaron was in middle school. Still, it's not a decision that a son can make with total clarity.

Early the next morning after the stroke, Aaron called the clinic and told them what had happened. About a week later, when he understood that his father would not recover, he told the doctors to extubate him and let him go. When he talks about what happened, he still leans on medical terminology to describe the events as a way of keeping his emotions in check.

After his father's death, it was clear to Aaron that he needed to accelerate his career. Some of his classmates openly celebrated his father's passing because of his career as an abortion provider, which hurt, of course, but it also cemented his determination to continue his work. In a place that put up as many challenges to abortion as it could, even the loss of one doctor was significant. He dropped the double major, downgrading his philosophy major to a minor to graduate a semester early, and transferred to medical school at East Tennessee State University (ETSU) in Johnson City, a little more than an hour and a half deeper into Appalachia.

In the meantime, he knew the clinic was in good hands with Dr. Susan Dodd, who worked with his father and stepped in as medical director of the Knoxville Center for Reproductive Health (KCRH) after Morris passed. As Aaron continued his studies and began rotations, he felt a deeper affirmation that he was on the right track, that this was the thing he could do to make the world a better place for the rest of his life. The determination was important: abortion stigma runs through the medical field as well, and in a part of the country where culture and religion are inextricable, it can be even more challenging to get the training necessary to provide abortion care. At ETSU, he founded a chapter of Medical Students for Choice, which helped him assemble a community of students with similar philosophies and career goals, while ruffling some feathers along the way.

As a fourth-year resident, he ran into trouble when he encountered a patient on his rounds who was eighteen weeks and five days into her pregnancy and clearly unhappy about it. "Even in medical school, I never would walk into a room and be like, congratulations, because it's not always a happy thing for people," he says. "So I would always ask people how they felt about it first." He asked her if the pregnancy was desired; she told him she didn't know. "Well, if you want to continue your pregnancy, we'll be happy to take care of you here," he said gently. "But if you don't, the closest place you can go at this point in your pregnancy is Atlanta." His senior resident was displeased, and she made her anger known in her evaluation of his performance. Though she did not explicitly mention the incident, Aaron is certain that it stemmed from his willingness to discuss abortion with a patient. A bad evaluation could have wrecked his career before it began, making it nearly impossible for him to be matched with a specialty residency program. Aaron fought the assessment and was eventually given a new evaluation, written instead by his clerkship director, which helped him get into a rotation at the Magee-Womens Hospital in Pittsburgh. In his applications, he made it clear that he intended to follow in his father's footsteps as an abortion provider. After four years, he was finally fully credentialed, and it was time to come home to KCRH. He graduated in May 2021, the board of KCRH appointed him medical director that June, and he was back in Knoxville, settled into an apartment near the clinic by the beginning of July.

DR. LEAH TORRES, too, was drawn to women's health care as an undergraduate at the University of Michigan. It was in "the obligatory liberal arts women's studies class that every female college student has to do," she jokes, that she learned a study at Rockefeller University in New York City on how obesity affects breast and uterine cancer had used only male subjects to study the diseases. Like Dr. Campbell, when she was in medical school, she found a home in the University of Illinois Chicago's College of Medicine's chapter of Medical Students for Choice. The organization helped her navigate the dissonance of studying obstetrics and gynecology in the United States, which is deeply influenced by what is known as the Church Amendments.

Enacted by Congress in 1973, the same year that abortion became legal through the *Roe v. Wade* ruling, the amendments are a set of provisions that protect anyone who declines reproductive care such as sterilization or abortion on the basis of their religious beliefs. Medical students, too, can opt out of training for these reasons, which perpetuates a knowledge gap in reproductive health care. Encountering practitioners and classmates who invoke protection under the Church Amendments while in medical school is common: Dr. Torres, for her part, recalls performing a tubal ligation as a second-year resident at a clinic in Pennsylvania, as another resident who was senior to her stepped back from the table and folded her hands because the patient was still of reproductive age and the procedure was voluntary. The other resident was Catholic, and any time a patient needed contraceptive services, she asked Dr. Torres to step in for her. "When you are in a position of power, you do not get to oppress others with your personal beliefs, and that is what physicians do [under the Church Amendments]," she explains. "They impose their personal beliefs on their patients. It causes harm, and it can get people killed."

As a result of cultural bias seeping into policy, abortion stigma has taken a toll on the number of providers in the United States. Over time, more and more barriers have sprung up between students and access to abortion provision as a routine part of their medical education. According to a study published in 2020 by researchers at Stanford University, half of all medical schools did not include abortion training in their curriculum, or they only provided a single lecture on the subject. "Abortion is one of the most common medical procedures," the researchers wrote. "Yet abortion-related topics are glaringly absent from medical school curricula."

Another survey shows that despite a requirement established by the Accreditation Council for Graduate Medical Education (ACGME) to offer standard abortion education, 5 percent of responding ob-gyn residency programs fail to do so, while 31 percent said the training was optional, which is out of compliance with ACGME requirements. As of 2017, among practicing obstetrician-gynecologists, only 24 percent of those surveyed performed abortions, even though the procedure is clearly in high demand: 72 percent of those doctors reported they had received requests for abortion care.

Here, too, geography matters. A 2020 study found that while nationally 57 percent of teaching hospitals have "institutional policies limited abortion [training] beyond state laws," the majority of these hospitals are concentrated in the South and Midwest, regions that have largely been post-*Roe* for years, long before the ruling was actually overturned. Those regions are also experiencing a decline in clinics, which means fewer employment opportunities (and that's before we factor in what it means to be an abortion provider in a state that is hostile to the procedure). According to the Guttmacher Institute, between 2014 and 2017, the number of clinics in the South decreased by 9 percent. In the Midwest, they decreased by 6 percent. Students in the states where abortion access arguably matters the most have the hardest road to getting abortion training.

As a student and later as a resident, when Dr. Torres would ask for specific training in abortion care, she was often hand-waved and told that miscarriage management via DNC was the same thing as abortion, and therefore she had all the knowledge necessary. "Not even close," she says now. "You are talking about a completely different patient. Sure, it's step-by-step the same procedure, but when you're talking to people and you're learning about them and about how to treat them and care for them, it is a very different scenario." She was adamant that she get that sort of training and experience, and so she applied for a fellowship specifically in abortion care. It took her to Salt Lake City, Utah, where she learned to provide abortion up to twenty-two weeks, which was about the gestational limit in the state at that time. Most importantly, she learned how to connect with people from all sorts of cultural and ideological backgrounds, including the "I need an abortion but I don't believe in it" sort of person who is wrestling with deep-set, internalized stigma.

Of course, to even get to the point where a doctor has to worry about the ever-mutating cost of ballooning state restrictions and the potential hostility of conservative neighbors, the initial stigma of marrying their identity with abortion care must be overcome first. Dr. Torres is regularly featured on antiabortion websites, some of which precede her name with dramatic descriptors like "notorious abortionist." This sort of title—"abortionist"—is outdated and clunky and conjures images of beefy, dirty men holding rusty speculums under flickering, near-dead light bulbs and cackling. The stigma lingers from pre-*Roe* days. In her book, *Doctors of Conscience: The Struggle to Provide Abortion Before and After* Roe v. Wade, sociologist Carole Joffe interviewed a New York abortion provider who is given the pseudonym Daniel Fieldstone (the protection is necessary because he provided abortion care before the state had legalized the procedure). He reflected on the language of the pre-*Roe* days, telling Joffe: "'Abortion' was such a dirty word then . . . and 'abortionist' was such a dirty word, it was one step above a pervert, or a child abuser . . . it was incredible, to be called an abortionist in the 1950s, you were the scum of the earth." It's also reductive, given that abortion providers tend to impart critical reproductive health care outside of abortion services. This is why antiabortion groups love to use the word. It drops like dead weight. Abortionist. Going into this field means reckoning with the likelihood that antiabortion activists will try to mine your personal data and publish it online, and that when your name is googled, sites like LifeNews.com and LiveAction.org will pop up with gruesome accusations, and not much can be done about it.

KNOXVILLE, WHERE DR. CAMPBELL has chosen to take over his father's former practice, is currently down to one clinic: KCRH. The Planned Parenthood in town was closed for renovations after someone set fire to the building on New Year's Eve 2021, destroying it. That it was ruled as an arson didn't come as a surprise, given that the clinic had been previously shot at in the hours before it opened less than a year before the arson. (No one was injured.) Before *Roe* was overturned, the other clinic that offered abortion care in the region was two hours away in Bristol, but it had a cutoff after fourteen weeks of pregnancy; Knoxville Center for Reproductive Health provided care up to eighteen weeks. Tennessee's law before the *Dobbs* ruling banned abortion at fetal viability, a somewhat fuzzy standard estimated to be around twenty-four weeks for most pregnancies. The law, as of this writing, bans abortion after about six weeks, and the state is on track to outlaw abortion entirely per its trigger law. Most of the patients KCRH serves are low-income Tennesseans; according to the clinic's operations director, more than half live at or below the poverty line. Forty-eight hours after their initial appointment, patients were required to make a return trip to the clinic for their abortion, in accordance with state law.

Dr. Campbell hadn't even been back in Knoxville for a full year before he was forced to reckon with the very real possibility that his home state could force him out of a job. In the 2021–2022 Tennessee legislative session, a bill to ban abortion outright was introduced. For an initial committee hearing on the bill, Campbell put on a purple paisley tie that belonged to his father, carefully combed his hair back, and drove three and a half hours west to Nashville to testify in the House Health Subcommittee in mid-March. On the floor, he spoke in a measured tone, reading from his iPhone well-known statistics that have been heard in this chamber and in many others— that one in four women in the United States will have an abortion in her lifetime, and that complications from abortion are markedly higher in countries where the procedure is heavily restricted. He glanced up intermittently, but he didn't seem to study the uninterested faces of the lawmakers in the chamber. Reason wouldn't sway them, nor would emotion. This is well-trod territory. But giving up, not appearing at all, was unthinkable. "Patient safety is paramount, and patient safety will be affected by this bill," he explained.

Solemnly, Campbell described scenarios in which patients may endure inevitable miscarriage, in which a fetus still has cardiac activity though a miscarriage is well underway, putting the pregnant person at risk of an intrauterine infection, which could lead to sepsis and death. He also referred to nonviable genetic fetal abnormalities. "These are not straightforward issues, and a blanket bill, like this bill, undermines the complexity of health care issues that may be experienced by pregnant women and their physicians," he told the lawmakers. There were no questions or comments, no response at all to his testimony. The rest of the session was devoted to questions about the legislation, most of which seemed to make the bill's sponsor, state representative Rebecca Alexander, uncomfortable. "My intent with this bill is to protect the unborn," she repeated in lieu of direct answers on the mechanics of the measure. It was approved and sent to full committee.

"On one hand, it feels very futile," Campbell said. "On the other hand, there is that part deep down that says you need to do the right thing." Though, ultimately, he added, "They don't give a shit what I have to say."

The legislature did eventually pull the bill from consideration, but only because they have a six-week ban on abortion making its way through the courts, and Republican leadership worried that passing another ban might hinder their previous effort, which is further along in the legal process. Now that the Supreme Court has overturned *Roe v. Wade*, that law is in effect. Campbell knows that his life doesn't have to be this complicated. "It would be a lot easier somewhere else. But that's not where people need to be," he said. "We need to be in states that are hostile to the provision of safe abortion." Still, he's put feelers out for work in other states—just in case he soon finds himself with too much time on his hands.

———

I N MARCH 2020, Dr. Torres was walking around downtown Louisville, Kentucky, taking a break from an Abortion Care Network meeting that she had traveled to the southeast for, when her phone rang. It was Robin Marty, an abortion rights journalist turned activist. "Hey, what are you doing these days?" Robin chirped into the phone. Dr. Torres answered in her usual sardonic monotone. "Uh, I'm in New Mexico," she replied. "I'm in a town in like No-bodysville and there are a bunch of MAGA people, and I hate them all, and I make good money, but it's corporate medicine, and I'm slowly dying a very slow, very painful death."

"Do you wanna be medical director of a clinic that focuses on comprehensive reproductive health, like doing all of the things including abortion and expanding services at an abortion clinic?"

Dr. Torres paused. "What plane am I getting on?" Robin laughed. "Don't you want to know where it is?" "Nope. What plane am I getting on?"

Robin had recently been brought on to handle communications at the Yellowhammer Fund, an Alabama abortion fund that saw a windfall of cash in 2019 after the state tried (and failed) to ban abortion. The fund was preparing to purchase the West Alabama Women's Center from Gloria Gray, who owned and operated the clinic for almost thirty years and was ready to retire and spend more time with her family. Besides, the work—the constant onslaught of new, expensive regulations and the everyday shouts of the protesters who liked to loudly apprise the carefully coiffed, made-up woman in her sixties that she was earning a living off dead-baby blood money—had been wearing on her. (Once, a protester tracked down her mother's phone number and called her to berate her for her daughter's employment.) The clinic's patient load had increased as well, and was at a point where the West Alabama Women's Center was providing more than half of all abortions in the state. Gloria was tired, and she had been looking for a buyer since 2017. So she went an unconventional route and approached Yellowhammer.

They accepted, and the two parties hashed out details for the sale and for the management transition. The deal was significant for a few reasons. Many clinic owners are of an older generation less bogged down by student debt and the consequences of the 2008 recession; they purchased their businesses when the economy was steadier and the wealth gap was less. Consequently, the younger generation of abortion rights activists has been less likely to work with or as abortion providers and more likely to work with abortion funds or in general activism, which have a lower economic barrier to entry. The Yellowhammer deal made it economically feasible for younger activists to purchase the clinic, enabling them to buy it as a collective rather than individually, and with ownership of the clinic, they were given a chance to change the model of the clinic to center reproductive justice and offer full-spectrum care, including gynecological care for transgender patients.

In July 2020, Dr. Torres made the move from New Mexico to Tuscaloosa, Alabama, also home to one of the state's lauded universities (and by "universities" I mean "football teams"). She came in to replace the clinic's physician of more than twenty-five years, Dr. Louis Payne, who was also retiring. Now, Dr. Torres works in a small back office she shares with Robin, who has become the clinic's director of operations and Jill-of-all-trades. When Dr. Torres isn't with patients, she can be found in that office, hunched over her computer filling out paperwork or answering emails or swearing at Twitter, usually while Robin cracks wise across from her and occasionally urges her to eat something with more nutritional value than a handful of Reese's Pieces from a nearby candy dispenser. Above Dr. Torres's head of cropped tousled curls is her framed Alabama medical license, stark against navy marbled wallpaper. It would be an unremarkable piece of doctor's office accoutrement, except for the homemade price tag affixed to it: $115,360.93.

When Dr. Torres came to Tuscaloosa, she had to first apply for a temporary Alabama medical license so she could practice medicine while waiting for her permanent license to clear. (The coronavirus pandemic complicated systems that were not exactly operating at the height of efficiency before the disaster.) Shortly after she began her new job, toward the end of August, two men from the Alabama medical board came into the clinic when Dr. Torres was in the middle of performing a dilation and curettage procedure on a patient who had come in with excessive bleeding and needed the tissue removed from her uterus. The clinic's staff told the men they would need to wait, despite their protestations. After Dr. Torres was done, the men informed her that they were revoking her temporary license. They handed her a letter saying as much, asked her to sign a paper confirming that she had received the information and understood its implications, and told her to surrender her temporary license. "Had they showed up five minutes earlier, I don't even want to think about what would happen to that patient if I couldn't see her," she says. "I also can't speak to the patients that we had to turn away, patients that were in the waiting room. I don't know what their stories were. I could have had another patient bleeding like that. I don't know." She estimates that the clinic staff was forced to turn away at least a hundred patients—maybe two hundred—as a result. "They compromised a lot of people's health that day."

The state was alleging that Dr. Torres made fraudulent statements in her application for an Alabama license. On her application, one of the questions the state asked was whether Dr. Torres had had any court action taken against her; she had answered no because although she had a malpractice lawsuit in another state, it had been settled and never made it to court. She knew about the error; she received an email in July that said the question was meant to inquire about any malpractice claim. Dr. Torres replied to apologize for the misunderstanding and included all the documents relevant to the case for the state to review. She never got a response, and so she assumed that all was well. She had made herself available to them and had included all the relevant documents, so what else was there to say? She had licenses in Vermont, New Mexico, and Iowa, and this had never tripped up the process. Plus, lawsuits happen all the time in the medical realm. These days, it's an inherent risk of choosing to be any kind of doctor.

The medical board's scrutiny of her application may have begun with a complaint that was filed against her by another physician— someone she's never met—just twelve days after she moved to the state. The complainant was taking issue with an interview she had done in 2019 while she was practicing in New Mexico, during which she instructed listeners on ways to end their pregnancies without their partners' knowledge. This physician cited an antiabortion blog post summarizing the discussion, which means it's unlikely that the complainant listened to the full interview. Robin suspects that the complaint was filed in tandem with antiabortion organizing around a patient who died an hour away in Birmingham after receiving abortion care and leaving the clinic, though Dr. Torres was not yet practicing at the clinic at the time. The incident was investigated by the Tuscaloosa County Sheriff's Office and the Alabama Board of Medical Examiners, and neither entity found a basis for criminal charges. A protest was held in the clinic parking lot on August 15; the complaint was filed the same day. That the clinic was not found to be at fault in the woman's death enraged antiabortion activists (often referred to simply as "antis" in abortion rights circles), and Robin ventures that the revocation of Dr. Torres's medical license and the drawn-out bureaucracy that followed was the state medical board's attempt to quench the outrage. "They're going to regret valuing the antis over my wrath, but it's cool," Dr. Torres remarks breezily. Her humor comes with an edge, but it's well-earned.

The letter informed her that there was a hearing set for December 21, which would be the earliest date at which she could appeal the revocation to the medical licensure commission. Such organizations are, by nature, nonpartisan, but given that they are comprised of professionals that were selected by elected officials, political slants all too often seep through. That four-month wait seemed laughable; indeed, Dr. Torres says that there were physicians who had their licenses revoked after she did, and their licenses were in the process of being reinstated before she even got the chance to defend herself. Notably, none of them were abortion providers. Additionally, she was summoned for a deposition in November.

The hearing was scheduled to begin at 10 A.M.; it did not start till 10:30 A.M. Dr. Torres, anxious to return to work, arrived early with her team, and they settled in around the long conference table. Dr. Torres and her legal team brought three character witnesses, but only one was permitted to speak. This expert witness testified that the question regarding whether Dr. Torres had any court action taken against her over the course of her career was unclear from a linguistics standpoint, but the commission rejected this testimony without justification.

She recalls being subjected to questions such as, "Are you a real doctor?" and "Do you speak English?" Dr. Torres's father's side of the family is Mexican American, though she is white (she is an adoptee), and her fluency in Spanish comes from a year and a half spent studying abroad in Spain. The question of her language was asked because of her last name. They went so far as to demand she read aloud in English and define words they chose at random to prove her fluency. The questioning escalated into accusations that she was lying by wearing her white coat, which is the professional standard, and that because her license had been suspended in Alabama, she was no longer a doctor. By donning her white coat, they argued, she was somehow continuing to practice medicine. She snorts, remembering. "Even if I decide to teach underwater basket weaving, I'm still a doctor," she says. "I will be a doctor till I die. It will be on my tombstone."

Even though being the object of racist assumptions and sexism has become a sort of pervasive baseline of her life, she tells me, the attacks on her character set her on edge. Adding to the insult was the meandering pace of the day—the majority white, male commission adjourned for a leisurely lunch break, and then insisted on ending the day at 5 P.M., naturally having not finished the business of the appeal. It would have to wait till after the holidays, when they next met, which wouldn't be until the end of January. Dr. Torres's lawyers fought the move to adjourn, arguing that she had been without her legal license for too long already and that innocent people were suffering because of it. The commission was not swayed.

Still, Dr. Torres and Robin and the rest of the clinic staff looked forward to the next hearing, scheduled for January 21, as a likely end to the turmoil. The West Alabama Women's Center had hired a provider on contract while Dr. Torres was out of commission, but for three weeks in January, they had been forced to suspend services because the interim provider had been exposed to COVID-19. Instead, they fundraised and worked to send as many patients as they could to other clinics.

The day of the meeting came and went—Dr. Torres was not permitted to attend this one, as it was for the board to deliberate, but her lawyers assured her that the decision would come in her favor—but there was no word on the outcome. After a couple of days, the lawyers called for the decision, but it wasn't the straightforward victory they had hoped for. Though her license was to be reinstated, it came with conditions. Time-consuming, expensive conditions. A $4,000 nondisciplinary fine, which of course was in addition to the ever-increasing legal fees, and a choice between two specific ethics courses: one that would require her to travel to Case Western University in Ohio, but the next available date was in September, and the other, an online course that began February 26. She paid the fine and registered for the online class, and her lawyers filed a motion to reinstate her license at the next month's board meeting, which was on February 23. The motion was denied, on the grounds that she had not completed the class yet.

They would not meet again until March, which also meant the clinic staff would have to do their best to reroute the hundred or so patients they had begun to book in anticipation of Dr. Torres's return. The days between the monthly dates when the medical board would engage with her case crawled. The anxious wait, the snarled bureaucracy, the inability to practice medicine made her feel like a criminal, like she had done something far more serious than misunderstand a question on a form.

The required ethics classes were tedious and exhausting. ("I called them my parole meetings," she remarks dryly.) There was an initial two-day course, and then they met for an hour each Thursday night for twelve weeks, and this, too, cost money. The board agreed to reinstate her license at their March meeting, before she had completed all twelve weeks of meetings, so long as the initial two-day class was under her belt. On March 24, her license was reinstated and she went back to work at the clinic.

It's not like abortion providers are compensated for the risk and the emotional labor that comes with the job. In a November 2021 survey of abortion providers in the South, one doctor says, "No one does this for the money or the lifestyle." Torres, too, is frank about money: she took a substantial pay cut to be able to practice the sort of medicine she's passionate about.

Neither Dr. Torres nor Dr. Campbell spend a lot of time fearing for their personal safety, but they are conscious of how they move through the world. "[Abortion providers] reasonably don't want to take the risk to live somewhere like here, or somewhere else in the Bible Belt, or the South in general," Dr. Campbell acknowledges. "It doesn't feel as safe." For his part, Dr. Campbell tries to walk a line between "theoretical risk" and "actual risk."

"Yeah, theoretically, I could walk out of my clinic and get shot. Is that gonna actually happen? Probably not. Could it happen? Yeah." He pauses briefly. "I hope I don't know about it. And I hope they do a good job. And it goes quickly."

While antiabortion violence is a real threat, it's been thirteen years since the last abortion provider was murdered in the United States, and besides, being afraid isn't a preventative measure, and they're practical people. Still, part of that practicality is taking some preventative measures. Dr. Torres has been speaking out for abortion rights for a long time, and she has a slew of antiabortion websites to prove that there are a lot of people out there who say they want to do her harm, at least from behind a keyboard. The first day she arrived at West Alabama Women's Center, her car still had New Mexico license plates, but when she stepped out of the vehicle, the protesters immediately turned their attention to her. "Hey, doc," they greeted her. The intent was clear: they were letting her know that they knew who she was and that they were watching. So, she's careful. She doesn't have mail delivered to her house. When a well-meaning friend meant to surprise her with a book, she started at seeing a package on her doorstep, heart hammering at a sight that would be benign to most people. Her house, by the way, is under a different name, and she doesn't put anything in the recycling that could identify her. "It's crazy, but this is how I live. I live in a state of vigilance," she explains, "because there are people who legit want to kill me. They want me murdered because I provide health care." She won't hide, she says. Instead, she describes herself as attentive. The risk and the stigma are part of why they do it; it's why it's *necessary*.

Now, of course, the stakes are higher. Torres and Campbell are both all too aware that their jobs, the careers that they pursued to better take care of patients, are on the line. Tennessee is Campbell's home, but he reckons that if his work becomes illegal, he'll pack up and move to a state where he can legally provide abortion and pitch in where the influx of patients who have traveled hundreds of miles for care is becoming too much. As for Torres, she says Alabama is stuck with her. There's plenty of reproductive health care she can provide if abortion is no longer legal. "Are you kidding me?" she says when I ask her if she'll leave the South. "I paid $115,000 for my license. I'm not going anywhere. I'm invested."

CHAPTER 12

In Defense

AT THE PLANNED PARENTHOOD clinic in Midtown, a retro boombox is blaring the familiar get-up-and-dance rhythm of the Spice Girls' hit song from the 1990s, "Wannabe."

The "girl power" playlist, which includes anthems from Kelly Clarkson and Britney Spears, is courtesy of a tiny blond lady in her fifties who sports a pink ball cap with the Planned Parenthood insignia, a neon pink traffic vest with a matching umbrella to shield patients from protesters, and demure pearl earrings. Her name is Mary Loveless, and she's a self-described southern debutante who has lived in Memphis all her life—well, except for her time as a student at Vanderbilt University up the road in Nashville and the five years she remained in Tennessee's capital after graduation. She works as a clinic escort, in part, because she remembers what it was like in the years before the *Roe v. Wade* ruling. Her classmates at the all-girls' private school she attended in Memphis would sometimes take trips to New York City after the state legalized abortion. "It was just kind of common knowledge, they'd go on these little trips to New York— that was the big place—they'd go to New York and, you know, have an abortion and see a couple of plays," she says. She knew there were girls that weren't so lucky. Mary speaks with the soft, precise southern accent of wealth and privilege, both factors that she sees clearly as having shaped her life.

Mary is sharing her shift with a white woman in her midthirties who I'll refer to as Joan, which is the code name the escorts share in honor of Jane in Chicago. She's been volunteering at the clinic for about a year, and she says her husband doesn't know that she does this. She comes to the clinic after he leaves for work and before her own job starts and sometimes on her lunch break, too. Joan is from a small town in Arkansas—she describes it as "very churchy"—but she identified as a feminist from a young age. While she was in college, she had a few pregnancy scares and suddenly the hurdles that she would have to overcome should she need an abortion came into sharper focus. "You start to realize that you don't really have anything close by, you don't really have anybody that you can lean on, because this topic is so politicized," she says, adding "and there's so many religious bigots that basically just make you feel like shit for even being sexually active." Planned Parenthood was a reliable hub for care, and she felt drawn to its mission, especially as donating and calling legislators began to feel like a paltry effort next to the growing threat that abortion rights could be lost.

When she began her work as a clinic escort, she was about five months pregnant, and she wore baggy clothes to hide her growing belly. Pregnancy toughened her resolve to do everything in her power to help fight for abortion rights. She had wanted to have a baby, and she felt strongly that everyone should be able to choose parenthood on their own terms. Every time she comes out for an escort shift, she admits, her nerves prickle. "You don't know what to expect," she says, and she worries about being "outed" as a clinic escort by the antiabortion protesters. But being here, ready to shield patients from the shouting and signs with a comically large umbrella to make them feel safe, is the most important thing.

The sun climbs in the sky as the morning slips away, and more protesters begin to cluster on the sidewalk. A black car pulls through the gate and into the parking lot, and the doors remain closed for a while after the engine cuts off. On the other side of the gate is a white man dressed in jeans and a black hoodie; he eyes the car and then walks toward it, lingering on the sidewalk in front of the car. As soon as the door opens, he starts his spiel about how he knows she doesn't want to do this, how they can help her if she'll just walk next door to the crisis pregnancy center. The woman who climbs out of the car is beautiful, with fine braids that hang down to her waist. She ignores the white man and opens the back door, lifting a little girl from a car seat. Joan rushes over, explains that she is there to help get the woman and her child safely inside and blocks them both from the man's sight using her umbrella. The group walks together a bit before the woman assures Joan that she's fine, she's just picking up test results anyway, and she strides toward the clinic on her own, head held high, her little girl's hand in hers. The man is still yelling about how perfect her child is, how she is made in the image of God, how he cannot bear the thought of her sibling being murdered. Won't she just come over to the sidewalk and come get a gift bag? The door closes with a soft hiss behind her. If the man is experiencing any emotion, it isn't discernible on his face. He merely shifts his gaze to busy Poplar Avenue, to wait for the next patient.

———

CLINIC ESCORTS FIRST began coalescing around clinic entrances in the 1970s as a response to the backlash forming against burgeoning abortion rights, which initially were in the form of relatively peaceful sit-ins. Early abortion protesters like John O'Keefe, a Maryland boy who was eventually dubbed the "father of rescue" by journalists James Risen and Judy L. Thomas, took their cues from antiwar protests and the civil rights movement. O'Keefe was particularly taken by the peaceful tactics and teachings of Dr. Martin Luther King Jr., though his application of Dr. King's rhetoric to picketing abortion clinics was more than a little cringey. He was drawn to the idea that Dr. King had opened white people's eyes to racism, and he felt he could do the same for people who failed to understand abortion as murder. In college, he held antiwar beliefs, though he was discouraged by the limited power of that movement, given that his brother, Roy, had died in the Vietnam War. O'Keefe was adamant that civil disobedience and direct action did not have to, and indeed, should not, involve violence.

He was deeply inspired by a protest that took place in the summer of 1975 at Sigma Reproductive Health Services in Rockville, Maryland, the only abortion clinic in town, led by fellow Catholic abortion opponent Burke Balch and Tom Mooney, a former antiwar activist. The men decided that only women should enter the clinic for the sit-in, and they sent in a group they called the Sigma Six, in hopes that it would catch on with the media (it didn't), to block the doors where patients entered procedure rooms from the waiting area. The women were instructed in passive resistance, meaning they were to go limp if anyone tried to move them physically; they were not to fight. "You had to get across something that would break the stereotype of misogynistic males who were trying to control women," Balch told Risen and Thomas in *Wrath of Angels,* their book investigating the rise of the antiabortion movement. A police officer showed up. For three hours, he, along with the clinic director, implored the women to move before they were ultimately arrested. Meanwhile, the men outside picketed and tried to divert patients from entering the clinic. The day marked the first sit-in at an abortion clinic in the United States. Tactics only escalated from there.

In the 1980s, as the antiabortion movement became more powerful and more emboldened, escorts became a growing necessity, particularly given the meager response from law enforcement (sometimes officers refused to show up at all). More and more clinics were sustaining damage as a result of the protests, and bombings and arson attempts were becoming more frequent. By 1983, there had been more than twenty such attacks. Antiabortion groups like Operation Rescue and the Pro-Life Action League were organizing protests that steadily grew in size and in tenor. The Army of God, the antiabortion terrorist group, had formed and was taking extreme action. In 1982, the group kidnapped Hector Zevallos, who was providing abortion care in Illinois, and his wife. The couple were held for eight days before they were ultimately released about a mile and

a half from their home. "We're all terribly frightened by the kidnaping [sic]," Ingrid Smith, executive director of the Ladies' Center,
told the *Washington Post*. "We know we're always in danger. I've had
threats on my life before." What happened to Zevallos and his wife
was only the beginning: abortion providers were attacked and shot
at; some were killed. Staff and patients needed some form of protection, something to make them feel less exposed and vulnerable.
There was also a practical reason. Crisis pregnancy centers became
more common, popping up across the nation in the 1980s. Their favorite places to set up shop were right next door to abortion clinics with ambiguous names like Hope Clinic for Women or Choices,
which is a tactic that persists today. Patients would get confused and
sometimes enter the wrong building; escorts helped to usher them
toward the correct door.

In her book about the people who take up the mission of escorting patients into clinics, *Bodies on the Line*, Lauren Rankin notes
that the simplicity of the act of walking a patient from their car into
a clinic is precisely what makes it so radical. "For many abortion
patients, from the moment they exit their car until the moment the
clinic doors close behind them, they are bombarded by dozens, hundreds, even thousands of people yelling at them, telling them to turn
around, handing them literature filled with junk science, shoving
cameras in their faces," she writes. "Even seeing one warm face, having one supportive body next to them, can help put a patient at ease,
or at the very least help them follow through on the choice they've
already made for themselves."

Some patients eagerly accept the emotional and physical support
of clinic escorts; others shrug it off, occasionally annoyed by the fuss.
While researching this book, I interviewed more than twenty clinic
escorts, and each one of them had a story of one patient they'll never
forget who told them that their protection meant something on a day
that was overwhelming enough without strangers bellowing at them
about circumstances they couldn't possibly know anything about.
The work comes with a toll: escorts are on the receiving end of sustained, often vicious, sometimes menacing abuse. As a result, their
stories often sound like they belong around a water cooler in a war

room rather than in casual conversation. Antiabortion protesters are simply referred to as "antis," unless they're a regular presence and their behavior is truly egregious, then they get nicknames like Lurch or Ouiser or Mall-Walker.

"You have to be a little off-kilter to be an escort," says Emily Berisso with a grin. She would know; she leads the volunteer escort program at the Memphis Planned Parenthood and has been volunteering in reproductive rights since she was fifteen years old. Even so, the vitriol clinic escorts face is very real, and it's nearly impossible to lay that burden down in between shifts. Escorts and protesters often develop an uneasy rapport, each side suspiciously gleaning what information they can about the other. Since the COVID-19 pandemic, the clashes have escalated. The Venn diagram between antimaskers and so-called pro-lifers resembles a near-perfect circle. Escorts have reported being approached and coughed on or spit at, which is dangerous during a pandemic, not to mention repulsive.

One of the key tenets of being a clinic escort, meaning someone whose primary goal is to make sure patients get from their cars into the clinic safely, is to not engage with the protesters. Patient comfort and safety is a priority, and addressing the antis only riles them further, potentially creating stress for the patient. (Escorts, though, are only human, and the ceaseless attacks would wear on even the most stoic volunteer. Most of the people I spoke with admitted to losing their composure with a protester at some point.) At the Memphis Planned Parenthood, this is the code escorts operate on, but they won't stop a patient from engaging if they wish. If a patient wants to get a gift bag, which usually includes some cheap nail polish, some candy, maybe a small rubber baby, they are welcome to do so. "But we also always make sure to tell them, 'The people on the sidewalk are protesters,'" Emily explains. "If they want to get a bag, we say, 'Absolutely, go ahead. But please know, the clinic they're telling you about is not a legitimate clinic and they'll want to talk to you for a long time to make sure you miss your appointment.'"

In some ways, escorting is a little easier than it once was. Prior to the FACE (Freedom of Access to Clinic Entrances) Act, which passed in 1994, protesters were within their rights to come right up to a clinic door or to hover outside windows and shout into exam rooms. In May 1992, abortion rights advocates began pushing for regulation at a House Subcommittee on Crime and Criminal Justice, which was chaired at the time by New York representative Chuck Schumer. Among them was a coalition known as WACDTF (Washington Area Clinic Defense Task Force), which issued a statement on behalf of its some three thousand members. The conclusion they came to sums it up: "A federal law is urgently needed to counter the efforts of a national organization that is delighted to use our legal system against itself. Operation Rescue leaders brag to their followers that they are 'above the law'; we need the U.S. Congress to prove that they are not." The campaign didn't gain enough traction to be pushed into law.

Then, on a spring day in 1993, abortion provider David Gunn was murdered outside Pensacola Women's Medical Services. Before shooting, the gunman reportedly yelled, "Don't kill any more babies." Two weeks later, Sen. Ted Kennedy introduced the FACE Act, which established federal penalties for any of three violations: using force, threat of force, or physical obstruction to intentionally injure, intimidate, or interfere with anyone obtaining or providing reproductive health services or anyone trying to exercise their First Amendment right of religious freedom at a place of religious worship, and the damage or destruction of clinic property or a place of religious worship. The law passed with bipartisan support in May 1994, a little more than a year after Gunn's death. Twenty-one years after the *Roe v. Wade* decision and nearly thirty years before *Roe* was gutted, it was the only time Congress passed a bill to protect abortion rights.

Though it was politically significant, the law proved to be weaker than abortion advocates had originally hoped. To be sure, less blood was shed in the name of curbing abortions, but protesters proved to be creative and resilient in their mission. At the Planned Parenthood in Nashville, for example, protesters regularly perch atop ladders that are propped against a fence meant to protect patients. Instead, they hear shouts from the sky, sometimes with the amplifying aid of bullhorns. At Reproductive Health Services in Montgomery,

Alabama, clinic escort Mia Raven says the shouting usually starts promptly at 5 A.M. In Louisville, Kentucky's EMW Women's Surgical Center, protesters cluster around the parking garage where patients are instructed to leave their cars—the clinic is downtown and has no lot of its own. "There's this one young guy, I think he was in the seminary—His name's Mark, and he looks very nice, clean," says Chris Ruben, a Louisville escort. "And he always spoke in a low, quiet voice, but he would bird-dog you. He wouldn't yell at you, but he would get right up in your face, and no matter how fast you walk, he would match pace. He's kind of tall, so he could hover over, and he was always like, 'Please don't do this, ma'am. I'm just trying to talk you out of killing your baby. Please don't do that,' and he would never stop talking." Once, he followed a patient all the way to the door; she was visibly shaken. He did not suffer any consequences.

CLINIC DEFENDERS ARE different from escorts in that they engage with the protesters, perhaps most famously in Jackson, Mississippi, at the state's lone abortion clinic that was also the plaintiff in the Supreme Court case that was used to overturn *Roe*. They call themselves the Pink House Defenders, a nod to the clinic's signature bubblegum-colored exterior. The cohort has also created a separate nonprofit, called We Engage, to articulate their mission and to educate the public about *why* they challenge the so-called sidewalk counselors.

"The sidewalks outside reproductive health clinics have been ceded to the antis for far too long, and they have used it as a place to spread their narratives of shame, stigma and propaganda," their mission statement proclaims. Engaging with the protesters, for the Pink House Defenders, is about pushing back against abortion stigma and not allowing disinformation to go unchecked. They make a compelling point, particularly in this era when a president comfortably lied from the White House about everything from abortion to election fraud, and when propaganda is spread easily through social media to a degree that it has irrevocably changed the face of democracy in the United States.

However, they are clear: patient safety and comfort comes first. As previously mentioned, patients enter the clinic in shifts. It's easier to make sure they are all safely inside that way, and it's more difficult for the protesters to zero in on a specific patient. During those shifts, the defenders' attention is on the patients and their physical, mental, and emotional protection. Defenders in rainbow vests walk alongside them, while others stand around the perimeter of the clinic, waving tambourines or loudly reciting Lewis Carroll's "Jabberwocky" to drown out the shouts of street preachers. Once everyone is safely inside the clinic or their vehicles, the defenders get back to engaging with the protesters, often posting clips of their interactions to TikTok. Their channel is popular, with more than 104,000 followers.

Within clinic escorting and defense, there is also a power dynamic at play that's important to name. Not only are the patients in a vulnerable position to begin with, but most of them are also people of color, while clinic escorts and their counterparts, clinic defenders, are overwhelmingly white. "Yes, there are clout chasers," Mia says. "If all you want to do is take pictures while you're there, you don't need to be there. And I will ask them not to come back if they're not there for the right reason. I don't need you there if you're not doing what you're supposed to be doing and helping the patients." While I do think the majority of escorts and defenders are volunteering for the right reasons, there are some who come across as performers who are more concerned with posting about their clashes with those on the opposite end of the political spectrum than with supporting people who are entering a space that has been stigmatized and villainized in American culture. Performative allyship has long been a thread that has run through white feminism, especially in reproductive rights, and it must be rooted out.

CHAPTER 13

Burnout

LATELY, WORK HAD been brutal. Dani was endlessly tired. It was beginning to seem impossible to stay on top of all the emails and the meetings. Tasks kept piling up. She was slogging through them at half speed, feeling like a bicycle that had lost its chain, pedals spinning helplessly. As the day wore on, her frustration enveloped her. A change of scenery would help, she decided. She threw her laptop into a shoulder bag and drove to her favorite coffee shop in Huntsville, Alabama, where she lived. It was midmorning in late October. The sun was making its lazy rise, and autumn was finally starting to gently shove aside the swelter of summer. She admired the way the filtered light glowed against her honeyed skin as she entered the café and ordered an iced chai with espresso. Balancing the drink in one hand, her shoulder hunched to support her bag, she walked to the back patio to enjoy the newness of the cool air. Maybe the drink would help energize her enough to get something done; she must be burned out, she reckoned, her mind was simply overburdened. She sipped her drink and settled into the iron chair. Then, she felt a jolt of comprehension. *Oh no. No no.* She pulled up her calendar on her phone, trying to reassure herself that she was mistaken.

She was not mistaken. Her period was late. She abandoned the near-full glass of chai and grabbed her bag, rushing toward her Subaru. There was a Walmart to the south; it was a straight shot down the parkway. Dani is not a woman who can rest in uncertainty; if there is action to be taken, she will take it. Fear gnawed at her as she drove, and a sense of uncontrollable urgency propelled her forward, faster and faster. Once she made it into the superstore, she went straight to the pharmacy section and picked up the first pregnancy test she saw; on the way to checkout, she detoured, reaching into the cold fluorescent light of a refrigerated beverage display to seize the biggest bottle of kombucha. She beelined toward self-checkout—it was fastest, and besides, she didn't need anyone searching her face, wondering. When she reached the safety of her car, she didn't pause. She twisted the cap off of the ginger berry kombucha, tossing it onto the floorboard, and took a long swig before twisting her key in the ignition and starting toward home. Driving, she tried not to spiral out about her potential pregnancy.

Instead, she focused on the road and on taking big, incremental gulps of the tea that tingled on her tongue. When she arrived at home, she left all her belongings in her car except the test and her phone, swept wordlessly past her roommate, and headed to the bathroom. When the two pink lines appeared, she felt her stomach drop. "It's like the fear that you have when you go, like, down a roller coaster where you're, like, I'm gonna die," she says. She couldn't think beyond, *I'm pregnant.* She exited the bathroom. Her roommate, Taylor, was in the kitchen. Dani stood, frozen, in the hallway. "Taylor," she said. "Taylor. Taylor. Taylor."

Taylor stepped into the hall. "What?"

Dani handed the pregnancy test to her roommate. It quavered in her hands. "Oh my god," Taylor murmured.

Dani's eyes burned and overflowed; her face crumpled with fear. Taylor straightened her spine. "OK. Let's think this through." First, she instructed, Dani should call her partner of nearly nine months, Alex. The two walked to the worn couch in the living room, and Dani tried to methodically fill her lungs with air, then empty them, over and over, until the rhythm steadied her. She picked up her phone, swiping past the home screen, tapping to command it to call her beloved. It rang. He didn't answer. Taylor settled in next to her with a laptop. She tried again. It rang. No answer. Again, again, again, again. He was at work, tending bar at the bierhaus across town, and she knew he couldn't pick up, but that knowledge wasn't much comfort. She gave up, staring into space while Taylor sifted through internet search results to cobble together some sort of action plan.

A mechanical buzz broke the silence. "Hey!" Dani gasped into her phone.

"What's going on?" Alex's voice was gentle, laden with concern. He had taken a short break from cleaning, and when he saw the number of missed calls filling his phone screen, he took advantage of the empty, midmorning bar he tended to call Dani back.

"I'm pregnant." She let the words hang; there was nothing else she could articulate beyond the fact of it.

Where he might have felt fear, he instead experienced stillness. "OK," he replied slowly. "What's our plan?"

So they talked. Yes, we love each other; yes, we want to be parents; yes, that's an adventure we want to embark on together. But no, not like this. We're not ready. The day before, Alex had put in his two weeks' notice. He wasn't sure what was next, but he knew this job was not right for him as someone who was dedicated to his sobriety. He had been steadily applying for work, but nothing had come through quite yet and the future was hazy, except for one thing: he wanted to be with her. As they spoke, Dani felt her fear dissipate.

"I think you're gonna be a great dad someday," Dani told him quietly. "And I want to do that with you."

Alex, who is white, smiled, his mustache twitching upward. "We don't have to be ready right now," he told her, "because we get to make our lives look the way we want them to. Together." The two resolved not to consider their unplanned pregnancy a mistake. A ten-minute heart-to-heart, and it was decided: they would release it. They knew time wasn't on their side. Dani was six weeks in, and though she was in Alabama, the recent ban in Texas on abortions past six weeks sparked alarm in her, and she didn't want to run the risk of not being able to get care for any reason.

Dani stared at the passing strip malls as Taylor drove her to the Alabama Women's Center. She had spent less than an hour with the knowledge that she was pregnant. Everything was happening so fast, and she felt off-kilter, certain in her decision to end the pregnancy but emotionally disoriented by the progression of what she had thought would be an ordinary Friday. When they arrived, she was careful not to look at the protesters across the street, white people with their signs and their assumptions. She trained her eyes on the pavement of the parking lot, one step at a time, until the two women reached the glass door. She pressed a button and felt eyes on her, and then she heard a click that signaled the door had been unlocked. A television in the corner blared the local news. Nervous, she stepped up to the receptionist's station, shielded by plexiglass. "Um, hi," she ventured. "I . . . need assistance?"

"Is this your first visit?" The woman looked bored.

"Well, yes . . ."

"You have to pay $150."

Dani looked puzzled. "For . . . ?"

The receptionist glanced up at her. "For your first visit. Is this your first visit? We take cash, card, whatever you got."

Urgency was still coursing through Dani. Her mind flickered to her bank account, doing the math from her last paycheck. "OK," she said uncertainly and handed over her credit card. The receptionist ran it and handed Dani a clipboard with medical forms. "Fill these out, please, and take a seat."

Dani settled into a squishy waiting room chair and filled out the forms. She flipped past the final form and saw one last sheet of paper that detailed the costs of abortion procedures. A medication abortion would set her back $700. "Taylor," she hissed. "Look at this."

Her roommate shifted to see. "Oh. Uh, OK, let's think about this. Maybe Alex could chip in for some. I can ask some of our friends . . . How much do you have?"

Dani stared. "Girl, collectively we don't have this kind of money. Be serious." She shook her head, curls bouncing. "All right, wait, let's just . . . hang on a sec." It was too much, too fast. She needed to think, a moment to put her big, complex emotions into a box and process everything that was happening, to examine the resources that she knew were and were not available to her.

The summer before, Dani had reached out to a network of abortion doulas because she was interested in learning more about their work and potentially joining their cause. A biracial Black farmer in a long line of farmers on her daddy's side, she felt a deep connection to the land and she believed in the magic of soil and seeds to provide food and medicine. She dreamt of fostering a community garden and advising people in her neighborhood about the herbs that could help soothe their physical ailments. So, too, was she interested in herbal abortion, but she had never done it, and she couldn't place her trust in faceless advice from the internet lest she accidentally poison herself. But she *could* use the internet to find someone she could come to trust.

Taylor remained in the waiting room while Dani stepped back through the door into the parking lot to call Talon, the Latinx doula she had spoken to over the summer, over an encrypted line. Talon, who is being identified here only by their network name and they/them pronouns to protect their privacy, answered her call. "Hi," Dani said shakily. "So, fun fact, I need your help."

Talon is used to these sorts of calls. "OK," they said. "First thing's first: I love you. You're loved. And you're OK." Her throat tightened with emotion and she found it hard to speak; here was the compassion she had not known she needed.

Talon let a beat pass, and then they got down to business, asking how far along Dani thought she was and what she wanted to happen. She responded, "Probably about six weeks. We want to release this pregnancy, but I'm at a clinic and we can't afford this."

"Where are you?"

"I'm at the Alabama Women's Center in Huntsville."

"OK, and what's the price?"

Dani hesitated. "$700."

Talon laughed. "Please don't try to pay that. I'll send you some pills in the mail for free. We're going to get through this together.

The thing about the network, though, is that we love free resources when we can get them. You've already paid them $150, so get your ultrasound and your blood work done so we can get all the facts and make sure everything is all set for your abortion."

"OK, I can do that," Dani told them, feeling slightly more in control.

She walked back to the door, and she was buzzed in again. She picked up the clipboard from Taylor and walked up to the desk to turn it over to the receptionist. "So, what happens now?" Dani asked.

"What do you mean?"

"I mean, now that I've done the paperwork, what happens?"

"Well, have you had your blood work?"

"No? I haven't been back yet, this is my first appointment." Dani was beginning to get irritated. Wasn't it obvious what she was there for? Why was this person making her work so hard to get information?

"Oh OK. Just sit down and they'll call you back for some counseling, and then they'll do some blood work and an ultrasound."

And so, she sat. For two hours, she waited. Patients were called back into the clinic, and a while later, they reappeared. Some seemed drowsy, others were still trying to manage their pain in the aftermath of their procedure. A swirling cauldron of frustration, dread, and resolve simmered inside her. Finally, she approached the desk again. "Hi," she said, offering what she hoped was a patient smile. "I'm just letting you know that I'm . . . still here."

The receptionist gave her a blank look. "Are you here for your first visit?"

Dani raised her eyebrows. "Yeah, we've been through this. I filled out the forms. I've been here for two hours."

Over her shoulder, the receptionist hollered. "Hey, can we get Dani in, what's going on?"

Dani started. She hadn't expected for her name to ring out like that, in this unfamiliar place. Another Black woman appeared behind the receptionist. "Yeah, hang on, we'll get you back," she told her.

After a few minutes, the woman opened the door to the waiting room and told Dani to follow her. In the back of the clinic, the energy was frenetic. The woman showed Dani into a dim room where an ultrasound machine sat, dormant, at the end of the exam table. A woman with braids fixed into a bun appeared at the door; she seemed harried. "OK, undress from your waist down. I'll be right back." She disappeared, closing the door behind her. Dani scanned the room for a sheet of tissue paper to cover herself. There was nothing.

But the woman who she assumed was an ultrasound tech had told her to undress, so Dani removed her pants and underwear and eased herself onto the exam table, suppressing a shiver. When the woman reentered the room, she recoiled and averted her eyes. "What are you doing? Oh gosh. You need to . . ." she said, pausing to reach into a drawer and retrieve a sheet. "You need these things—here."

Dani burned with shame and draped the sheet over her waist. "You didn't give me these," she mumbled. The tech didn't respond and instead pushed a button, prompting the table to lift with a metallic groan. "OK, so what are you getting done?"

Dani's frustration was mounting. Everyone around her seemed to be speaking in a shorthand she didn't understand. She had only learned she was pregnant a few hours ago. "What do you mean?" she asked, trying to keep her tone neutral.

"Are you doing the pill or the procedure?" The tech seemed distracted, pushing more buttons, and Dani continued to rise toward a bright light, legs parted, feet in stirrups.

"I don't know," she replied.

The table stilled. The tech moved to Dani's feet. She held an instrument that was shaped like a curling iron in her gloved hands. "What have you had done? Have they done counseling with you yet?"

"No."

"Have they done blood work with you yet?"

"No."

"Huh. OK." Without warning, the tech inserted the wand into Dani. On the table, Dani went rigid and hot, angry tears sprang to her eyes. She blinked them back furiously, staring at the ceiling. "OK, I've got you clocked in at six weeks and three days," the tech said briskly, withdrawing the instrument and removing her gloves.

The table lowered. "Get dressed, and someone will be along to help you."

She left the room, and Dani sat up and tried to steady herself, shifting off the table and pulling her underwear and pants back on. The feeling of cotton, snug on her skin, comforted her. But soon another woman appeared at the door and ushered her into another room. "We're going to take your blood now," she said.

Dani had reached her limit. "Can someone please just talk to me first? In complete sentences? Can I have a conversation? Names?" The woman gave her a beleaguered look. "Just come into this room, please." Dani's shoulders slumped, but she followed. The nurse indicated a plastic chair where she should sit and set about getting her supplies in order. She set a roll of fabric bandages on the countertop next to Dani. "Oh, actually, do you just have a regular Band-Aid or something? The fabric bandages irritate my skin a little," Dani said.

"I didn't see an allergy on your paperwork," the nurse replied.

"Oh, well it's not a full-blown allergy. It's just kind of uncomfortable?" she said, her last syllable rising in her surprise that this seemed to be a problem.

"You're going to have to fill out your paperwork over again."

"Wait, seriously? It's not a full-blown allergic reaction; it just itches a little. I was just wondering if there was an alternative."

The nurse sighed. "I'll be right back," she said and closed the door behind her. Seconds later, she returned, this time with an older Black nurse. "You didn't put down your allergy on the medical history report," the older nurse said, surveying Dani.

"At this point, just use the fabric bandages. I don't care. I don't care." It seemed absurd to Dani to try and hide her exasperation.

"Oh OK!" The older nurse left the room.

The nurse scooted her stool closer to Dani and began preparing to draw her blood. She wrapped a bright blue tourniquet around Dani's arm and began prodding with her gloved fingers to find the vein. Tears were beginning to fall in earnest, trailing down Dani's cheeks. "Oh," the nurse said, untying the tourniquet. "Are you OK? What's wrong?"

The floodgates opened and sobs overtook her.

"I can stop. We can do this later," the nurse assured her.

Dani regained some control. "No, let's get this over with, get it done. I want to leave."

The nurse apologized and explained that Fridays are procedure days, which often means the staff is working hard and trying to quickly accommodate as many patients as they can. The abortion ban in Texas that had gone into effect a couple of months earlier had made procedure days even more intense because the clinic was dealing with overflow from surrounding states and turning away patients was gutting. They were overwhelmed and understaffed.

Dani nodded. She understood. But she could not reconcile the reality of business demands with what she had been experiencing in her own body. The tears would not stop. The nurse drew her blood. "Why don't I give you just a moment, and I'll come back," the nurse said gently and eased out of the room.

Soon, the older nurse knocked and entered. "What's wrong with you? Why you crying?" she asked, putting her hand on Dani's shoulder and lowering herself to look into Dani's eyes. This was the connection she had needed. Her auntie is a nurse, and in the strange cold of unfamiliar surroundings, she desperately wanted the warmth of familiarity.

Dani began to cry harder.

"What's wrong, what's wrong," the nurse murmured. "Oh honey, you just need a hug, don't you?" She wrapped Dani in her arms, and Dani reveled in the affection.

"Listen, we are not going to judge you for anything you decide to do," the nurse said. "If you don't want to do this, you don't have to do this. What grade are you in, honey?"

Dani tugged at her mask and wiped fluids from her face. "I'm twenty-eight. I haven't been in school in a long time," she replied.

"Aw, OK, you're gonna be OK," the older nurse said. She turned and left. Dani felt like she had been slaking a wild thirst, only for the faucet to be abruptly turned off.

Another woman came into the room for the counseling session, but Dani doesn't remember much of it. It was a blur of medical terms, and the woman was reading from a sheet of paper. Dani had accepted that she would not find any more human connection here. "So, what do you want to do?" the white counselor asked.

"I don't know yet," Dani said dully. She was so tired.

"Well, we have a forty-eight-hour waiting period that's mandated by the state anyway before you can get a procedure, so you just give us a call when you decide and let us know," she said.

Dani grabbed her bag and left. Taylor drove her home. Once there, she collapsed into the couch, and Alex brought her some pizza. After they took some time to watch TV and think about something other than abortion, they decided to call Talon together to talk through their plan to self-manage Dani's abortion. Talon asked how they were both feeling, and then began to explain the medication abortion process. It would take some time for the package of mifepristone and misoprostol to arrive in her mailbox, but it works better at around eight or nine weeks' gestation anyway, Talon told them. That also gave the couple some time to plan out when and how Dani would have her abortion. With Talon, Dani felt like her abortion was happening on her terms. At the clinic, she sensed her bodily autonomy was not the priority, and when she tried to exercise it, she understood herself to be a problem, a hitch in a system that left little room for her as an entire human being.

Throughout her abortion process, Dani says she was most frightened and ill at ease in the clinic. Her experience, unfortunately, isn't so unique. Abortion clinics are important and necessary, but they've been under attack and overburdened for so long that sometimes the quality of care suffers—particularly in states that have long been hostile to abortion. There is a cost to unending strain and to the embattled nature of abortion rights work. Clinic staff go to work each day, and they never know if it may be their last: clinics are always at risk of shutting down with the whims of the state's legislature. There are fewer and fewer abortion providers because the work is far from lucrative, and the work comes with substantial risk. Clinic workers deal with trauma daily, be it sexual assault victims or from pregnant people they have to turn away because they're just over the gestational limit or menacing protesters who scream threats and write down their license plate numbers.

This is all in addition to the weighty morality that comes with abortion care, that the work is mission-driven rather than "just a job." Work like this can't be left at the threshold of the workplace. There is always the potential for the work to bleed over dramatically into one's personal life, like in 2015, when antiabortion activist David Daleiden released a series of covertly recorded "sting" videos with Planned Parenthood employees that were manipulated to fit his grotesque agenda to claim that the health care provider was selling baby parts for profit. The employees who spoke with him were tricked into believing that Daleiden was a representative from a (fake) medical company called Biomax, for which he claimed to be working to procure fetal tissue for research. Anyone who works in abortion care knows to be cautious with strangers, and the caution can take an added emotional toll. Clinic workers, too, have admitted to me over the course of reporting that they're sick of talking to reporters, and it makes sense. Dealing with the media should never have become part of their job.

A few days later, at home, nausea began to overtake Dani. Whenever it lifted, she craved red meat with a ferocity that she had never known. She felt tired and scrambled. "Pregnancy brain is *real*," she says. The couple experienced the weight of the situation, and they grieved it in their own way, but they also found humor and joy in discovering the changes in Dani's body. "I had to eat constantly or I would turn into a gremlin," she remembers, giggling. "I had an *iconic* meltdown in the parking lot of a Wahlburgers." From then on, Alex took special care to make sure she ate and to prioritize her hunger. Perhaps more than anything, more than the fear or trepidation, they felt wonder at what they could create together.

They planned to release the pregnancy on November 2. That's the word Dani uses most for her abortion—*release*. There are days where she uses the word *abortion*, but there are also days when the word feels somehow too big, "too heavy in my mouth."

"Honestly, a release is more encompassing of the entire process and how we felt," she explains. "It wasn't just a physiological thing. We accepted and then we let go of a lot of things about ourselves. It was not just tissue. We had to release things about our perceptions of each other, our perceptions of ourselves."

She felt prepared. She had typed out a care plan in a Google doc, detailing what teas and tinctures she would ingest to ease her discomfort at what time. In an earlier conversation with Talon, they gave her a warning that has remained with her. In Spanish, they told her: *You have to treat these feelings that blow through you as wind. You feel them. They're there. But their purpose is not to stay—you must let them go, or they will make you sick.* The pills were encased in a small, plastic container with a heart drawn over the lid in orange marker, and the package included a candle, Emergen-C tablets, and tea. Alex had to work that day, but she assured him that she would be fine.

Late morning light peeked through the blinds, and the pills rattled as she counted them out to take her first dose of mifepristone. Muscle memory took over and she swallowed them whole, forgetting to let them melt slowly in the sides of her cheeks. Next, she swallowed the misoprostol, though the two medications are meant to be taken twenty-four hours apart, and she made a cup of tea with mugwort, chamomile, and ginger, and settled into her bedroom to wait. After about an hour, her uterus began to cramp. Nausea overwhelmed her, and she rushed to the bathroom, where she began to vomit uncontrollably. The next few hours were spent curled up against the cold tile next to the toilet, moving only to expel more liquid. She began to bleed, but not much. She reckons she threw up some of the medication before it had a chance to work. Around 9 P.M., she began to pass tissue, but it was far less than the amount she had been told to expect.

When she awoke the next morning, she felt fine. It was almost as if the previous day had never happened, except for some light spotting. But she tired easily, and a few days later, her throat began to tickle and she developed a cough. She had an upper respiratory infection that was separate from her abortion, though later she wondered if terminating her pregnancy had affected her immune system, given the hormones in the medication. Still, she recovered, and she thought the ordeal was over.

Twenty days later, she went to her gynecologist to follow up on an abnormal Pap smear from a couple months prior. Her doctor, a no-nonsense Black woman named Sanithia Williams, came in the exam room where Dani was waiting. They greeted each other, and Dr. Williams settled onto her stool. "OK, so I'm gonna assume that you already know that you're pregnant," she said.

"No, I'm not," Dani said, eyes widening. Her mind raced. Was it safe to tell Dr. Williams that she had self-managed her abortion? She knew Dr. Williams was an abortion provider at the clinic she had visited, but she had gone outside the limits of the law. Could she trust this doctor who she'd only seen twice with that information? She quickly decided not to risk it. "I . . . miscarried," she said slowly.

Dr. Williams raised her eyebrows slightly. "You *miscarried*? Did you miscarry at our . . . other clinic?" She gave Dani a knowing look, and Dani realized that Dr. Williams must have seen the record of her clinic visit in her patient file.

"Well, I went there, and I couldn't afford what the clinic was charging, so I went through my friend who was a doctor and they sent me pills for free," she said instead, skirting the truth in an effort to protect herself and Talon.

Dr. Williams explained that Dani's urine sample had shown that she still had pregnancy hormones, which meant that it was likely she had retained tissue, which could pose a risk of infection if the tissue wasn't removed. They would do an ultrasound to be sure, and it was all going to be fine—incomplete abortions and miscarriages are very common. After Dani left, Dr. Williams called and confirmed that there were still products of conception in Dani's uterus, and they would need to do a DNC to remove it.

"Because we live in Alabama," Dr. Williams told her at her next visit, "You have to come in for another ultrasound, but after that, we can perform what is considered here as abortive services, either at the hospital, where we can administer anesthesia, or at the clinic." Dani started to cry; Dr. Williams put her hand on Dani's knee. "We are here for you, and to make sure you're safe, and we want what's best for you," she said firmly.

Fuck, I thought this was over. She told Dr. Williams she would get back to her to schedule the procedure. It was the week of Thanksgiving, and she wanted to have time with her family before she dove back into managing her body. She didn't tell her doctor that she was afraid. She had never had surgery, and her one experience witnessing surgery had been frightening. Earlier that year, when she and Alex had started dating, he had needed a rhinoplasty surgery to correct a deviated septum. It was a common procedure, and they weren't worried. But he had an adverse reaction to anesthesia during the surgery: when the doctors tried to wake him after the procedure, he aspirated and went into shock. He was in the cardiac care unit for forty-eight hours, and his doctors weren't sure he would survive. He was then on a breathing tube for another twenty hours. Doubling Dani's anxiety was that she had only had health insurance for about a year. It had been several years since she had been able to access routine medical care, and she was finding her reentry to the fluorescent world of doctors' offices and inscrutable medical terminology overwhelming and frightening.

She talked to her doula and to Alex about her fear and frustration. "They were, like, 'This is your time, baby—call in your plant allies, call in your plant medicine, call in the things you know about your body,'" she remembers. She told them she would think about it, confessing that taking that approach felt more accessible to her. A couple days after Thanksgiving, she went to visit family in Tennessee, soaking in time with her dad and her aunts and her cousins after being separated for long stretches due to the pandemic. After all the emotional turmoil, being with her people was a balm. "I was there with my aunties and my cousins, and we kiki-in' and yellin' at kids, and all the sudden I just feel this twinge in my uterus," she says. "I was like, 'Yes ma'am, can I help you?'" She pulled out her phone to text Talon. "My uterus is talkative today!" she typed. "How likely is it that I could start releasing tissue based on my body's cycle?" Dani was between ten and fourteen days away from the beginning of her regular menstrual cycle; she keeps careful track of her menstruation and her body's reactions to shedding its uterine lining. "Well, it's possible, but your body would need some help," Talon replied. "It's also possible that you would still need tissue extracted manually by a doctor."

She decided that if there was any chance that she could finish her release on her own terms, she had to try. She began by incorporating more vigorous movement into her routine—power walking around Big Spring Park downtown, lifting heavy objects, working out at the gym. She brewed pennyroyal tea, drinking it for two days. A few days later, she noticed the familiar smell that signaled to her that her period was coming. Just in case, she went back to Dr. Williams's office on a Tuesday for the second ultrasound and scheduled the procedure for Friday. She told Dr. Williams that she was hoping to pass the products of conception on her own, but Dr. Williams told her that it was unlikely she would be able to. Still, Dr. Williams expressed sympathy for her situation, for the way her problem was consuming months of her life. "Look, if we were in California, the day you found out you were pregnant, you could have come to my office, and we would have literally been able to do it that day or the next," the doctor told her gently. "But we live in Alabama, and it's all political. And it sucks." Dani nodded, grateful to have found a connection with her doctor. She reviewed her insurance and found that it would cover a DNC performed at a hospital, and so she began to accept that she would likely have to take that route.

On Thursday morning, her alarm went off, and she sleepily trudged to the bathroom. She looked down and noticed a reddish-brown stain in her underwear. "I was right," she whispered, grinning to herself. She called Dr. Williams to cancel her procedure for Friday, but the doctor cautioned her. She was concerned that Dani might be at risk for infection. They rescheduled for Tuesday, just in case. For the next several days, Dani continued to see spotting, but she knew it was not enough. Once again, she resigned herself to getting the procedure. She spent Sunday morning in leisure, taking a walk downtown, picking up a sandwich, and settling into the park to enjoy the unseasonably warm weather and read a novel. When she began to walk back to her car, her breath began to shorten. A cramp seized her uterus. *Maybe I'm just tired.* When she arrived home, she snuggled up in her bed and put on PBS *Masterpiece Theater*, and it wasn't long before she fell fast asleep.

She awoke to a full bladder. She settled onto the cold toilet, noticing the blood in her underwear had turned lipstick red, and while she was relieving herself, she felt an unfamiliar sensation and heard a *plonk*. Startled, she rose up and turned to look down. *Oh my God, that was it, that was the pregnancy.* She cleaned herself up and went to the kitchen to get a utensil so she could inspect the tissue to try to get an idea of where she was in the process of release. It reminded her of a jellyfish; she thinks it was either the placenta or the amniotic sac. Seeing it moved her—this was a piece of her, of Alex, made in love. She texted him and Talon to let them know what was happening, and then she decided to have a ceremony over it for her own closure. She lit some sage and a candle and meditated, thanking the spirit of this being for the lessons it had taught her, for all that it had brought into her and Alex's lives.

"I can't wait to meet you again," she said softly, "when the wheel brings us back together."

From there, she assumed she would start a normal period. She padded into the kitchen and made some nettle and dandelion tea. When she sat down with her tea, she started when she felt warmth seep between her legs. "It was like someone had turned on a faucet," she says. She texted Alex and asked if he could come. He had recently started a new job at a market across town, but she was starting to feel light-headed, and the amount of blood seeping from her body was alarming her. She called Talon, and they advised her to eat warm, nourishing, hydrating foods—beef stew, bone broth, iron-rich foods that could replace the nutrients she was losing. She called to her roommate. "Taylor, do we have any beef stew?" Her eyes blurred.

"I don't think so, but I can call Alex and ask him to bring some," Taylor said, walking into Dani's bedroom. She pulled out her phone to make the call; the line rang, and Dani wore a disoriented expression. Dani could hear Taylor talking, but her roommate's voice was distorted and fading; her vision dimmed until it was cloaked in dark green. She crumpled.

"Hey, Alex, can you bring some sort of beef stew or something with you when you come over, Dani needs . . . she passed out, just get beef stew," Taylor said, ending the call and rushing forward. Alex, who was already en route, hit the gas—he was only a couple minutes away. When he arrived, he slung his Honda Civic into the driveway, yanked it into park, and hurried into the house. Dani was awake, but she was confused and slick with sweat. Taylor had called Talon, who was on speakerphone, instructing Dani to drink water. "Go get her some food," they said to Alex. "She absolutely has to eat." He had his marching orders. He drove to Walmart, where he filled a cart with ingredients to make stew and broth. Stopping by the pharmacy section, he grabbed a thermometer and maxi pads.

Back at the house, Taylor lifted Dani off the floor and put her into bed. "Cold," Dani mumbled. Taylor piled blankets over her and coaxed her to drink water. Dani feared that she would have to go to the hospital, but given her past experiences, she was reluctant. More doctors was a last resort. As the night deepened, as she was able to replenish her body, she began to feel better. She passed more tissue, and for three days, she rested, but she and Alex describe that time as beautiful, a time for them to connect and care for each other, process the release, and dream of the future. "I lost a part of him. I had to let go what we made together. And what I let go of was just as much him as it was me," she says. Still, "it was important to choose me and to choose us."

"We didn't make a mistake," she says firmly. "It came out of love."

———

I N 2014, MARS WOOD was about to turn twenty-two. Mars, who is Black and nonbinary, was in their last year of college at the University of North Carolina at Chapel Hill when they discovered that they were pregnant. They knew, even before they knew for sure. After a week or two, they summoned up the nerve to head to the CVS near their house, where they bought three pregnancy tests and tried to ignore the cashier's look at the check-out counter. When they arrived at the tiny cottage they shared with two other roommates, they found that no one else was home. *Good, one less thing to worry about*, they thought. It was going to be hard enough to manage their own reaction and to prepare for the reaction of their partner of two and a half years. They climbed the stairs and wedged themselves into the bathroom to take the test. When the pink lines appeared, they stared, convinced that there was a mistake, that they

were somehow reading it wrong. Briefly, they wished for the appear-
ance of the roommate they were closest to, for another set of eyes
to confirm that this was happening. Two more tests dissolved any
remaining uncertainty. "I was, like, 100 percent, I cannot—this is
not the time. I'm not even sure I want to parent at all," Mars recalls.
"I come from a line of women who became parents when they didn't
want to, and we're all around the same age—my mom had me when
she was twenty-three, her mom had her when she was twenty-two."
They called their partner and headed over, a plastic Ziploc bag full of
positive pregnancy tests in tow. When they arrived, they handed the
bag to their partner.

Overwhelmed, they simply blurted out, "I'm getting an abortion."
She looked at Mars, and nodded. The two were in agreement.

There was a Planned Parenthood clinic in town that provided
abortion care, but their partner, a transgender woman, was also a
student, so they had little money and no transportation with the exception of Mars's trusty orange bike—named Rapidash in homage
to a Pokémon character—that Mars had won in a student auction
for a dollar and rode around town with a black milk crate strapped
to the back. For the couple, the clinic was the last resort, partly due
to resources and partly because they didn't want to have to explain
their sexuality or correct medical professionals' assumptions about
their gender identities. "I want to come with you," their partner told
them, "but I don't want to go into that clinic." Mars understood.
They had been to that clinic before for gynecological care and knew
it wasn't trans friendly at the time. Being in the South, even at a university where folks tended to be a bit more open-minded, was hard
enough. Still, they scheduled an appointment just in case because
they wanted an abortion as soon as possible; at the time, they were
uncomfortable with the idea of an abortion past twelve weeks' gestation. Mars reached out to herbalists and midwives they knew and
sought guidance on herbal methods of abortion, scanning websites
like Sister Zeus, a popular source for instructions on how to manage
fertility through plants. From those conversations and from online
research, they carefully concocted teas and tinctures with herbs like
pennyroyal and black and blue cohosh. With the pennyroyal, they

used particular caution, as the herb can be toxic if too much is ingested. Besides, the pungent taste of the pennyroyal was off-putting on its own. The drink was thick and muddy and tasted of earth; the cohosh tincture had a pleasant sharpness as it slid along their tongue.

They bled, but like Dani, they knew it wasn't enough. Looking back, they say they may have been overcautious with the pennyroyal dosage, but still, better to err on the side of not dying from poison. It sort of defeats the purpose of getting an abortion. The couple borrowed a friend's car to get to their Planned Parenthood appointment, where an ultrasound confirmed that the pregnancy had stalled but tissue needed to be extracted. They did not disclose that they had attempted to self-manage their abortion—it didn't feel safe. The ultrasound tech turned the screen to show them; Mars flinched. They were not asked whether they wished to see it. And, as predicted, both Mars and their partner were misgendered, despite repeated corrections.

The doctor recommended the use of medication to complete the abortion, which would cost them $450. The two agreed to split the cost, putting the burden on credit cards so they could pay it off slowly. They were living completely on their own, working part-time as full-time students. There was not any financial wiggle room in their lives for an abortion, so they just hoped that bit by bit they could outpace the interest that would accrue.

When it was over, and Mars was able to expel the pregnancy at home, easing the cramps with a warm bath until the water turned scarlet. For them, the process was over in just a few hours. They went back to Planned Parenthood for a follow-up exam, to be certain their uterus was empty and there was no risk of infection. After it was confirmed that Mars was in the clear, the nurse suggested they get an IUD. "We can put it in for free. We could do it right now," she chirped. A wave of shame washed over Mars—*this lady must think I'm such an idiot for getting pregnant.* "Um, all right," they replied. The insertion was excruciating for them, and they felt they were not given the space to make a truly autonomous decision about contraception, which made it traumatic.

"I look back and I recognize that saying yes to that was a form of self-harm," they told me. They knew they didn't want hormonal contraception—it could worsen the gender dysphoria they had already experienced as a nonbinary person, which had escalated during pregnancy—so they opted for the copper IUD, which in their body provoked vicious menstruation cycles, rendering them unable to walk some days out of each month. Nearly five years later, they could no longer bear it, and they went back to the clinic to get it removed, but they were informed that because the IUD was not expired, they would have to pay full price to have it removed, setting them back at least $200, which they didn't have.

This part of Mars's story echoes a long, dark history of the American government and the nonprofit sector using contraception as a means to control Black birthing bodies that were understood by white politicians and medical professionals to be unruly and too prone to producing children, unfit for their lily-gilded visions of motherhood. "Mississippi appendectomies" as a euphemism for forced sterilization in the Jim Crow era, when there was the push to entangle contraceptive requirements with welfare eligibility, the coordinated campaign in the 1990s to coerce Black people with uteruses to allow a contraceptive called Norplant to be embedded in their upper arms without clear disclosure of potential side effects.

Except Mars experienced this in 2019, at a time when there's no excuse to not be cognizant of this history and the trauma it has inflicted. Instead, they sought help from a midwife friend, who removed the IUD in exchange for a couple of hours of childcare. Still, Mars is adamant that the Planned Parenthood they went to is a good place, and they know that the clinic has come a long way over the years, putting effort and resources to become more trans-friendly and more intentional about consent and communication with patients. "Bless Planned Parenthood and bless that clinic for how much they've grown since then," they say.

Mars is also very clear that they carry no regret with them about their choice, but they don't feel represented by narrow political campaigns that reduce all abortion experiences to a sunny catchphrase or hashtag. "Emotionally and spiritually, it hurt," they tell me. "I really approached that pregnancy where I was like, 'This is my baby.' I know not everyone comes to that, but for me, I felt like I could see a life where I could potentially do this, but that's not the track that I want." They experienced grief and sadness after their abortion, and it weighed on them that their experience didn't seem to fit the pro-choice political rhetoric. "I just felt like a traitor to pro-choice, where I was, like, 'Oh, the rhetoric is you're supposed to feel relief and happiness, and I feel all these emotions that the antis outside the clinic are telling me that I was gonna feel.' What does that mean?" Now, as an abortion rights advocate and the former director of the Carolina Abortion Fund, they are transparent about their own experience, that it's normal to experience a spectrum of emotion.

————

THE PRO-CHOICE RHETORIC that Mars alludes to is well intentioned but can ultimately be damaging and delegitimizing for patients. As Katrina Kimport, a researcher for Advancing New Standards in Reproductive Health, points out, "with over 850,000 abortions performed in the US, annually, there is no such thing as a typical abortion patient." Humans are complex beings who don't easily fit into straightforward narratives, no matter how politically useful simplicity may be. The antiabortion movement is powerful and well funded, and abortion rights organizations are often so caught up in their fear of losing more ground that they unintentionally wind up causing harm. In some extreme cases, this also means a pedestal for doctors who are not providing the sort of care that patients deserve and who may even be taking advantage of the dynamic created by this idea that for abortion rights to remain legal, the entire operation must be unimpeachable. Anything less is swept under the rug, because to the mainstream, the hurt of a few is not worth risking legal abortion.

For decades, national abortion rights movements, led largely by wealthy white women, have centered abortion as the object of the fight. As a result, other aspects of reproductive freedom have suffered and been deprioritized, and the realities of the majority of Americans have taken a back seat to political rhetoric. "The harsh reality is that an utter disregard for the reality of Black women's lives—and, by extension, all Indigenous people, people of color, queer and trans folks, and disabled people—has led us to this moment," wrote Renee Bracey Sherman, founder and executive director of We Testify, and Dr. Tracy Weitz, cofounder of Advancing New Standards in Reproductive Health, in a 2022 article for Rewire News Group. "Because of its own internal racism, the reproductive rights movement is ill-equipped to meet the challenge of this moment." This dynamic has created disparities in care for as long as the reproductive rights movement—which focuses on abortion rights over other forms of reproductive health care—has existed.

Ann, a white woman who worked as a counselor at a Planned Parenthood clinic in Indianapolis in the early aughts, says she was disturbed by the churn of the clinic. Patients had a precise ten minutes with her; any longer, and she would be scolded for holding up the day's process. Some twenty years later, she still identifies as pro-choice, but then, she was a twenty-one-year-old fresh-faced feminist, a young white woman straight out of college, with little experience comparable to that of the patients she was counseling. She held brand-new degrees in gender studies and English literature, and she had never had an abortion. When she applied for the job, she didn't bother to temper her enthusiasm: she faxed her résumé to the clinic no less than five times (in part because she wasn't sure how to work the fax machine). When Ann was seventeen, she became sexually active, like many of her peers. The Centers for Disease Control and Prevention reported in 2017 that more than half of American teens have had sex by their eighteenth birthday. She turned to Planned Parenthood to help her stay healthy and safe. The level of care she received there was significant to her, especially as a midwesterner steeped in a culture that was overwhelmingly sex negative, though she was from a liberal family that was much more open-minded. She wanted to give that gift to someone else, and she was surprised when the counselor she interviewed with gave her a hard look. "You know we only provide abortions at this location, right?" She had not known, but she knew where she stood. She affixed a bright smile to her face. "Yes!" When she was offered the position as counselor, her moral conviction accepted it for her. She figured she'd never been squeamish, and she believed in abortion rights, so all should be well.

When she began the new job, she was taken aback by the bare-bones training given to her and the dim dustiness of the clinic. She has a hazy memory of shadowing another counselor before she officially started her job, along with informal conversations with the clinic administrator that covered some of the do's and don'ts of the work. The clinic, situated in a drab strip mall, was operating under considerable strain. The protesters were belligerent and occasionally violent, abortion providers were scarce, resources were in short supply. Ann had little guidance when it came to how to do her job well; she mostly found she had to go with her sense of morality, and sometimes, that wasn't enough. The staff was in survival mode.

An administrative office in the back smelled of cigarettes; the staff would sometimes come in on Saturdays when the clinic was closed to clean it themselves, to save money on janitorial staff. (According to a spokesperson for Planned Parenthood Great Northwest Hawai'i, Alaska, Indiana, Kentucky, two employees who worked in Indianapolis, though not necessarily in the same clinic, said they never cleaned on days off.) She recalls the place being properly sanitized and absolutely up to health standards but not necessarily clean. "It did not have the kind of feel you expect when you walk into a doctor's office," she says. "I felt a sense of kind of shame because you want to help these women during what, for some of them, was a really difficult moment. You just realize that the standard is really not high, and there's this defeatist attitude of *there's only so much you can do*." Once, in a procedure room, she accidentally stepped on a blood clot, and no amount of sanitizing spray could make her feel like her shoe wasn't somehow forever tainted. The carpets were stained; the clinic doctor liked to joke that it looked like a bloody body had been dragged down the hallway. He didn't seem to notice—or care—that his quip never got a laugh.

One day, not long after she started her job, another clinic worker accidentally stuck herself with a used needle. The lab room she worked in was small, and the space limitation combined with the frenetic pace of the work meant that it was only a matter of time before there was an accident. The clinic reached out to the patient and asked if they would take an HIV test, but the patient refused, so the worker wound up on medication meant to ward off the virus but that also weakened her birth control. Consequently, she found herself pregnant, and gave birth to a baby she had not planned.

Nowhere was the survival mode mentality more evident than in the unchecked behavior of the lone abortion provider at the clinic, a graying white man in his fifties with an unnaturally dark tan, a sports car, and a fondness for pushing boundaries. He called her "honey" and played with her hair, and when she needed him to do something, he would respond by telling her he had been waiting all his life to hear her say that, thrusting his pelvis so there could be no mistaking his insinuation. He requested that she attend a pool party at his house wearing a bikini, and he was rumored to have watched porn on computers at the clinic (for this, it was said, he was reprimanded so that he no longer did that). When he overheard Ann discussing her cat's ailments with a coworker, he did not hesitate to interject: "Damn, Ann, don't you know I hear enough all day about sick pussy?"

It was his interactions with patients that disturbed Ann the most. The doctor seemed to have a special disdain for any sign of weakness. To a young patient who was shaking from fright, he said, "Are you going to be a pain in the tail about this or are you going to act like a big girl and take it?" Sometimes he would ask a patient to "smile pretty" for him and he would "make it nice and easy" for them. She suspected that he was harder on patients who did not speak English, and she fought for privileges as the only Spanish speaker on staff to accompany Latinx patients into the procedure room so she could answer their questions and advocate for them if necessary.

Still, he was an abortion provider in a hostile state, which meant he was afforded a certain kind of reverence that was layered upon his racial and class privilege. He spoke openly of the handgun that he carried in his glove compartment, and he liked to tell of his constant awareness that he could be in danger, explaining to staff that he always checked for that "little red dot on his chest" that meant he was in the sights of a rifle. These comments were delivered with machismo and fueled by a savior complex that does sometimes show

up in abortion providers, made worse by his perceived status as the
so-called rooster in the henhouse. Like in any other field, when the
work is heralded as heroic, it can go to a man's head. This is partly
our fault for giving in to that human inclination to heap too much
symbolism on a single person, for wanting narratives to be simple
when they are always complex and flawed.

Ann filed multiple complaints against him, acting on the advice
of her mother, who told her to keep a written record of everything
that happened. Before she left the clinic, in part due to emotional exhaustion, she was assured that her complaints were being taken seriously, and she was forbidden to ever speak of his behavior. After all,
he was risking his life to provide abortion care. Better to let the clinic
handle it than to risk handing the antiabortion movement a weapon
they would not hesitate to use. It was as if she had become the threat
instead of the man who was causing harm, all due to the embattled
nature of the work, the feeling that any slight misstep could be used
to sink the clinic and narrow resources for patient care even further.

He retired years later. Still, he is far from the only provider in his
field who has enjoyed a bizarre reverse protection by way of the antiabortion movement. The abortion rights movement, like any other
social movement, has flaws. Its central mission of abortion access is
a noble one, but it is shot through with ego and white feminism and
capitalist values and a fear of the attacks of the antiabortion movement that is so deep that sometimes it overpowers deserved scrutiny
and justice. In this moment, as the Supreme Court ruling that legalized abortion in the United States has been overturned, leaders of
the movement must carefully interrogate the current power dynamics in any future efforts to build a new road toward legal reproductive autonomy. There is no such path forward that does not center
reproductive justice and the voices of those who have been harmed
by the inequalities that have persisted in the years since 1973. *Roe*
was the floor, not the ceiling, as activists have often said. To continue
with the current dynamics of the traditionally white reproductive
rights movement is to repeat history, and it's not good enough.

CHAPTER 14

Banned

BY MIDMORNING ON an early October day in 2021, the parking lot is full at the Trust Women clinic in Wichita, Kansas. Cars have been pulling in steadily for hours under a slate sky, droplets from the unpredictable autumn showers pimpling their shiny surfaces. Black iron gates frame the entrance to the lot, and in between bursts of rain, protesters pace back and forth, pleading with cars to stop and writing down license plate information when they refuse. A yellow box truck sits, engine off, across the street. The cab identifies itself as property of the Kansas Coalition for Life, and it's hooked to a white cargo area splashed with gruesome images of torn, fragmented fetuses. "EVERY Abortion is an Act of Violence! Violence is NOT the Answer," proclaims the text. The truck stays parked there, one in a pair owned by the antiabortion group, but the maintenance is costly. Every now and again, the mirrors are smashed, and someone has been periodically stealing the catalytic converter out of it. But never mind, it makes its point just fine there on the side of the street. A plastic baby doll that has clearly seen better days rests in a weather-worn bouncer on the other side of the entrance to the parking lot, hoping to evoke in the pregnant people who pass it some deep sense of maternal responsibility and guilt. As the day continues, more protesters shuffle up and down the sidewalk that runs along the iron gate. A tall wooden fence surrounds the clinic itself to protect patients from hostile gazes. Where the fence meets the corner of the building, a sign advises anyone who has been sexually abused by a priest or clergy to call a hotline. Next door to the clinic is a benign-looking crisis pregnancy center, simply called Choices Medical Clinic.

Black-and-white Texas license plates flash as they turn into the lot. October is just beginning, and for the past month, Texans have been living under an abortion ban that makes the procedure illegal after roughly six weeks' gestation. The courts have failed to intervene, despite precedent and the clear unconstitutionality of the law, and months have passed since it went into effect, forcing more and more pregnant people to leave the state to seek abortion care. In Texas, on this day, *Roe* is dead. The Wichita clinic, along with others in the Midwest and the Southeast, is feeling the strain of an influx of patients. Some parked cars hold men, waiting, seats leaned back, the glow of a phone casting their faces in a blueish light. They may be here for the first time, or for the second appointment, when patients can actually get care. Kansas, too, has a twenty-four-hour waiting period between the initial appointment, when patients receive state-mandated counseling, and an abortion procedure.

To enter the clinic, patients must first step into a bright room and pass through a metal detector, helmed by a wizened security guard who is quick with a mischievous grin, which usually appears on the heels of a joke reminiscent of something that might have come out of the writers' room of *The Andy Griffith Show*. His clear blue eyes are kind, shadowed by snow-white caterpillar eyebrows, and his voice is gravelly, softened by the country twang of a man who was born in Kansas and raised in the Oregon mountains. Passing through this in-between, some patients indulge the guard named Carl Swinney by returning a smile; others stare blankly, unable or unwilling to muster the energy for banter because what would be the point. They want to get medical care and then leave.

Carl is somewhat protected from the sometimes overwhelming patient trauma that can come to a head in the clinic. The staff is not. Around 10:30 A.M., there is a commotion near the front desk. A patient is weeping as she is leaving the clinic, begging for abortion care, and the receptionist is gently repeating to her that she's over the state's gestational limit and they cannot help her. The patient is familiar: she's a grandmother, and she has come to the clinic before seeking birth control. Originally, she requested long-acting reversible contraception in the form of an IUD, but complications arose when they tried to place it, so she settled for pills instead. Recently, she made an appointment for an abortion. When she came in and got an ultrasound, she was further along than she originally thought, past twenty-one weeks and six days. Nurses and other staff who knew the patient from past visits weep with her, and they go through the list of clinics that could help her. None of them are in Kansas. They also reach out to abortion funds to try and alleviate the financial burden. Still, everyone involved knows it will be an uphill battle for her to get the care she needs. When she leaves, clinic director Ashley Brink goes to comfort the staff. "If you need a break, take it," she advises. Instead, they make plans to contact the patient the following week to check on her and ask what else she needs.

Ashley knows the staff at Trust Women are exhausted; she is, too. They're seeing about thirty-seven patients a day now, which is twice the normal load. Two people have called in sick. All the abortion providers are fly-ins, which means none of the physicians live locally. In September, the month the Texas ban went into effect, they saw fifty-one patients from the Lone Star State, and their sister clinic in Oklahoma City has added a procedure day to the workweek. Ashley's fine brown hair stays pulled hastily into a top knot, or maybe a ponytail. It changes throughout the day. She lives in scrubs, usually paired with a T-shirt, and most mornings she clutches a purple-and-gold coffee mug that says, "Everyone loves someone who has had an abortion," a nod to abortion storytelling nonprofit We Testify. She has an affinity for ink, and her tattoos belie her passion for her work and the history of abortion access. One says "Call Jane," with the phone number for the service underneath, in the style of the fliers

Jane used to distribute. Another tattoo is a reference to Margaret Atwood's dystopian novel *The Handmaid's Tale*. It reads, *Nolite te bastardes carborundorum*, a faux-Latin phrase, which translates to "Don't let the bastards grind you down." Two and a half months have passed since Ashley began her job as clinic director, and her office bookshelves remain mostly bare as a result of the running start she found herself taking. Peppy indie pop-rock streams out of her computer intermittently throughout the day, and she is rarely seen in the clinic without her worn pink Nike sneakers—that is, unless she's sporting her black Vans. Most importantly, she's a Kansan through and through, born and raised in a small town in the northeastern part of the state.

The pace of her days has only increased in the aftermath of Texas's ban. "We could work providing abortions till midnight every night, but that's not sustainable," she says. The situation in Texas feels like it's escalating the longer the law remains in effect, which not only means more Texan patients but more patients from other states who are facing lengthy waiting lists to get abortion care because of increased demand. The law itself is frightening and draconian and encourages citizens to report their peers if they have done anything to "aid or abet" an abortion. Physicians are afraid to provide abortion care at any stage lest they get hit with a lawsuit and the threatened fine of $10,000—minimum. One Texas patient called to make an appointment at Trust Women and said she was under the six-week limit, but cardiac activity was detected during her ultrasound, and the clinic was afraid the presence of a so-called heartbeat could be at odds with the law.

Abortion is an extremely safe and common medical procedure. But it is still a medical procedure, and the body still undergoes the stress that comes with that. Ideally, a patient shows up well rested and well nourished. If the patient is forced away from their home, if they must travel by car or plane and make all the attendant arrangements that come with that—airfare, gas money, hotel stays, childcare, time off work—they are unlikely to arrive for their appointment in a relaxed state. The uncertainty, too, breeds fear and panic. Alarming headlines and fast-changing laws that confront different panels of judges and appeals processes are difficult to keep up with, and it's even more challenging for people who are navigating the bureaucracy and economic burdens of being low income in the United States. Some juggle multiple jobs to make ends meet, making any necessary time off that much more complicated.

The crew at Trust Women has put a lot into trying to make the clinic seem less, well, clinical. A small fountain in the corner of the lamp-lit front waiting room babbles quietly to itself, next to a water cooler and a sign that promises hot water for tea and coffee, available on request. The bathrooms feature quotes from Dolly Parton: "If you want the rainbow, you've got to put up with the rain." A post-counseling waiting room in the back has a desk with pens and note-cards for patients to leave words of encouragement for one another, pinning their words to a bulletin board for those who come after. Staticky guitar riffs from The Killers' "Somebody Told Me" cough out of an old radio in the back of the room, and an oil diffuser glows on a side table.

Even the cavernous, sterile procedure rooms come with some small adjustments, some of which aren't obvious. Lamps are set up for more light control, eliminating any blinding overhead light. The brown vinyl surface that patients lie on for their procedures is always referred to as a table, never a bed, to be sensitive to people who have experienced sexual assault. When I ask Ashley how she and the staff are doing, she laughs a little, shooting me a beleaguered look. "We're here," she says. "We're seeing patients. We're doing the thing, and everyone shows up every day ready to do this, and that's more than I could ask because it's hard."

THE TRUST WOMEN CLINIC in Wichita carries extra baggage. It was once called simply Women's Health Care Services and was led by Dr. George Tiller, a doctor who gained notoriety among antiabortion activists for being one of the few doctors in the nation who would provide abortion care in the third trimester. Dr. Tiller was preparing to exit the US Navy, where he was serving on a tour of duty as a surgeon, and start a residency in dermatology when his parents, along with his sister and brother-and-law, died unexpectedly when a private plane piloted by Dr. Tiller's father crashed in the summer of 1970. At twenty-nine years old, he found himself the legal guardian of his year-old nephew and responsible for a sprawling family practice in Wichita that his father ran. He returned home with the intent to get his family's affairs in order over the course of six months, which would include winding down his father's clinic, but he soon realized that there weren't enough doctors in Wichita who could take on his father's patient load. He had the medical credentials necessary to provide care as his fathers' patients searched for a new physician, and he shifted to a three-year plan to offload his father's practice and get back to his own career.

"After I had been there for a little while, patients in the practice began to ask me if I was going to do abortions like my father did," Tiller recalled in a 2001 interview. "I was outraged. Why would these nice people say that he was a scumbag kind of a physician?" Over time, he came to understand. Conversations with patients led him to a story he hadn't heard before, about a woman who came to his father for an abortion. He had delivered two of her babies, and she was pregnant again, too soon after the birth of her last child. She begged him for an illegal abortion and he refused, telling her it would all be alright once the baby arrived. She died soon after because when she was forced to seek care elsewhere, she found someone who was incompetent.

Tiller knew that loss must have devastated his father; it certainly seemed to change his convictions. He never knew how many abortions his father performed, but he learned from that story and others that abortion access was a human rights issue, and he could not ignore his moral responsibility to care for his patients to the best of his ability. When abortion became legal in 1973, he decided he would provide the procedure and he would continue to work in Wichita. At first, he provided abortion care at a local hospital, Wesley Medical Center, but hospital abortion care ran around $1,000, and Tiller could do the procedure for $250 at his clinic. (There were two other hospitals in Wichita, but both were Catholic and therefore did not provide abortion care.) The former family practice became Women's Health Care Services, and the clinic primarily offered abortion care, alongside two other providers in the small city.

Dr. Tiller had a reputation for being exacting. He demanded perfection from himself and his staff, and anyone who couldn't live up to that needed to get the hell out of the way. On his watch, there were no shortcuts. That's not to say he was a saint: he could be belligerent, he had a mild savior complex, and he wrestled with alcoholism and drug use. Early on in the days of legalized abortion, Dr. Tiller was among only a handful of doctors in the US who provided abortion care later on in gestation, and as such, he grew intimately familiar with the myriad ways pregnancy can go horribly, horribly wrong. Women who desperately wanted babies came to him under wrenching circumstances in which a chromosomal fluke meant they were forced to terminate their pregnancies. Other patients were very young and frightened by what was happening to them. A natural consequence of this sort of exposure was that it expanded his compassion, and many of his patients vividly remember his kindness and care during some of the worst moments of their lives.

Krista, a white woman who now volunteers with Planned Parenthood in Memphis, was fifteen years old when she and her mother went to Dr. Tiller seeking his help. At fourteen, she and her boyfriend became sexually active, and while they used protection most of the time, it wasn't exactly readily available to the Illinois teens. It was 1985, and when she realized she was pregnant, she shut down and went into deep denial. *It can't happen to me, this can't be happening*, she told herself over and over. Finally, she summoned the courage to go, alone, to a supermarket to buy a pregnancy test, and the positive result shattered her young certainty that she was an exception, that she could not possibly be pregnant. She braced herself and told her parents, and the family was in agreement that fifteen was much too young to have a baby. First, they went to Peoria to seek care, but Krista was turned away. She was too far along for them to be able to help her. Wichita was the only option.

Her mother made the travel arrangements, and they made the journey together. Mother and daughter found themselves in a group of patients who would be back and forth between the clinic and a nearby hotel for a few days. She remembers a couple who had tried to have a child before, only to lose the child to a genetic abnormality. They had discovered that their second pregnancy would be the same, and they could not bear to watch their baby suffer all over again for the few days it would be able to survive outside the womb. There was a woman who was competing to become Miss America, and her pregnancy would have rendered her ineligible despite years of training and significant expense. Krista remembers a little girl the most, a few years younger than she was, maybe around eleven years old. The girl was Hispanic, and she didn't speak any English, but her face was contorted in terror every time Krista encountered her. The group had a counseling session with Dr. Tiller that was based on one he had come across in Alcoholics Anonymous during his battle with substance abuse.

For patients further in their pregnancy, Dr. Tiller preferred an abortion method that required an injection that stopped the fetus's heart before miscarriage was induced. After the injection, Dr. Tiller would counsel his patients once more before dilating their cervixes, and in those conversations, he would also ask their wishes regarding what should be done with the fetal remains. Some women wanted photos made of the babies they had fervently wanted, while others wanted baptism before laying their child to rest in a tiny casket. Some simply wished to have nothing to do with what came out of their bodies. They waited for labor to begin at the hotel, and Krista has a fuzzy recollection of a nurse stopping by to check on her. When the process began to reach its natural conclusion, she went back to the clinic and Dr. Tiller, who was kind and reassuring throughout her abortion. Before she left, he peered down at her through wire-rimmed glasses and told her that she reminded him of his daughter. "He very much believed that this was a health care issue and very much believed that this made a difference in women's lives," she says. "And he laid down his life for that belief."

Dr. Tiller was not one to take guff from anyone, much less mouthy antiabortion protesters. Protests began in earnest in 1975, and they were fiery, fueled by outrage at the range of abortion care offered at the clinic. In 1986, not long after Krista went to Women's Health Care Services for abortion care, a pipe bomb went off at the clinic, causing more than $100,000 in damage. The perpetrator was never discovered. Amid the damage, Dr. Tiller fashioned a sign: it said, "Hell No! We Won't Go!" His next step was to install extra security: bulletproof glass, gate and fencing, a metal detector, and armed guards, which came to include Carl, who incorporated a bulletproof vest into his uniform. Carl remembers him as "a good man" who "didn't have any fear." As the protests escalated and employees began to face targeted harassment, Dr. Tiller also began issuing regular staff bonuses, which he dryly referred to as "combat pay," in addition to a heightened effort to be extra-generous with praise and small trinkets of appreciation. Sometimes he would tell them that "the only requirement for evil to triumph is for good people to do nothing." And to him, the people who chose to continue doing what was necessary to help women were the best people of all. The people outside who were making it their life mission to frighten his patients and his staff were the worst. Occasionally, he would shout back at the protesters who harassed him daily. He once told Operation Rescue leader Randall Terry that he was sorry Terry's mother hadn't aborted him. Another time, a television camera recorded an antiabortion protester waving a sign in Dr. Tiller's face, who turned and growled, "Why don't you stick that someplace where the sun doesn't shine?"

The first time an antiabortion protester tried to kill Dr. Tiller was in the summer of 1993. A housewife and mother named Shelley Shannon—who had been radicalized by a group called the Army of God that told its members murdering abortion providers was morally justifiable to protect the "unborn"—took a bus from her home in Oregon to Wichita. It wasn't her first act of violence—she was responsible for a string of clinic arsons that had not yet been connected to her, following instructions laid out in the Army of God's handbook—but this trip would be different. She approached Dr. Tiller in the clinic parking lot as he was beginning to drive away in his 1989 Chevy Suburban, and he thought she was going to try to make him take some antiabortion pamphlets, so he raised his middle finger at her. She shot him in both arms. He managed to get back inside the clinic, and his staff treated his wounds as Shelley Shannon sped off. Dr. Tiller's nurse assistant at the clinic had the presence of mind to chase Shannon for long enough to jot down Shannon's license plate number as she drove away in a rental car, and the police picked her up when she arrived in Oklahoma City to return the vehicle. The next day, Dr. Tiller was back at work, and for good measure, he posted another sign outside: "Women Need Abortions and I'm Going to Provide Them."

Sixteen years later, Dr. Tiller was hunted by another antiabortion extremist: this time, a slender, bald white man named Scott Roeder, who homed in on Tiller's church as the place where he would be most vulnerable. Twice, Roeder went to Sunday services in search of Dr. Tiller, but the physician was nowhere to be found. On Roeder's third visit, Tiller was serving as an usher at Reformation Lutheran Church. With head bowed, the man approached Dr. Tiller, who was talking with other congregants. He pulled a gun from his pocket and shot the abortion provider point-blank in the head in his house of worship. He did not survive.

It's been more than a decade since Dr. Tiller was murdered, but at Trust Women, which reopened and rebranded under his former protégé Julie Burkhart, the past has a habit of lingering, sometimes right outside the gates. Wichita has been at the heart of the so-called pro-life movement since the Summer of Mercy, a six-week-long protest organized by Operation Rescue in 1991 that focused on George "Killer" Tiller, as they called him, and his clinic. That summer was the group's largest and most lucrative effort, lasting forty-two days, resulting in nearly 2,700 arrests, and bringing in an estimated $177,000. It's difficult to pin down precisely why Wichita has remained such a battleground over time. "If we want to get really real, the reason why antiabortion extremism exists is because of white supremacy," Ashley says. "We're in the Midwest. There's a lot of Christian religious extremism. And racism, which is interesting, because Kansas was a free state. I'm like, y'all, what are we doing with the Confederate flags here?"

A S THE MORNING begins to fade into midday, the rain has stopped, though thick gray clouds remained, stubborn, overhead. Just outside the gate, two graying white men who look to be around retirement age stand by a sagging card table that holds antiabortion pamphlets and a curling pile of paper with an impressive list of license plate information. One of the men, Mike Hagan, tells me he's been setting up outside the clinic since 1992. He strikes me as earnest and thoughtful, if paternalistic, open to engaging with my questions and criticisms, though we are clearly operating from fundamentally different ideologies. His partner is curt and frosty, that is, until he begins to berate me for my profession—"the media is such a liar, I would put them on the lowest respect of anything that I trust these days in the United States"—and starts ranting, something about a conspiracy theory involving President Joe Biden in a basement, before stalking off. Mike smiles apologetically and goes on to explain that they are both affiliated with Kansas Coalition for Life, which is led by Mark Gietzen, an antiabortion activist who has protested at the clinic since 1978. During Dr. Tiller's tenure, Geitzen had a fondness for reaching out to Fox News personality Bill O'Reilly with inflammatory "tips" about Tiller's work, and he cultivated a deep network of antiabortion activists across the Midwest who had no problem making the trek to Wichita for protesting.

Mike says Kansas Coalition for Life has made a commitment to financially supporting each mother and subsequent "youngster" who is saved through the child's eighteenth birthday. This pledge is advertised on the pamphlets he distributes, but the mechanics of the program are unclear. Mike talks about abortion with sorrow that does not read as contrived. He's not bombastic, like many of his peers on the sidewalk: his voice is soft, and it's clear that he believes in what he's doing. He acknowledges that, as a man, he cannot truly understand what it's like to experience pregnancy, and he certainly can't understand what it's like to give birth. Women who work as "sidewalk counselors," as he calls it, are more effective. Still, he feels he cannot sit on his hands while what he sees as a life-and-death situation plays out. He has to enter the fray, but he'll do it in his way— quietly, gently. That doesn't mean, however, that he shies away from the group's violent depictions of abortion, like the so-called Truth Truck on display across the street.

We continue to talk, now two instead of three, and cars interrupt our conversation every now and then, prompting Mike to scramble, imploring them to stop, scribbling down their license plate information when they roll past into the lot. He admits that his note taking is likely intimidating for people. "I'd be worried about it myself if somebody did [the same]," he says, but, he shrugs, it's public information, and anyway, their intent is to offer a protective measure in case anything goes wrong inside the clinic. In this way, they fancy themselves an asset to law enforcement: Mike explains that if someone inside dies or is maimed from a botched abortion, their information could help identify the victim, or if a minor gets abortion care and it isn't reported to the state per the law (though Kansas requires all informed consent forms to be reported to the state, which means the ages of all abortion patients are tracked), they can testify in court that they saw the minor enter the gates. The record also gives them standing in court, he says, because it shows "commitment and responsibility." "Nobody ever looks at this stuff ever," he promises, "until something bad happens." (It bears repeating here that abortion is an extremely safe, common, and simple medical procedure.) He believes, at the very least, that that used to happen with some regularity. "When Tiller was operating here, you know, they'd often have a botch situation and they'd take it to the hospital and try to hide it, put all kinds of pressure on these people, pay 'em off so they didn't say anything negative," he tells me. Over the course of our conversation, he brings up the list of license plate numbers a few times on his own, perhaps sensing my discomfort with it.

Inside the clinic, multiple employees mentioned that the practice made them feel watched and uneasy. Recording license plate numbers is not an unusual tactic; it was first popularized by antiabortion activist Joseph Schiedler as an intimidation method in his manual *Closed: 99 Ways to Stop Abortion*. (Schiedler is known as a godfather of the antiabortion movement and one of the leaders of the direct-action approach to abortion protest.) If Mike has indeed been a presence at the clinic since the 1990s, he knows that the group's dedication to recording license plates has not historically been harmless. In 2004, for instance, the Wichita-based antiabortion group known as Operation Rescue organized a campaign to harass anyone who worked at the clinic to such a degree that they would quit their jobs. They used the license plate numbers of the employees to make sure they had the right homes before they began picketing their homes or digging through their garbage. A *Rolling Stone* feature profiling Troy Newman, an antiabortion activist who was heading up Operation Rescue at the time and still leads the organization today, detailed the results of the campaign as they played out. Writer Kimberley Sevcik described Operation Rescue's effort to intimidate administrative assistant Sara Phares like this: "Before long, protesters from Operation Rescue showed up at her house. They parked a tractor-trailer across the street, plastered with twenty-foot-long images of dismembered fetuses. From its speakers came the kind of sweet, tinkling music that lures children from their backyards in pursuit of Dreamsicles. One protester, a somber man in a tan windbreaker with a three-foot crucifix thrust before him, performed an exorcism on Phares' front lawn, sprinkling holy water on the grass to cast demons from the property." The prelude to this action involved a letter-writing campaign in which hundreds of Phares's neighbors received a series of postcards that encouraged them to seek out Phares and let her know exactly what they think of her work "killing babies."

Newman was not the first to decide that intimidating doctors and clinic staff was a good approach. Schiedler is largely credited with identifying doctors as a "weak link" of abortion and trying to convert them to the "pro-life" side. When that didn't work, he set about organizing harassment campaigns similar in spirit to those of Operation Rescue. In short, Schiedler walked so that Newman could run. Now, Newman is also an adviser for Kansas Coalition for Life, according to its website.

A woman in purple scrubs with long brown hair and an air of excitement approaches. Earlier, Mike had flagged down a van that was approaching the clinic and passed the driver some of their pamphlets. The driver worked for a ride share, but the woman, Jennifer McCoy, had recognized that he was on "our side," as she says—a vanity plate on the van said "Blessed," and he wore a shirt with imagery from a crowdfunded Christian TV show called *The Chosen*, which chronicles the life of Jesus. She had beckoned the driver to roll down his window, and he did. "Can I do anything to help you?" she asked. Peering into the van, she could see a woman in the back, reading the leaflets that insist: "If you are pregnant, you *are already* a mother. *No one* can change that. An abortion decision will only make you the mother of a dead child—*forever.*" The driver told her that they were going to Choices, the crisis pregnancy center, instead. Jennifer had come over to celebrate.

"That's what we do," Mike says, looking intently at me. Jennifer's presence seems to sharpen Mike's conviction. There's an edge to his voice that wasn't there before as they discuss the windowless design of the building, which, combined with the fence, does give the place the feel of a fortress. The conversation quickly turns gruesome, and I can't shake the feeling that they are watching my face to see if I would blanch. "They used to have an incinerator and they'd take the baby parts and incinerate 'em, and we would walk out here and you would actually get the little black flecks and the aroma," he says matter-of-factly. "They had to stop it eventually because too many people associated it with the Holocaust." (The antiabortion movement commonly remarks on their perceived parallel between the Holocaust and abortion, which is deeply offensive to people who are Jewish.) Jennifer adds that the burning would take place at two o'clock in the morning, and they would be on the sidewalk still, holding twenty-four-hour prayer vigils. "After the ash would build up on the roof, when it would rain, the gutters, the downspouts would shoot out ash," she says. "It'd be foamy and always bothered me."

A few minutes later, the van pulls up again, and Jennifer goes to talk to the driver. He tells her that his wife used to work for Choices, the crisis pregnancy center next door, and that he talked to the woman in the back seat and prayed with her. She had traveled to get to Wichita, hence the need for a ride share driver, and she was staying at a nearby hotel. She agreed to let the driver take her to Choices, which is next door to the Trust Women clinic. Jennifer gave the driver her information and asked him to pass it along to the woman after she was done at Choices. "I want to let her know no matter where you're at, I know people who will help you with whatever your situation is, whatever state you come from," she says. "I got friends everywhere."

The van is blocking the entrance to the clinic parking lot, and Carl is pedaling toward us on a bicycle that's much too small for his large frame, a look of irritation crinkling his face. Off to the side, Mike says Carl comes out any time they're blocking traffic (which, he admits, is something they've tried to do to keep people from getting to their appointments). Jennifer sees Carl, too, and she bids the driver farewell with a quick "take care," before she crows at Carl, "Ya lost another one!"

"Oh, he's pissed," she says to me. Carl tells the van to move on, glares at Jennifer and Mike, and pedals back toward the clinic.

Jennifer McCoy adheres to the Catholic faith. A mother of twelve children—only one was adopted, she tells me, the rest she gave birth to—she has a girlish voice, though she's scrappy as hell. She has a bright, friendly demeanor, but she is not harmless. A deep conviction lies behind everything she does and colors the way she sees the world, maybe even more sharply than it does for most. At twenty-four years old, she was convicted of attempted arson. According to a press release from the Department of Justice, she tried to set fire to two clinics in southeastern Virginia, first by placing a lit flare through the mail slot at Peninsula Medical Center for Women in Newport News in 1994 and then breaking a window at the Tidewater Women's Health Clinic in Norfolk, entering the clinic, pouring two gallons of kerosene inside, and setting it aflame in 1996. When she appeared before a judge, she had a cross of ashes on her forehead in observance of Ash Wednesday and the beginning of Lent. "I didn't want anyone to get hurt, and I didn't want children to die," she said in court. "If the babies don't get justice, why should anyone else?" She served two and a half years in prison and reportedly paid $1,335 in restitution.

"She was too stupid—those are her words," Mike tells me. "She was enticed into it. She went through an abortion. She's had the pain she went through afterwards. It hurt so much, she turned to hatred because of what went on, and somebody talked her into it. She paid a heck of a price for it."

When I ask her about it, she agrees to tell me about it but then shies away, talking instead about the Clinton administration's infringement on First Amendment rights by passing the FACE Act, which made blocking the entrance to a clinic through force, the threat of force, or physical obstruction a federal crime. "At that time, there were a lot of the abortionists that were doing damages to their own buildings to collect the insurance money because they were sometimes having problems with business, and so there were a lot of unsolved crimes," she says. "There were people doing things; I'm not saying there weren't. One of my best friends burned down like seven abortion clinics when nobody was in them, and he's a minister." She chuckles and then veers into a series of stories that I don't quite follow as to how they fit together.

Still, she tells me she became pregnant with her ROTC instructor's child when she was sixteen and he was in his thirties, married and with children. Legally, the relationship was not consensual, but she says she was in love. Her mother coerced her into an abortion by telling her they were going for a simple obstetrician appointment. She wanted Jennifer to think that she had come around to support her decision to parent, despite Jennifer's mother's original insistence that she have an abortion. "There was no one on the sidewalk that day," she says. "Had there been one person outside telling me that that was an abortion clinic, I never would have gone in."

The "had there been" keeps her outside the clinic, and it's kept her in this line of work for nearly thirty years. It's also taken her inside abortion clinics, where she would pretend to be a patient in need of a pregnancy test, usually with her infant in tow to help persuade other women in the waiting room that motherhood was feasible and, indeed, well worth it. Sometimes, they followed her out of the clinic. "I feel like this is where God wants me to be," she says. "And I don't want any one of these people—not one of them—to ever have to go through everything that comes along with going in this place."

Jennifer's words, I think, are genuine. What's harder to swallow are some of her actions, like the attempted arsons and the company she keeps. A photo of her surrounded by her children at a clinic protest in 2009 shows the family decked out in black T-shirts that proclaim, in white and red letters, "Visualize Abortionists on Trial." The phrase is a slogan that was invoked often by a website called the Nuremberg Files, created by militant antiabortion activist Neal Horsley, who used the platform to publish the names, addresses, and other personal information of roughly two hundred abortion providers in the United States, who were referred to as "baby butchers." Names of those who had been murdered were struck through—"the butchered," the site said—and the names of those who had been wounded by antiabortion violence were listed in gray. The Nuremberg Files explained itself thusly: "A coalition of concerned citizens throughout the U.S.A. is cooperating in collecting dossiers on abortionists in anticipation that one day we may be able to hold them on trial for crimes against humanity. We anticipate the day when these people will be charged in perfectly legal courts once the tide of this nation's opinion turns against the wanton slaughter of God's children." These dossiers were connected to the deaths of three abortion providers, including Dr. Barnett Slepian, who was gunned down at his Amherst home by a sniper named James C. Kopp. Hours after Dr. Slepian's death, his name was crossed off the list, though Horsley insisted he had no prior knowledge of the murder, saying he merely updated the website after seeing a TV report. Clayton Waagner, an antiabortion terrorist who sent fake anthrax threats to clinics in the early aughts and told Horsley he had plans to kill some forty-two clinic workers, also said he closely monitored the information posted on Horsley's sites. Waagner is currently in prison, and he is expected to remain there until 2045. The Nuremberg Files was shut down in 2002 after a court deemed it a "true threat," overriding any free speech claims. Even so, the internet is vast and impossible to police, and versions of the website can still be found (though the information—and the retro, cartoonish graphics of dripping blood—are outdated).

Jennifer told a reporter at Vice News that she counts Rev. Donald Spitz, who operates the website for the Army of God, which explicitly supports the murder of abortion providers, among her friends, calling him "quite a character." The two met at a clinic in Norfolk,

Virginia, where she was trying to "save" a friend who was seeking an abortion. "When I pulled into the driveway, he was there," she said to reporter Matt Ramos. "He thought I was going to go to the clinic. I didn't know anything about the inner workings of pro-life work. He's truly the one who showed me. I have always felt called to be at the clinic, but he showed me how." Spitz touts Dr. Tiller's murderer, Scott Roeder, and Paul Hill, who shot and killed both Dr. John Britton and his bodyguard, James Barrett, as "American heroes."

When Roeder was arrested, McCoy's name came up as one of his frequent visitors in jail. The FBI investigated Roeder's visitors out of an initial concern that Tiller's death had been part of a conspiracy among antiabortion activists: this was not proven. On the day of Tiller's funeral, McCoy showed up, as usual, on the sidewalk by the clinic. She held a sign that read: "George Tiller—Murderer Not Martyr."

For now at least, the "sidewalk counselors" remain on the sidewalk, and they are low on the list of worries inside Trust Women. But they are tough to ignore, and there's no question that their tactics upset patients. Ashley says that the concept of providing abortion care—"killing babies," as the folks outside would put it—is not the tough part of her job. "The hard part is listening to the stories and hearing what [patients] went through to get here," she says. "The hard part is listening to them cry because of them feeling harassed by the protesters and the emotional toll that that took on them. And we face that every day coming into work."

On my last day visiting the clinic, I linger, chatting and saying good-bye to the staff members I've met, walking back through the clinic to make sure I have all the detail I need, that I've asked all the questions I meant to. The front waiting room is almost dark. All the lights in the clinic have been turned off except for the bright overhead light in the receptionist area. A Black woman sits in the waiting room, alone, looking at her phone. She's from Texas, and her flight got in early that morning. She's passing time before her flight home leaves at 6 P.M.

PART THREE

Post-*Roe*

CHAPTER 15

The Race

A **S OF THIS WRITING,** it appears that the right to abortion as established in the *Roe v. Wade* ruling is dead.

Many people will say something along the lines of, *We should have seen this coming.* That's true. The spirit of the *Roe v. Wade* ruling has been dead for a long time in vast regions of the South and the Midwest, and grassroots abortion rights activists have been warning about this moment for at least a decade, but it has seemed like an uphill battle to get anyone to care. In 2020, journalist Marie Solis wrote a piece for Jezebel that was headlined, "This Is a Story About Abortion, No One Will Read It." As a reporter who also covers access to reproductive health care, it resonated with me deeply. She wrote:

This story was supposed to be about abortion pills. I intended to write about how a federal judge temporarily suspended the Food and Drug Administration rule that forced patients to pick up the pills in person, from either a hospital or clinic—a significant barrier to early abortion. But when I pitched the editor this story, she wrote back to tell me that it was a good idea, and important to cover, but difficult to get anyone to read about. Even on a site like Jezebel, where a large swath of the audience is ostensibly interested in the topic, a reported piece on abortion was likely to get little engagement. Why was that, she asked, and how could we get readers to care about something like an FDA regulation?

This question stung at first, but it was the sting of recognition: I've written about reproductive rights for years, and rarely has it been the boon to readership my editors hoped. I wanted to find a satisfying answer not so I could get more people to click on my stories, but to solve a problem that I'm positive is structural.

Even within our own newsrooms, even with our own readers, we have struggled to get anyone to listen. And now, what we have been warning of has come to pass. But no one, of course, can entirely predict the future—not reporters, not activists, not even Supreme Court justices. But they—the latter—can alter it. And they have.

In 2018, Mississippi enacted a law banning abortion after fifteen weeks' gestation, with narrow exceptions—cases of severe fetal abnormality or in medical emergencies that threaten the life of the pregnant person or creates "substantial and irreversible impairment of a major bodily function." The gestational limit therein is about two months less than the standard set by the *Roe* ruling. It has never actually gone into effect. Federal judge Carlton Reeves immediately issued a temporary restraining order blocking the measure after the Jackson Women's Health Organization, the state's only abortion clinic, challenged the law. In November, Reeves issued a permanent injunction against the law, which explained that a fifteen-week ban clearly "disregards" the Fourteenth Amendment's constitutional right to autonomy on which the *Roe* ruling was partly established. Reeves, who has gained something of a reputation for his sharp rebukes of the state's efforts to ban abortion, added in a footnote that legislators' "professed interest in 'women's health' is pure gaslighting," and he scolded the efforts to curb abortion access when lawmakers "choose not to lift a finger to address the tragedies lurking on the other side of the delivery room: our alarming infant and maternal mortality rates." Now, the Supreme Court has overruled Reeves, likely changing the legal landscape for reproductive rights for at least a generation.

Mississippi, as Reeves alluded to, has been an active player in the long game to overturn abortion access. Gov. Phil Bryant, who held office when the fifteen-week ban was passed, vowed to work to "end abortion" in the state. Bryant's successor, Tate Reeves, has not committed to protecting contraception rights for Mississippians with uteruses. In 2019, Mississippi, too, was among a slew of states that attempted to pass heartbeat bans, so-called for the point in pregnancy when the electrical currents that may eventually become a fetal heartbeat begin to circulate, which happens at around six weeks' gestation.

The law worked its way up through the courts and had been in wait on the Supreme Court's docket since 2020. It moved up to the Supreme Court not long after Justice Ginsberg's death and the appointment of Justice Amy Coney Barrett by President Trump to replace her. Much of Coney Barrett's confirmation hearings surrounded the issue of whether or not the judge considered *Roe v. Wade* to be established precedent. During her hearing, she insisted that she had "no agenda" regarding abortion. Still, she had a history of using her power and privilege that seemed to contradict her claim. In 2006, Barrett and her husband, both ardent Catholics, signed a two-page newspaper ad that ran in the *South Bend Tribune,* which described the *Roe v. Wade* decision as "an exercise of raw judicial power" in a nod to Justice Byron White's dissent in the 1973 decision, and called for "an end to the barbaric legacy" established therein. A second "right to life" ad, which was not dated but referred to the fortieth anniversary of *Roe v. Wade* and pledged to "renew our call for the unborn to be protected in law," appeared in a supplemental filing disclosed by the Senate Judiciary Committee. The ad was signed by University of Notre Dame faculty and staff, including Barrett. According to a letter submitted to the filing, Barrett said her name was included as a member of the university's Faculty for Life group, which sponsored the advertisement. And in 2013, she gave two talks—a lecture and a seminar—at Notre Dame hosted by an anti-abortion student group and a Catholic Center within the university that also submitted an amicus brief supporting Mississippi in the *Dobbs* case. Her lecture, entitled, "The Supreme Court's Abortion Jurisprudence," was advertised in a faculty newsletter as examining, "*Roe v. Wade* and the cases that followed it, concluding with a look at the cases that are currently being litigated in the lower courts." (The precise content of the talks is not known.)

In response to the question of her legal views on abortion posed by Sen. Dianne Feinstein, Coney Barrett answered, "Senator, what I will commit is that I will obey all the rules of stare decisis," referring to the weight with which justices are supposedly bound to regard precedent. She did, however, hedge some. "I think in an area where precedent has been pressed and litigated, as is true of *Casey*, it would actually be wrong and a violation of the canons for me to [grade precedent] as a sitting judge," she said. "So if I express a view on a precedent one way or another, whether I say I love it or I hate it, it signals to litigants that I might tilt one way or another in a pending case."

Initially, there was a great deal of speculation that perhaps Chief Justice John Roberts would be the unlikely stopgap on the bench, acting as a moderating force to balance the three Trump-appointed justices who feel less bound by precedent. Perhaps Roberts's concern with his legacy on the Supreme Court would keep the rights of people with uteruses intact. In retrospect, this was foolish—when has male ego ever served us? When has it ever brought us anything other than destruction and ill-formed opinions about the inner workings of our bodies and distrust in our abilities? Desperation can give way to belief in almost anything.

As time went on, the Court's intentions became increasingly apparent. When Texas banned abortion and the Court refused to do anything despite the clear contradiction to prior Supreme Court rulings, it seemed a sign that *Roe* had lost its power with the new bench. Even during oral arguments in *Dobbs v. Jackson Women's Health Organization* in December 2021, it had been apparent that the case would not go well for abortion rights. Justice Clarence Thomas came in early with an eagerness to test the waters on consideration of fetal personhood—which was not an issue that *Dobbs* put to the Court—specifically probing whether or not child abuse laws could be enforced against pregnant people who use drugs before viability. Justice Amy Coney Barrett was concerned with safe-haven laws, which allow a parent to anonymously surrender an infant without fear of prosecution, suggesting that women can and should carry unwanted pregnancies to term, give birth, and then relinquish the child if they so choose. Justice Brett Kavanaugh repeatedly expressed that he feels the legality of abortion is not one for the Supreme Court at all but rather for the states, so he can wash his hands of the whole thing and avoid the hypocrisy of declaring that *Roe v. Wade* is established precedent while also overturning *Roe v. Wade*. Justice Samuel Alito tried to draw a comparison between *Roe* and *Plessy v. Ferguson*, which upheld state segregation and was later overturned in *Brown v. Board of Education*, on the basis that the prior decision violated the Fourteenth Amendment guaranteeing citizens' equal protection under the law. Alito also offered up this tidbit of judicial wisdom: "The fetus has an interest in having a life." Justice Neil Gorsuch was fairly quiet, but when he did speak, he groped around for a way to frame undue burden, the standard for protecting abortion access that's been in place since *Planned Parenthood v. Casey*'s 1992 decision, as unworkable and to banish *Roe*'s viability standard altogether. Roberts hewed closely to a "what's the harm in a fifteen-week limit?" frame, carefully not engaging with issues of personhood.

By closing arguments, Scott Stewart, the Mississippi solicitor general representing the petitioners, or the defenders from the lower court case, made clear that the antis' fight won't end here, even with a victory on the fifteen-week law or a reversal of *Roe*. "There are interests here on both sides," he declared. "There are interests for everyone involved. This is unique for the woman. It's unique for the unborn child too whose life is at stake in all of these decisions." This is nothing if not an argument for his—and, by extension, Mississippi's—belief in fetal personhood. Not all the conservative justices seemed game to debate when life begins, but enough did. In addition to Thomas's apparent interest, Alito literally asked, "Are there secular philosophers and bioethicists who take the position that the rights of personhood begin at conception or at some point other than viability?"

On May 2, 2022, Politico published a leaked first draft of Justice Samuel Alito's opinion in the forthcoming *Dobbs v. Jackson Women's Health Organization* case. The draft was devastating in its total rejection of the precedent established in both *Roe v. Wade* and *Planned Parenthood v. Casey*. "*Roe* was egregiously wrong from the start," Alito wrote, calling the legal reasoning behind the landmark ruling "exceptionally weak." Repeatedly, the justice referred to the rulings as incompatible with "this Nation's history and tradition," to which he must have been taking an extremely narrow point of view that is more about the history of Americans who look like him than the nation itself. There was, of course, no mention of Native or Black communities' traditions around abortion, nor any mention of the reproductive atrocities that were inflicted upon nonwhite bodies that are irrevocable from our history.

The leaked draft changed everything. Seeing the dissolution of reproductive autonomy for people with uteruses laid out in the stark black-and-white format of a Supreme Court decision, woke up those who had been (naïvely) insisting that *Roe* could never die. It spurred rage that ultimately led to protests in all fifty states, vigils in front of the Supreme Court, pleas scrawled in chalk on the streets where the conservative justices reside, outside of Susan Collins's house in Bangor, Maine, outside crisis pregnancy centers and churches and statehouses. When city workers came with pressure washers to erase the messages, it felt personal. Like they were erasing us.

Abortion patients are among the most disempowered and disenfranchised in this country, meaning they don't always have access to reliable news or to the sort of education that would allow them to understand the complex machinations of our legal system. Clinics and funds have been overwhelmed with calls from people who were confused about whether they could still get abortions, made worse by reporters who were suddenly thrown into coverage that had long been deprioritized in their newsrooms and therefore did not understand the reproductive health beat, further clogging up the phone lines asking for interviews and clinic tours. Male pundits who didn't seem to care at all about the loss of bodily autonomy pontificated on Twitter and news channels about what the leak meant for the

Supreme Court itself and the ramifications for elections, never mind that pregnant people would soon be forced to give birth in direct conflict with their personal desires.

Even amid the shock and the grief, many organizations had been preparing for something like Alito's draft opinion in *Jackson Women's Health Organization v. Dobbs*. Oriaku Njoku, a cofounder of the Black-led, Atlanta-based abortion fund Access Reproductive Care (ARC)-Southeast, chuckles a little when she thinks about the timing. The day of the leak, the team was working on scenario planning, mapping out what could possibly happen and how they could best prepare to continue to serve their community. "There are three things that could happen: *Roe* could stay the same, *Roe* could be gutted, *Roe* could be overturned," they recall (Oriaku uses she/they pronouns interchangeably). "But one thing that we acknowledge is that *Roe* never guaranteed abortion access; that just made abortion legal." In many ways, the work in the South was going to stay the same. "So regardless of what was going to happen, we already knew access was still going to be an issue."

For Ashley Brink and the team at Trust Women, the goal is simply to keep providing care for as long as possible. After they continued to see an increase in patients from Texas, the Trust Women outpost in Oklahoma City expanded their hours and their staff, scheduling more procedures than they once did. "It's kind of like seeing as many people as we can in a safe and sustainable manner," she told me in May 2022, after the Supreme Court leak. "It's a marathon." Still, she hopes that with the death of *Roe*, the right people step up to help those who are most vulnerable with practical support. "People with privilege need to use it and need to be willing to be the ones to get arrested for driving across state lines to take someone to their appointment or paying for someone's abortion," she said.

The Supreme Court's ruling has not only made it possible for abortion-hostile states to outlaw the procedure within their own borders—it also paves the way for a federal ban on abortion, should Republicans gain control of Congress and the White House. The party is already mobilizing.

CHAPTER 16

After the Fall

EVERYONE WILL FEEL the effects of post-*Roe* America. There are no exceptions, especially given the implications Alito's opinion is likely to have on privacy law. Low-income birthing people, however, will suffer the most acute consequences because of their economic constraints. Those with more resources may be able to travel out of state or even out of the country for care if necessary, though even for people with a solid middle-class income, those costs add up quickly; and travel in and of itself is a burden. None of this is speculation. Even if the Supreme Court ruling is relatively recent, before the ruling was issued, *Roe* had been dead in Texas for eight months.

For the tiny team at Frontera Fund in Texas's Rio Grande Valley, the impact was immediate. The phones continued to ring, and emails avalanched into the group's inbox—from pregnant people asking for help, from people who were unsure of what the law meant, from too-eager reporters who, in the furor of the moment, did not take the time to read the fund's media guidelines and reach out through the designated channels. Overnight, the fund's direct tried-and-true processes were rendered useless. They had prepared contingencies for the law to take effect, but the jump from reliable access hubs in-state to coordinating care and travel out of state, particularly from the southernmost tip of a place known for its vast sprawl, could never be an easy one. The costs quickly add up: there's the travel out of state and back by plane or car, food and drink, lodging, and, in some cases, childcare. Requests for financial and logistical aid swelled.

Cathy Torres, the organizing manager of the Frontera Fund, wears her hair, a striking mix of blue and gray curls, in a cloud piled atop her head. Large black glasses perch on her sculpted brown face. Unsurprisingly, she looks weary, but she also has that steely glint in her eye that's familiar to anyone who has been up against a wall but refuses to back down. She comes by it natural.

Cathy was raised to hold tight to her rights to participate in de-mocracy. Born and raised in the Rio Grande Valley, she was obsessed with Nickelodeon as a kid, and the advertisements to get online and vote for president through their website thrilled her. Of course, even as a child, she knew it wasn't an official voting mechanism, but it still felt significant, like she could have a voice with a push of a button. Her first time logging on to "vote" was in 2004; she voted for John Kerry. In 2008, she voted for Barack Obama, then a senator from Chicago who went on to become the nation's first Black president. (For him, she voted twice on the website.) The first election she was able to vote in legally was the 2014 midterms, mere months after she started college: she voted Wendy Davis for governor, who lost to Re-publican candidate Greg Abbott. Cathy's first presidential election was in 2016, and the outcome—a president who lost the popular vote and was not subtle about his racism and misogyny—devastated her. Still, she's not one to keep count of the losses.

As a freshman in college, she knew she wanted to find a space where she could make a difference, and she cared deeply about social justice and human rights. Getting involved in a student organiza-tion seemed like a good place to start, and the moment she found the Young Democrats, she likens to the scene in *Pitch Perfect* when Anna Kendrick's character comes upon the a cappella group in a similar setting. She felt like she had finally found her people. It was the beginning of a dedication to organizing that would eventually lead her to abortion rights. "I always naïvely thought everyone was pro-choice," she explains. "I had no idea there was an opposition because it just didn't make sense to me to be against it."

As a student, she made friends who were hindered by Texas's restrictions on abortion access, and if there's one way to fire her up, it's to see the people she loves face injustice. She learned about Frontera Fund and was drawn to the way they directly aided people who needed abortion care, so she began pitching in on their fundraising campaigns. Soon, she was volunteering for them, helping book travel for patients and do intake, and her duties continued to escalate in that special, nonprofit way, until she was brought on as full-time staff, just as the six-week ban, also known as SB8, was beginning to take effect. There wasn't much time for grief, but she went home to visit her parents. She wanted to feel safe, just for a day, to be able to cry it out and to enjoy the small comfort of her dad making her favorite food. The group is staffed and led solely by people who are from the Valley, which is crucial, because in conversations about Texas politics or inequality in the state, Cathy says the Valley gets left out. "We *know* what it is our community needs," she says with pride. "There's nothing like actually being there, funding someone's abortion, and making sure that they get there with as little barriers as possible."

Cathy and the group at Frontera Fund know that not all of the people who contact them for help can travel. Some residents of the Rio Grande Valley are undocumented, and it's impossible to leave the Valley without going through a domestic border patrol checkpoint. "Not only is SB8 a major attack on people who can be pregnant, but it's also straight-up racist because it's just more systems of oppression impacting an immigrant person's ability to access abortion care," Cathy explains. Orange-and-white traffic cones divert cars from the dusty highway toward a structure that looks like it could be a toll plaza. Cameras often record cars that pass through and interactions between agents and drivers. At the checkpoint, armed US Customs and Border Protection agents inspect vehicles one at a time, sometimes aided by hulking German shepherds, whose "alerts" constitute probable cause to search a vehicle (no matter that the dogs have about a 50 percent accuracy rate, as determined by multiple analyses). Motorists are asked if they are US citizens, and if they answer in the affirmative, they are permitted to pass through, so long as the agent does not have "reasonable suspicion" that there are either illegal substances in the vehicle or any of the people inside are in the country illegally. By passing through these checkpoints, undocumented people are risking the very thing they are likely seeking—abortion care to protect their families and their lives. "If [people seeking abortions] are undocumented, they either stay here and are forced into parenthood, or they cross the checkpoint, risking deportation," Cathy says. "Undocumented people in the Valley are essentially landlocked between the checkpoint and the border itself."

Under such circumstances, it's possible that pregnant people seeking abortion may reach out to Frontera Fund about how they can self-manage their abortions safely. Perhaps they have already begun the process of self-managing an abortion, and they're afraid that something isn't right. The fund will share resources with those people to make sure they have access to knowledge that keeps them safe throughout the process.

Self-managed abortion through medication is safe and common, and in a post-*Roe* America, it is the most accessible, practical option for those living in areas where abortion is outlawed. For one, medication abortion looks precisely the same as a miscarriage: physicians cannot tell a difference, which means patients have a way to get care should they experience abnormal bleeding or tissue retention from the pregnancy. It is not, however, a solution for everyone, and like abortion access in general, there are vast inequalities in who can get access to misoprostol and mifepristone. Not everyone has access to the internet. Not everyone knows what their rights are. Not everyone has the money to pay for the pills. Not everyone wants to self-manage their abortion. Not everyone can take the legal risk, especially under our current criminal justice system, which disproportionately punishes Black and brown folks for a wide variety of infractions. The future of abortion access is dynamic.

"The post-*Roe* reality that folks talk about is actually the lived experience of southerners every single day. The reality is that wealthy white women are always going to get their abortions. It's never an issue, you know," Oriaku says. "Even the idea of *just order the pills and take the pills*—they're not thinking about how Black and brown bodies are consistently criminalized, and the idea of ordering pills is, one, not something a lot of people do, but two, you just have $250 on hand to immediately pay for medication. That's not people's lived realities."

We also know what happens when pregnant people are denied the abortions they need. A landmark study from a team of researchers at the University of California, San Francisco's Advancing New Standards in Reproductive Health, tracked one thousand women who were either denied abortion care or received abortion care over a decade and found that being turned away caused devastating long-term harm. For one, they were less likely to survive childbirth than the average American woman, according to the national maternal death rate, and many experienced delivery complications. These women suffered depression and low self-esteem as a result of being unable to access abortion care, and six months after giving birth, they were four times more likely to be living below the federal poverty line than women who recieved abortion care, which also directly impacts the ability to parent. These women saw their credit scores plummet, and they were more likely to develop chronic migraines. They were more likely to remain in contact with an abusive partner. These women were trapped in lives they did not want, and lives that were ultimately poorer and more challenging than perhaps what they had dreamt of. Being denied an abortion was a violation of a human right that altered the rest of their days.

CHAPTER 17

A New Network

I N AN ERA without *Roe v. Wade*, there will be no coat hanger abortions. We are not entering the world depicted in Margaret Atwood's dystopian novel, *The Handmaid's Tale*, published in 1985: there will be no scarlet cloaks, no white "wings" to cover our faces, no demure, oblique expressions—"may the Lord open" and "under His Eye." Sure, there are broad, frightening parallels to the iconic book that has been adapted into a popular TV series, but it is a work of fiction written from one (white, cisgendered) woman's perspective, and the reality of what has happened, what has *been* happening, and what could still happen is frightening enough.

Abortion rights groups have been preparing for the end of *Roe* for a very long time, especially in those communities that already face disproportionate criminalization regarding pregnancy outcomes and have endured abject racism in the medical system. White women, in particular, must learn from our past and step aside, taking direction from leaders whose lived experiences are most relevant in this moment. In the United States, white feminism has been a force that has shaped the bent of women's rights and has consistently upheld white supremacist values. To be clear, when I refer to white feminism, I am not referring to white women broadly who are feminists. I'm referring to a power dynamic in which white women use the surface ideals of feminism to achieve their own agendas, ignoring the needs of women of color and ultimately upholding white supremacy. It is the antithesis of intersectionality, a term coined by Black professor Kimberlé Crenshaw in 1989, which observes that society creates multiple ways to marginalize people—race, class, gender, sexual orientation, physical ability, age—and that it's important to take all of these factors, and the ways they interact, into account.

Author and journalist Koa Beck, a queer woman of mixed race, explains white feminism as "an ideology, and a very specific approach to achieving gender equality that inherits its strategy from white supremacy. This idea that you are hurtling towards the accumulation of power, which white feminism has always been on board with—more women in this position, more women in this department, more women in Congress—but there's no real reinterpretation of that power or consideration of how to redistribute it." This dynamic has been apparent within the reproductive rights movement historically—the passage of the Hyde Amendment, for example, and before that the "pro-choice" framing by white women who sought to use what we would now call respectability politics to gain legitimacy and hold onto it—and it persists to this day. As Mikki Kendall writes in her book *Hood Feminism*: "Since its inception, mainstream feminism has been insisting that some women have to wait longer for equality, that once one group (usually white women) achieves equality then that opens the way for all other women . . . white feminism tends to forget that a movement that claims to be for all women has to engage with the obstacles women who are not white face."

The white feminist–led approach to abortion rights had become complacent before the fall of *Roe* because abortion was technically legal and accessible to certain privileged populations. As the Hyde Amendment became a barrier for low-income people and as anti-abortion model legislation gave state lawmakers an easy, assembly-line approach to chipping away at access, *Roe* still stood, and abortion rights leaders clung to the 1973 ruling as the bottom line, often glossing over the stark reality that *Roe* was always the floor, not the ceiling. It came to a point, observes Dr. Tracy Weitz, in which the mainstream movement was protecting abortion in law only, not for those who truly needed it.

Now, because white women have enjoyed a degree of privilege, they can sometimes assume that they are, as the well-worn mantras say, the only ones who can "get shit done." But abortion funds, particularly those run by people of color, are feeling the strain. "We love the energy, we love the want to alleviate the distress," Cathy Torres says. "But we would really appreciate it if folks would educate themselves a little bit." Instead of giving in to a savior impulse, she says, the best thing that white women of means can do is to support the existing networks that were built by those who are intimately familiar with the terrain. In Texas and in much of the Southeast, for example, the vast majority of abortion funds are led by people of color, and the work they've done to provide aid to their community in the aftermath of the six-week abortion ban passed in 2021 speaks for itself.

Oriaku Njoku suggests privileged white women think about it like this: "Instead of being an ally and standing in solidarity, how can you be an accomplice or co-conspirator to make sure that the material conditions of people who are also in your community are being met? How can you make sure that you come to this work not with the white savior complex, but because you're invested in everyone in your community being able to thrive?"

"As long as the privileges that white women get to have and move through the world are intact, they can stand and they can have deep reflection and a tear can fall for us," says Rev. Cherisse Scott, CEO of SisterReach, a reproductive justice organization based in Memphis, Tennessee. "But we are out here literally trying to save our lives and the lives of our children and our families and communities, and I just don't see the same level of commitment [from our white counterparts]." The inequality Rev. Scott is referring to is a power imbalance that has all too often been ignored, and it has exacerbated the gaping divide regarding who gets quality care. White women are elevated to lead, but they don't take the time to learn what is necessary for those with different lived experiences.

The fight for abortion rights has had a white feminism problem for as long as it's been around in the United States. White women have largely been comfortable with the idea of abortion as a stand-alone issue: "reproductive rights" largely has meant "abortion rights" only and has been presented as a binary choice. It has never been so simple for people of color, which is why, in 1994, the reproductive justice movement was formed, which articulated abortion rights as only one aspect of reproductive autonomy. The foremothers of the movement "recognized that the women's rights movement, led by and representing middle class and wealthy white women, could not defend the needs of women of color and other marginalized women and trans people," explains SisterSong, the nonprofit that formed out of the reproductive justice framework. "We needed to lead our own national movement to uplift the needs of the most marginalized women, families, and communities." So reproductive justice spans the breadth of reproductive decision-making—to give birth or not and to raise any children in an environment that is safe, healthy, and conducive to a good quality of life. The movement also examined and laid out why restrictions on abortion, which are most often rooted in racism and classism, are harmful to the health and well-being of all people. "It's necessary to grasp and articulate what's wrong with restrictions on abortion," acknowledges Dorothy Roberts, a prominent Black scholar who uses the reproductive justice framework to study inequality in reproduction. "Forced pregnancy is part of a broader devaluation of women and attempts to control women's lives, which is a very gendered form of social control. We make a stronger claim to the right to abortion if we understand these connections, and the broader societal implications, as well as building a stronger movement, when we can be in solidarity with people who are fighting for these various aspects of reproductive freedom."

It is necessary, too, for abortion rights organizations and those purporting to speak for the most marginalized in this country to articulate clear goals. National abortion rights organizations like NARAL and Planned Parenthood traditionally—though not exclusively—have been led and overwhelmingly staffed by upper-middle-class white women. These groups have been well-funded for years—for so many Americans with expendable income, the reaction to any large-scale assault on abortion rights has translated to "time to donate to Planned Parenthood." What most folks don't understand is that if they donate by default to Planned Parenthood at the national level, that money isn't being used to help people directly access abortion care. It's used for lobbying. It goes to fund conversations between people who have resources and power, whose experiences are far removed from those who have experienced limited reproductive autonomy in this country. When the Supreme Court announced it would take up the *Dobbs* case, "everybody and they mama sent out emails," fundraising off the new immediate threat at the federal level, Laurie Bertram Roberts says, exasperated. "[Mississippi Reproductive Freedom Fund] has been funding Mississippians the longest: we were the first abortion fund on the ground here. And you know who gets the least amount of funding for abortion?

"What kills me is that it's because we're not big and we're not sophisticated. We're not the right kind of Black people. We don't have degrees. Our parents weren't doctors and lawyers. We're not bougie in the right kind of way. I might be light skinned, but I ain't the right kind of light-skinned person. We don't get that kind of attention. And the thing that kills me about that is people will run and give money to Planned Parenthood every time something happens in Mississippi, but Planned Parenthood don't perform abortions in Mississippi."

Maybe to the people who live in hotbeds of political power, Laurie doesn't look like the "right kind of" abortion advocate. But she does look like (and, most importantly, she has the lived experience of) a lot of folks who seek abortion care.

Groups like the Planned Parenthood Action Fund, NARAL Pro-Choice America, and EMILY's List offer endorsements for candidates, and grades and rating systems for members of Congress, but it doesn't seem to take much beyond lip service to supporting abortion rights, or votes on certain bills, for candidates and politicians to get their seal of approval from these organizations. "They don't actually have people who are having abortions at heart," says Renee Bracey Sherman. "They're mini corporations."

Now, we're facing the consequences of that approach. Even legislative attempts to head off a Supreme Court reversal of *Roe* have seemed half-hearted. The Women's Health Protection Act first failed in the Senate in February 2022, a few months before Justice Alito's draft opinion in the *Dobbs* case was leaked. It was then reintroduced—with all references to reproductive justice removed—after the leak, only for it to, of course, fail once more. Joe Biden, the president of the United States who ran for office pledging to protect "reproductive health care," has said the word *abortion* once as of nearly two years into his tenure, according to We Testify. And for all the marches and pink pussy hats in the world, there has been little in the way of clear demands. "It becomes very self-evident to those of us who study social movements that there's no power here," Dr. Weitz says of the majority of mainstream women's rights organizing. "There's outrage, but there's no power."

This has been a sore point for local, grassroots organizations who *do* practice direct aid and whose leadership is likely to reflect the communities they serve. "I've done the research. I've talked to my community. My community says, 'This is what they need,'" says Rachael Lorenzo, who has Mescalero Apache, Laguna Pueblo, and Xicana roots and is the executive director of Indigenous Women Rising. "And I am here to provide that."

Now, as the federal right to abortion has been shattered, the folks doing direct-aid work hope this means that the movement can take an honest look at where its power has been concentrated and redistribute it according to true need.

The death of *Roe* offers an opportunity to right these wrongs and to make sure power is redistributed to those who have been consistently and systematically disempowered. If we do it right, we could build a stronger future that considers and values the full spectrum of everyone's reproductive needs.

Afterword

I THOUGHT, HAVING written this book, having spent most of my career warning of the end of the constitutional right to abortion, that I would be prepared when the *Dobbs* ruling came down.

After living through a presidency that seemed almost assured not to happen, an insurrection, a global pandemic, I should know by now that to assume to know anything about what is still to come is only arrogance.

On the morning of June 24, I walked my dog, made my coffee, and settled in with my laptop by 9 A.M. to monitor SCOTUSblog and see whether the Supreme Court would issue the *Dobbs* ruling. I had been doing this for weeks—tabbing between Twitter and Slack and SCOTUSblog, buckling up for the swells of anxiety that came in ten-minute increments as the Court released the orders of the day. "I have a bad feeling," my *Mother Jones* editor typed into our Slack chat. "I mean, I do every decision day, but idk." I shrugged, assuming that it wouldn't come until the end of the month, which was the end of the term. That the justices would want to drop the controversial ruling and then get the hell outta Dodge. That there was still time. Then, of course, at 9:11 A.M., it happened.

The following hours and days are lost in a blur of adrenaline. Not knowing what else to do after publishing the immediate news, I got in my car and drove to the local Planned Parenthood here in Nashville. The lot was empty, save for a TV news crew and a gaggle of very happy white men in blue shirts who frequented the sidewalk to "counsel" women who were seeking abortions. Three of the men wore long-sleeved sun-protective blue shirts that featured an insignia of a pair of baby's feet with a heart in between. "Missionary to the Pre-Born," the white lettering said. "Scott Hord Ministries." Honks punctuated the noise of the road with regularity, usually from rumbling delivery trucks, celebrating the Supreme Court's decision to overturn the right to abortion. One man drove by, right hand on the wheel, his upper body hanging out of the open window of his pickup truck. "Roe versus Wade!" he crowed, honking. He wore a jubilant grin. The men on the sidewalk waved and cheered in response.[1]

Over the course of our conversation, after I had introduced myself and explained why I was there, they made it very clear that they did not feel that their work was done. Scott Hord, the leader of the group, spoke of plans to train up and organize even more antiabortion protesters in the states that have pledged to keep abortion legal, like Illinois. He hopes for a day in which abortion is abolished, full stop. When it comes to issues like pregnancy as a product of sexual violence, he is clear that he thinks rape is abominable, but he says he defines the act as "the forcing of one's will against another to bring harm." He then drew a parallel between that and abortion. "What is abortion? Unfortunately, it's the forcing of one's will against another, not to bring harm, to bring death."

I must admit that as someone who has been assaulted,[2] as someone who knows and loves so many women who have had similar and more horrific experiences, I had to set my jaw against my own nausea at this point in the conversation. I drove home, numb, wrote and filed my stories, and tried to prepare for a new world—one in which the damage and trauma I've been covering is much, much more severe.

After that morning, abortion bans went into effect across the country at a dizzying rate. Oklahoma was ahead of the curve—a full month before the *Dobbs* ruling, the state banned abortion[3] for pregnant people who are about six weeks along, effectively shuttering one of Trust Women's two clinics. Alabama, Arkansas, Texas, Missouri, and South Dakota were among the first[4] to follow suit once they officially had the judicial branch's blessing.

Two days after the ruling, I drove to Alabama's capital, Montgomery, to try to start to wrap my head around post-*Roe* America. On Monday morning, when I arrived at Reproductive Health Services, a red truck pulled into the near-empty parking lot of the city's only abortion clinic. The driver, a woman from Birmingham, an hour and a half away, rolled down her window as a petite white woman with a pink ponytail, wearing a bright rainbow vest, strode across the cracked asphalt to meet her. When she reached the truck, Mia Raven began to gently explain that her appointment was canceled, that the unthinkable had happened, that abortion was now illegal in Alabama.

The woman inside the truck was dumbfounded. She told Mia that she had called the clinic in Montgomery that morning before she left her home and had been assured that the doors were open, that she should come on down. It didn't take long for Mia to piece together what had happened. She pointed across the street to a lot where people lingered among signs advertising free ultrasounds.

A man had also walked up to the truck from that direction, but he stayed on the sidewalk, looking at the duo and loudly droning a sermon he had clearly given many times.

"You spoke to the crisis pregnancy center," Mia said flatly. "They won't help you get an abortion."

"But they have the word *choice* in the name . . . ," the woman explained.

Mia nodded sympathetically. "I know, baby, that's how they confuse you."

She pulled a sheet of paper off the clipboard she'd been clutching and handed it through the window of the truck. At the top of the paper, it read: "As of June 24, 2022, abortion is now illegal in Alabama. We hope you find this list of resources & information helpful." Below, there was a list of resources for continuing a pregnancy, the information for a pro-choice adoption agency, and a list of states where abortion is legal (with caveats about gestational bans and that the landscape is shifting quickly). Within moments, the window was rolled back up, and the truck slowly pulled out of the parking lot and out of sight.

In the next half hour or so, this basic series of events repeated twice more. Then, by around 10 a.m., there were no more cars.[5] The expressions on the faces of the women have stayed with me, the way they flashed from insistence, then anger, then fear, then . . . nothing.

For Alabama clinic staff, abortion providers, and escorts, the pace at which their state banned abortion, paired with the fluidity of the law, meant they were mired in confusion, heartbreak, and fury. In mere hours after the *Dobbs* ruling, the state had filed an emergency motion to reinstate the 2019 Human Life Protection Act, which had been deemed unconstitutional three years ago, when the right to abortion was protected by precedent. Judge Myron Thompson responded to the state's motion by lifting the injunction.[6] Abortion funds and clinics suddenly found themselves in meetings with criminal lawyers who advised them all to practice extreme caution, given the hostility of Alabama to abortion and the state's clear intent to restrict the medical procedure as much as possible, as quickly as possible. Mia and Reproductive Health Services in Montgomery, along with the Yellowhammer Fund, the West Alabama Women's Center in Tuscaloosa, and Alabama Women's Center in Huntsville, all received similar legal advice: to tell patients that abortion was illegal in Alabama but to not make any specific recommendations regarding where they should go for care. The lawyer that consulted with Mia went so far as to tell her to include adoption and ob-gyn information in the pamphlet she was distributing to people who came to the clinic seeking help so that it wouldn't appear that she was prioritizing abortion as an option when she listed the states where the procedure was still legal.[7]

The clinic in Huntsville is a mainstay of the community. It's been around for more than two decades, and it's where many low-income folks go to get reproductive health care even beyond abortion. It must stay open, and in order for it to do that, the people who make it run must be there and able to focus on their patients. Providing abortion care is a calling for Dr. Sanithia Williams, who practiced out of the Huntsville clinic. Now, she provides all the reproductive health care she has before, except abortion. In the week after the *Dobbs* decision, she saw one of her regular patients at the private practice she shares with Dr. Yashica Robinson. The woman came in, told Dr. Williams she thought she was having a miscarriage, and rattled off a list of symptoms. "Well, those all sound like very common pregnancy symptoms, but let's take a look and see what's going on," Dr. Williams told her. The ultrasound confirmed that all was well, and when Dr. Williams said as much, her patient broke down into tears. She had found out she was pregnant only a couple of days earlier, after *Roe* was overturned, and she had hoped she was miscarrying so that she wouldn't be forced to give birth. Normally, this is where Dr. Williams could tell her that abortion was an option and talk her through what that procedure might look like, should she wish to pursue it. Now, she could only let her know that there were places in the United States where abortion was still legal, but that as her doctor, she could not provide that care. Instead of going through this with someone she knew and trusted, the patient would have to get abortion care with a complete stranger, if she was able to travel out of state in the first place.

"It's hard enough to not be able to actually provide the service, but it's an extra kick in the teeth to not understand exactly what the laws are and not even be able to help someone navigate finding the next clinic or making an appointment, things like that," she says. "To be so unclear on what exactly we can and cannot say to patients—I feel amputated as a provider."

Dr. Williams is forced to contend with another factor—she is a Black woman who has been providing abortion care in a country that is governed by a criminal justice system that has proved itself to be disproportionately harsh on people of color. The owner of the clinic is a Black man, and the other doctor, Dr. Robinson, is a Black woman. They feel a heightened sense of the stakes when it comes to potentially misinterpreting the law, and they have every reason to be wary. "As a Black woman, I'm really familiar with the idea of what happens to Black folks when they interact with the criminal justice system," Dr. Williams told NPR.[8] "I'm well aware, as a Black woman, that I want to be careful about the types of decisions that I'm making and making sure that I'm doing everything according to the letter of the law." That pressure, too, goes beyond the simple binary of whether abortion care is offered. Both Williams and Robinson are ob-gyns, which means they guide people through pregnancies and, of course, all the complications that can come with that.

Before the *Dobbs* ruling, in states like Texas where abortion was banned after roughly six weeks, pregnant people who needed abortion care for medical reasons—maybe the fetus was not viable—were often told to travel out of state even under those circumstances by doctors who feared accidentally challenging the law. Dr. Ghazaleh Moayedi, who is an ob-gyn in Texas, has been navigating the conflict between the law and her job as a physician for months. "The law makes it seem like medicine can be objective," she said. "The reality is that medicine is not a science at all, right? No person's body is an algorithm that follows a direct course. Medicine is an art that is *informed* by science." Dr. Moayedi and her colleagues have been forced to work in the fuzziness of that art with increasingly dire legal consequences hovering overhead. "I've had to have discussions in an obstetric setting of like, 'Well, is this life-threatening *enough*? Well, no, we think her heart function is okay enough to live right now,' meaning it's not deadly enough to warrant an exception to the emergency clause," she said. "We have to constantly have conversations with other physicians about where that line falls."[9]

To be sure, there have also been examples of people in the reproductive care space using their privilege to take on more risk. In Tuscaloosa, those in leadership at the clinic decided that they would refer people to specific clinics to get the care they needed because the law did not explicitly bar them from doing so. Robin Marty, who is white, says that she felt a moral obligation to continue care in whatever legal way that she was able. "We did not encourage them to continue with their abortion, we did not discourage them and tell them that they shouldn't, we simply listened to them," she says. "We told them that this was an option that if they wish to continue their abortion they could still do that, and then we made sure that they understood that they could not get an abortion here with us."[10] To protect the staff from any legal retribution, Robin told them all that if they didn't comply, she would fire them—not to make them do anything they didn't want to, but rather to keep the responsibility on her shoulders.

As abortion bans continue to go into effect across the country, some clinics are packing up shop and working to move their practices to states that are pledging to protect abortion rights, in part to help handle the massive patient influx that those states are experiencing. CHOICES, a full-spectrum reproductive care clinic in Memphis, Tennessee, is opening a clinic in Illinois. The Pink House in Jackson, Mississippi, and Texas's Whole Woman's Health clinics have plans to move to New Mexico. Some abortion funds are taking time off to recuperate in the immediate aftermath of the *Dobbs* ruling, regrouping while the legal landscape stabilizes. They know their work is, in some ways, beginning anew.

A future in which reproductive justice is at the heart of the law and our culture has never seemed farther away. But activists, abortion funds, and abortion providers all insist with wholehearted passion that they are not done, that they will continue to work toward a day when all people and their families have access to full-spectrum health care, nutritious food and clean water, and the freedom to live their lives without fear of harm levied by hate.

"*Roe* was before, and we can build something better, something that is more intersectional," says Imani Gandy, senior editor of Law and Policy for Rewire News Group and a true expert on all things abortion. "And I think because reproductive rights as a framework is sort of ceding ground to reproductive justice, we are in a better position as a movement to build something that works for everyone. And it might take twenty-five, thirty years, but at least hopefully at the end of those thirty years, we won't be in a situation where only people who can afford it can get abortions."

Acknowledgments

I FEEL FORTUNATE to have been able to write this book, and above all, I am grateful to the generosity and trust of those who chose to speak with me, who patiently told me their stories, corrected my assumptions, and explained this complex, quickly changing landscape. Not all of their names and experiences appear in this book, but those conversations shaped the text and are the foundation of what you've read. In particular, I feel indebted to those who shared their abortion stories with me. The greatest honor of my life has been to bear witness to the wide spectrum of abortion stories that have been entrusted to me over the course of my career. Thank you is not enough.

My agent, Jill Grinberg, took a call from me out of the blue and guided me through the process of proposing and publishing a book with kindness and humor. She is a fierce advocate, and I am extraordinarily lucky to have her in my corner. Colleen Lawrie is the book editor of my dreams. She believed I could write a book before I did, and she has not wavered in that belief, even when we drastically stepped up the time line of *No Choice*. I'm not convinced I could have made it work with anyone else. Her thoughtful comments and empathetic approach are the backbone of this text. The team at PublicAffairs has supported this effort in every way possible. Johanna Dickson made it her mission to promote the hell out of *No Choice* and somehow made the publicity side of this whole thing less daunting. Christine Marra, Jane Raese, Kate Mueller, Jeff Georgeson, Donna Riggs, and Melissa Raymond kept the trains running on time and whipped the manuscript into shape with precise copy edits and style changes. They are superstars.

To Laura Thompson, my gal Friday, who fact-checked the bulk of this work with immense care and dedication. Thank you for your labor, your candor, and your friendship: I mean it when I tell you this could not have happened without you. To Sara Krolewski, who came on at the last minute to pitch in on the final sections of the book, I am so grateful that the publishing gods brought us together. You are a true hero. Any inaccuracy within these pages is an error of my own making and happened in spite of the work of these two women, not because of them. It is my responsibility alone.

To Vauhini Vara, who took me through two years of the book-writing process via the Book Project of the Lighthouse Writers Workshop. Thank you for talking me down over and over, for puzzling out structural solutions, for cheering me on relentlessly. To Renee Bracey Sherman, who made time for my work over and over, even when she truly did not have the time, and who challenged me to be better. You will always be my Beyoncé. Emily Rapp Black read an early chapter of *No Choice* in a workshop and has been a champion of it and me ever since, and it still stuns me to be able to say that. Her tender heart and righteous fury kept me going even when the writing process got really, really dark.

This book was made possible with the support of the Lighthouse Writers Workshop, the Nashville Public Library, and the Virginia Center for Creative Arts. My Book Project cohort offered tremendous feedback over the past two years, and I am thankful for those comments from Sabrina Sarro, Melissa Alvarado Sierra, Simone Stolzoff, John J. Lennon, Nami Thompson, and Jeffrey Darst. At VCCA, James Kennedy, Janly Jaggard, Fiona Donovan, Sharon Charde, Boris Torres, Lisa Eunice Reisman, and Martha Anne Toll, among others, consistently listened to me despair and told me to snap out of it when I needed that. Thank you.

The following institutions allowed me to access their archives and granted me knowledge and detail that brought so many characters to life. They are: the Graduate Theological Union at Berkeley, McCormick Special Collections and Archives at Northwestern University, the Schlesinger Library at Harvard University (with a special shout-out to research librarian Sarah Hutcheon). Long live libraries and librarians. Isabela Dias, too, assisted with research at the Library of Congress.

I am fortunate to have an incredibly loving community, friends who have celebrated me and pushed me and engaged with these pages. The women at *Mother Jones* (#staff-lady-chat forever), past and present, were a source of support and friendship and laughter for seven years, and I love them all furiously. Christopher Merchant, Eddie Rios, Celeste Mora, Amanda Silverman, Nina Liss-Schultz, Caitlin Cruz, Lauren Markham, and Emily West generously read pieces of this book and took the time to talk through ways to make it better. My writing group—Diana Dresser, Sarah Dealy, H. R. Hegenaur (and honorary member, Monette)—did the same and somehow made me feel safe doing the scariest thing of my career. Special thanks to Kara Voght for the gift of noise-cancelling headphones early in the process, her unending support, and for giving me a place to stay on several trips to DC (thanks, also, to her generous husband, Ben Cushing).

It's difficult to put into words what Amanda Silverman means to me. At *Mother Jones,* she was my editor for nearly five years, and not only have her relentless questions and persistent pushing made me a better writer, reporter, and investigator, but she has also become one of my dearest friends. Sharing my work (and, sometimes, a brain) with her has been the privilege of my career. Eddie Rios read my pages and gave me feedback, *and* he sent me the greatest series of care packages of all time, while reminding me to do basic things like drink water, not just coffee, and to move my body. Eddie, thank you for being family to me.

To my teachers: Leon Alligood was the first to teach me that journalism does not mean sacrificing beautiful writing. Sonny Rawls taught me to walk confidently into places I am not supposed to be and how to make trouble in the best way. Deborah Gump taught me the value of an iron will and that exclamation points do have a (very rare) place. Dr. Jenna Gray-Hildenbrand blew open my world with her women and religion class and showed me that feminism and faith do not have to be at odds. Jane Marcellus has always been an inexhaustible fountain of support and research knowledge, and without her, I would probably not have started dating my husband. Jennifer Kahn took me seriously at a time when it really, truly mattered and changed my life forever. Lea Ann Atherton told me in the sixth grade that I could be a writer and gave me permission to chase that dream, impossible though it seemed to a small-town southern girl.

I have long been buoyed by the encouragement and support of Amanda Haggard, Rainesford Stauffer, Lexi Marshall, Noelle Anderson, Sarah Mimms, Heather Mimms, Nancy DeVille, Brittany Patterson, Nausheen Husain, Samantha Masunaga, Lara King, Adam Hochschild, Kim Green and Hal Humphrey, the Havner family (Trista, Charlie, Cal, and Charlie Grey), Dalton Rardin, and so many more. Peter Quick believed in me when we were just kids, many years before I figured out how to do that for myself. Pete, I love you and I miss you, and there's a piece of you in every single second of every single day.

I have the best in-laws on the face of the earth. Drew and Lisa Potter are the older siblings I always wanted: Lisa is pure sunshine, and Drew is the only person I've ever met whose stubbornness rivals my own. I adore them and look up to them. Andrew and Libby Potter are less in-laws and more parents to me, and my God, how lucky am I to write books with two former librarians on my side. I love you two immensely, and I'm proud to be your daughter.

Mark and Janet Andrews, my sweet, wonderful parents, have always supported me without question and have never made me feel anything short of beloved, even when I have been difficult to understand. Never, not once, have they asked me to be anything other than myself. Lauren Andrews, my sister, my best friend, has been a gift my entire life and has taught me to see the world with wonder and awe. Also, she curated TikTok selections to make me laugh in the final months of edits, and it truly kept me sane.

Finally, Daniel Potter. Every Hallmark cliché and beyond applies to you. My life partner, my creative partner, the love of my life. Thank you for seeing me through it all, even the "Norman Mailer" phase of authoring. Until the sun explodes.

Notes

1. B. Andrews, "I Watched Them Celebrate," *Mother Jones*, June 24, 2022, https://www.motherjones.com/politics/2022/06/roe-pro-life -protesters-nashville-abortion-planned-parenthood/.

2. B. Andrews, "Evangelical Purity Culture Taught Me to Rationalize My Sexual Assault," *Mother Jones*, September/October, 2018, https://www .motherjones.com/politics/2018/08/evangelical-purity-culture-taught-me -to-rationalize-my-sexual-assault/.

3. Associated Press, "Oklahoma Governor Signs Nation's Strictest Abortion Ban," Politico, May 24, 2022, https://www.politico.com/news /2022/05/25/oklahoma-strictest-abortion-ban-stitt-00035302.

4. Guttmacher Institute, "Alabama," July 8, 2022, https://states .guttmacher.org/policies/alabama/abortion-policies.

5. B. Andrews, "Mourning in Montana," *Mother Jones*, June 27, 2022, https://www.motherjones.com/politics/2022/06/abortion-clinic-shut -down-montgomery-alabama-what-happened/.

6. A. Yurkanin, "Supreme Court Abortion Ban: Alabama Abortion Advocates Regroup After Roe v. Wade Decision," Al.com, June 24, 2022, https://www.al.com/news/2022/06/supreme-court-abortion-ban-alabama -abortion-advocates-regroup-after-scotus-decision.html.

7. B. Andrews, "220627_Mia_Raven," Otter, June 27, 2022, https:// otter.ai/u/OKZ41C4AADV7Ag43u1ZdAy-JEwQ.

8. S. Bond, "One Black Abortion Clinic Fears Being Further Targeted by the Justice System," NPR, July 3, 2022, https://www.npr.org/2022/07/0 3/1109607660/one-black-abortion-clinic-fears-being-further-targeted-by -the-justice-system.

9. G. Moayedi, "I'm an Abortion Provider in Texas and I'm Forced to Consider: Is 'This Life-Threatening Enough?'," as told to B. Andrews, *Mother Jones*, June 30, 202, https://www.motherjones.com/politics/2022 /06/abortion-providers-forced-decisions-life-of-mother-exception-texas/.

10. B. Becca, "Robin 22," Otter, June 28, 2022, https://otter.ai/u/LTEb EED1to3BfVWSvYzjctI_TME.

Bibliography

Abma, Joyce C., and Gladys M. Martinez. "Sexual Activity and Contraceptive Use Among Teenagers in the United States, 2011–2015." *National Health Statistics Report* 104 (2017).

Andrews, B. "Amy Coney Barrett Keeps Insisting She Has 'No Agenda' When It Comes to Abortion Law." *Mother Jones*, October 13, 2020.

———. "As a Girl, I Went Through Abstinence Ed. As a Woman, I'm Trying to Understand the Damage Done." *Mother Jones*, September 28, 2016.

———. "The Infuriating and Inspiring Story Behind the Opening of a Red-State Abortion Clinic." *Mother Jones*, August 1, 2016.

———. "When Choice Is 221 Miles Away: The Nightmare of Getting an Abortion in the South." *Mother Jones*, September/October 2019.

———. "White Ladies: Curl Up in Your 'The Future Is Female' Sweatshirt and Read This Book." Interview with K. Beck. *Mother Jones*, February 2, 2021.

———. "Why the Sale of a Tuscaloosa Abortion Clinic Could Signal a Massive Change in Abortion Care." *Mother Jones*, May 15, 2020.

Angyal, C. "Selling an Abortion Clinic Might Be Even Harder Than Running One." HuffPost, August 31, 2017.

Arcana, J. 2020. *Hello. This is Jane.* O'Brien, OR : Left Fork.

Arcana, J., J. Galatzer-Levy, R. Surgal, M. Stern, CSLU Herstory Project, and Jane. *Jane: Documents from Chicago's Clandestine Abortion Service, 1968–1973.* Portland, OR: Eberhardt Press, 2007.

Arons, J. "The Last Clinics Standing" (web page). American Civil Liberties Union, 2018.

Baehr, N. *Abortion Without Apology: A Radical History for the 1990s.* Boston: South End Press, 1999.

Barnett, R., and D. Baker. 1978. *They Weep on My Doorstep.* Medford, OR: Pacific Northwest Books Co.

BBC. "Historical Attitudes to Abortion" (web page).

———. "New Life for Texas Abortion Bill Blocked by Wendy Davis," June 26, 2013.

Beck, K. *White Feminism: From the Suffragettes to Influencers and Who They Leave Behind*. New York: Atria/Simon and Schuster, 2021.

Beery, Z. "What Abortion Access Looks Like in Mississippi: One Person at a Time." *New York Times*, June 13, 2019.

Bonow, A., E. Nokes, and L. West. *Shout Your Abortion*. Oakland, CA: PM Press, 2018.

Boston Women's Health Book Collective. *Our Bodies, Ourselves*. New York: Atria/Simon and Schuster, 2011.

Bristol Regional Women's Center. "Welcome to Bristol Regional Women's Center." www.bristolregionalwomenscenter.com/.

Brown, J. *Without Apology: The Abortion Struggle Now*. London; New York: Verso, 2019.

Brownmiller, S. "Abortion Counseling: Service Beyond Sermons." *New York Magazine*, August 4, 1969.

Burns, R. M., and K. A. Shaw. "Standardizing Abortion Education: What Medical Schools Can Learn from Residency Programs." *Current Opinion in Obstetrics and Gynecology* 32, no. 6 (2020): 387–392.

Caplan-Bricker, N. "The Five Worst Things About Texas's Abortion Law—and Three Ways to Fight It." *New Republic*, July 17, 2013.

Carmen, A. *Family Planning Oral History Project Interviews*, 1973–1977. OH-1; T-25; M-138; A1-3, Interview V. Schlesinger Library, Radcliffe Institute. Cambridge, MA: Harvard University.

Carmen, A., and H. Moody. *Abortion Counseling and Social Change from Illegal Act to Medical Practice: The Story of the Clergy Consultation Service on Abortion*. Valley Forge, PA: Judson Press, 1973.

Cates, W., Jr. "Legal Abortion: The Public Health Record." *Science* 215, no. 4540 (1982): 1,586–1,590.

Cha, A. E., and R. Roubein. "Fetal Viability Is at the Center of Mississippi Abortion Case. Here's Why." *Washington Post*, December 1, 2021.

Chen, S. "Hundreds of Children Died in Native American Boarding Schools, Report Finds." Axios, May 11, 2022.

Chowdhary, P., A. Newton-Levinson, and R. Rochat. "'No One Does This for the Money or Lifestyle': Abortion Providers' Perspectives on Factors Affecting Workforce Recruitment and Retention in the Southern United States." *Maternal and Child Health Journal* 26, no. 6 (2022): 1,350–1,357.

Cohen, D. S., and C. Joffe. *Obstacle Course: The Everyday Struggle to*

Get an Abortion in America. Oakland, CA: University of California Press,2021.

Conradt, S. "5 Famous Filibusters." *Mental Floss*, March 8, 2013.

Cook, L., and K. Leonard. "Explaining the Whole Woman's Health v. Hellerstedt Abortion Case." *U.S. News and World Report*, January 11, 2016.

Crockett, E. "Mississippi Gov. Phil Bryant: 'My Goal Is to End Abortion in Mississippi.'" Rewire News Group, 2014.

———. "Study: Women Had to Drive 4 Times Farther After Texas Laws Closed Abortion Clinics." Vox, March 20, 2016.

———. *Whole Woman's Health v. Hellerstedt*. Chicago-Kent College of Law, Illinois Institute of Technology, 2016.

Cross, E., and L. Cross. "26 States Are Certain or Likely to Ban Abortion Without Roe: Here's Which Ones and Why." Guttmacher Institute, October 28, 2021.

Cruz, Ted. "Sen. Ted Cruz Reads Shakespeare on the Senate Floor During Rand Paul Filibuster." Published by Charlie Spiering. YouTube video, 2:12, March 27, 2013.

Currie, B., D. Eubanks, A. Gipson, J. Ford, L. Carpenter, N. Bain, D. Scoggin, et al. House Bill 1510. Regular session 2018, Mississippi Legislature.

Davis, F. *Moving the Mountain: The Women's Movement in America Since 1960*. Urbana: University of Illinois Press, 1999.

Davis, W. *Forgetting to Be Afraid: A Memoir*. New York: Penguin, 2015.

Dean, S. "The Mother of Socrates: Priestess, Pharmacist, Obstetrician." Feminism & Religion (website), November 5, 2015.

Dioscorides Pedanius, W. M. *Pedanii Dioscuridis Anazarbei De materia medica libri quinque*. Hildesheim, Germany: Weidmann, 2004.

Dirks, D. A. *To Offer Compassion: A History of the Clergy Consultation Service on Abortion*. Madison: University of Wisconsin Press, 2019.

Douglas, S. J., and M. W. Michaels. *The Mommy Myth: The Idealization of Motherhood and How It Has Undermined Women*. New York: Free Press, 2004.

Ehrenreich, B., and D. English. *Witches, Midwives, and Nurses: A History of Women Healers*. 2nd ed. New York: Feminist Press, 2016.

Ekland-Olson, S. *Who Lives, Who Dies, Who Decides?: Abortion, Neonatal Care, Assisted Dying, and Capital Punishment*. Oxfordshire, UK: Taylor and Francis, 2014.

Endicott, M. "After a Flood of Donations, an Alabama Group Can Now Fund Three Times as Many Abortions as Last Year." *Mother Jones*, May 21, 2019.

Espey, E., T. Ogburn, A. Chavez, C. Quails, and M. Leyba. "Abortion Education in Medical Schools: A National Survey." *American Journal of Obstetrics and Gynecology* 192, no. 2 (2005): 640–643.

Euripides, M. S. *Medea*. Translated by P. Vellacott. New York: Penguin Classics, 1963, 2021.

Fadiman, D., dir. *From Danger to Dignity: The Fight for Safe Abortion*. Documentary, 57 mins. Menlo Park, CA: Concentric Media, 1995.

Farmer, B. "Tennessee Senate Leaders Try to Slam the Brakes on Texas-Style Abortion Ban Advancing in the House." WPLN, March 17, 2022.

Faux, M. *Crusaders: Voices from the Abortion Front*. New York: Carol Publishing Group, 1990.

Federici, S. B. *Caliban and the Witch*. New York: Autonomedia, 2014.

Feuer, A. "The Texas Abortion Law Creates a Kind of Bounty Hunter. Here's How It Works." *New York Times*, November 1, 2021.

Fiske, E. B. "Clergymen Offer Abortion Advice." *New York Times*, May 22, 1967.

Foster, D. G. *The Turnaway Study: Ten Years, a Thousand Women, and the Consequences of Having—or Being Denied—an Abortion*. New York: Simon and Schuster, 2021.

Frankfort, E. F. *Rosie: The Investigation of a Wrongful Death*. New York: Dial Press, 1979.

Garcia-Ditta, Alexa. "Reckoning with Rosie." *Texas Observer*. November 3, 2015.

Gerstein, J., and A. Ward. "Supreme Court Has Voted to Overturn Abortion Rights, Draft Opinion Shows." Politico, May 3, 2022.

Ginsburg, F. D. *Contested Lives: The Abortion Debate in an American Community*. Berkeley: University of California Press, 2006.

Ginsburg, R. B. "A Look at . . . Roe v. Wade v. Ginsburg: The Case Against the Case." *Washington Post*, June 20, 1993.

———. "Speaking in a Judicial Voice." New York University Law School lecture, 1992.

Goldman, E. *Anarchism and Other Essays*. New York: Mother Earth, 1910.

Goodwin, M. *Policing the Womb: Invisible Women and the Criminalization of Motherhood*. Cambridge, UK; New York: Cambridge University Press, 2020.

Goodwyn, W. "Gov. Perry Cut Funds for Women's Health in Texas." NPR, September 20, 2011.

Gorney, C. *Articles of Faith: A Frontline History of the Abortion Wars*. New York: Simon and Schuster, 1998.

Goyal, V., I. H. M. Brooks, and D. A. Powers. "Differences in Abortion Rates by Race-Ethnicity After Implementation of a Restrictive Texas Law." *Contraception* 102, no. 2 (2020): 109–114.

Greenhouse, L., and R. Siegel. *Before Roe v. Wade: Voices That Shaped the Abortion Debate Before the Supreme Court's Ruling.* New Haven, CT: Yale Law School, 2012.

Gurr, B. A. *Reproductive Justice: The Politics of Health Care for Native American Women.* New Brunswick, NJ: Rutgers University Press, 2015.

Gutierrez-Romine, A. *From Back Alley to the Border: Criminal Abortion in California, 1920–1969.* Lincoln: University of Nebraska Press, 2020.

Guttmacher Institute. "Maternal Mortality Review Committees," 2022.

———. "State Facts About Abortion: Alabama," 2022.

———. "State Facts About Abortion: Arkansas," 2022.

———. "State Facts About Abortion: Mississippi," 2022.

———. "State Facts About Abortion: Tennessee," 2022.

———. "State Facts About Abortion: Texas," 2022.

———. "State Facts About Abortion: Utah," 2022.

———. "Targeted Regulation of Abortion Providers (TRAP) Laws," 2020.

Hall, R. *Abortion in a Changing World.* Vol. 2. New York: Columbia University Press, 1970.

Hartmann K. E., C. Fonnesbeck, T. Surawicz, S. Krishnaswami, J. C. Andrews, J. E. Wilson, D. Velez-Edwards, S. Kugley, and N. A. Sathe. "Management of Uterine Fibroids." *Comparative Effectiveness Review,* no. 195 (December 2017).

Hill, A. B. Senate Bill 2116. 2019 regular session, Mississippi Legislature.

Hippolytus. *Didache.* Baden-Württemberg, Germany: Herder, 2000.

Holpuch, A. "Arson Destroyed Knoxville Planned Parenthood Clinic, Officials Say." *New York Times,* January 7, 2022.

hooks, b. *All About Love: New Visions.* New York: HarperCollins, 2018.

Hopkins, K. *Contraception in the Roman Empire.* The Hague, Netherlands: Mouton, 1965.

HuffPost (@Huffpost). "Thanks to Ted Cruz, 'Green Eggs and Ham' is now printed in the Congressional Record (via @bycoffe)." Twitter, September 25, 2013. https://twitter.com/HuffPost/status/382869208582725632?s =20&t=46_JYkLoDhyLfBl4MoFHl.

Hunter, N. D. "Justice Blackmun, Abortion, and the Myth of Medical Independence." *Brooklyn Law Review* 72, no. 1 (2006): 147–197.

Institoris, H. *Hammer of the Witches: A Complete Translation of the Malleus Maleficarum.* Translated by C. S. Mackay. Cambridge, UK: Cambridge University Press, 2011.

Jacobs, J. "Remembering an Era Before Roe, When New York Had the 'Most Liberal' Abortion Law." *New York Times*, July 19, 2018.

Joffe, C. "Failing to Embed Abortion Care in Mainstream Medicine Made It Politically Vulnerable." *Washington Post*, January 11, 2022.

Joffe, C. E. *Doctors of Conscience: The Struggle to Provide Abortion Before and After Roe v. Wade.* Boston: Beacon Press, 2001.

Jones R. K., E. Witwer, and J. Jerman. *Abortion Incidence and Service Availability in the United States, 2017.* New York: Guttmacher Institute, 2019. https://www.guttmacher.org/report/abortion-incidence-service-availability-us-2017.

Jones, R. K., and J. Jerman. "Population Group Abortion Rates and Lifetime Incidence of Abortion: United States, 2008–2014." *American Journal of Public Health* 107, no. 12 (2017): 1,904–1,909.

Jones, R. K., E. Witwer, and J. Jeman. "Abortion Incidence and Service Availability in the United States, 2017." Guttmacher Institute, September 2019.

Judge, P. "The Procedure." Criminal Productions (podcast). Vox Media Podcast Network, 2017.

Kanno-Youngs, Z. "A Battle over How to Battle over Roe: Protests at Justices' Homes Fuel Rancor." *New York Times*, May 12, 2022.

Kaplan, L. *The Story of Jane: The Legendary Underground Feminist Abortion Service.* Chicago: University of Chicago Press, 2019.

Kendall, M. *Hood Feminism: Notes from the Women That a Movement Forgot.* New York: Viking, 2020.

Kimport, K. *No Real Choice: How Culture and Politics Matter for Reproductive Autonomy.* New Brunswick: Rutgers University Press, 2022.

Kissling, F., and E. Frankfort. "Investigation of a Wrongful Death." *Conscience* 17, no. 3 (1996): 23–24.

Knoxville Center for Reproductive Health. Knoxville, TN. https://kcrh.com.

Kolbert, K., and J. F. Kay. *Controlling Women: What We Must Do Now to Save Reproductive Freedom.* New York: Hachette Books, 2021.

Lader, L. *Abortion.* Boston: Beacon Press, 1970.

Lai, K. K. R. "Abortion Bans: 9 States Have Passed Bills to Limit the Procedure This Year." *New York Times*, May 29, 2019.

Lawrence, J. "The Indian Health Service and the Sterilization of Native American Women." *American Indian Quarterly* 24, no. 3 (2000): 400–419.

Lee, S. J., H. J. P. Ralston, E. A. Drey, J. C. Partridge, and M. A. Rosen.

"Fetal Pain: A Systematic Multidisciplinary Review of the Evidence." *JAMA* 294, no. 8 (2005): 947–954.

Lenz, L. *Belabored: A Vindication of the Rights of Pregnant Women.* New York: Bold Type Books, 2020.

Levin, J. *The Queen: The Forgotten Life Behind an American Myth.* New York: Little, Brown, 2019.

Levintova, H. "Up to 240,000 Women Have Tried to Give Themselves Abortions in Texas." *Mother Jones,* November 17, 2015.

Littlejohn, K. E. *Just Get on the Pill: The Uneven Burden of Reproductive Politics.* Oakland: University of California Press, 2021.

Loofbourow, L. "They Called Her 'the Che Guevara of Abortion Reformers.'" *Slate,* December 4, 2018.

Maginnis, P. Family Planning Oral History Project Interviews, 1973–1977. OH-1; T-25; M-138; A1-3, Interview XIV. Schlesinger Library, Radcliffe Institute. Cambridge, MA: Harvard University.

Martínez, E. S. *De Colores Means All of Us: Latina Views for a Multi-Colored Century.* London: Verso Books, 2017.

Marty, R., and A. Palmer. *New Handbook for a Post-Roe America.* New York: Seven Stories Press, 2021.

Marty, R., and J. M. Pieklo. *The End of Roe v. Wade: Inside the Right's Plan to Destroy Legal Abortion.* New York: IG Publishing, 2019.

Mason, C. *Killing for Life: The Apocalyptic Narrative of Pro-Life Politics.* Ithaca: Cornell University Press, 2002.

McClure, L. K. *Women in Classical Antiquity: From Birth to Death.* Hoboken, NJ: John Wiley, 2020.

McNamee, G. L. "Texas state, United States." *Britannica.* https://www.britannica.com/place/Texas-state.

Messer, E., and K. E. May. *Back Rooms: Voices from the Illegal Abortion Era.* Buffalo, NY: Prometheus Books, 1994.

Metress, C. *The Lynching of Emmett Till: A Documentary Narrative.* Charlottesville: University of Virginia Press, 2002.

Mississippi State Department of Health. "Health Department Changes Clinic Hours, Shifts Focus to Preventive Health," 2016.

———. Title 15; Part 16: Health Facilities; Subpart 1: Health Facilities and Certification. "Minimum Standards of Operation for Ambulatory Surgical Facilities," November 12, 2016.

Mohr, J. C. *Abortion in America: The Origins and Evolution of National Policy, 1800–1900.* Oxford [Oxfordshire]: Oxford University Press, 1979.

Nathanson, S. *Soul Crisis: One Woman's Journey Through Abortion to Renewal.* New York: Penguin, 1990.

National Women's Law Center. "Women and Medicaid in Mississippi," 2010.

Nelson, J. *Women of Color and the Reproductive Rights Movement.* New York: New York University Press, 2003.

Noble, K. B. "Key Abortion Plaintiff Now Denies She Was Raped." *New York Times,* September 9, 1987.

Oyez Project. *Planned Parenthood of Southeastern Pennsylvania v. Casey,* 1992. Chicago-Kent College of Law, Illinois Institute of Technology.

———. *Roe v. Wade,* 1972. Chicago-Kent College of Law, Illinois Institute of Technology.

Papers of the Clergy Consultation Service. Manuscript Series CXXVIII, Charles Deering McCormick Library of Special Collections, Northwestern University Library, Evanston, IL.

Pastena, J. A. "Women in Surgery: An Ancient Tradition." *Archives of Surgery* 128, no. 6 (1993): 622–626.

PBS. "Anthony Comstock's 'Chastity' Laws." *The Pill* (series), *American Experience,* 2003.

Peck, P. "'I Felt Like No One Truly Listened': The Invisible Toll of Fibroids on Black Women." *New York Times,* December 13, 2021.

Pender, G. "State Health Department Closing Two-Thirds of Regional Offices." *Clarion Ledger,* June 12, 2017.

Pender, G., and B. Harris. "'Here We Go Again.' Federal Judge Blocks Mississippi's 'Heartbeat' Abortion Law." *Clarion Ledger,* May 24, 2019.

Peterson, B. "Kidnaping Focuses Tensions and Fears on Abortion Clinics." *Washington Post,* August 22, 1982.

Phelan, L. C. Family Planning Oral History Project Interviews, 1973–1977. OH-1; T-25; M-138; A1-3, Interview XVIII. Schlesinger Library, Radcliffe Institute. Cambridge, MA: Harvard University.

Phelan, L., and P. T. Maginnis. *The Abortion Handbook for Responsible Women.* North Hollywood, CA: Contact Books, 1969.

Plato. *Plato's Theory of Knowledge: The Theaetetus and the Sophist of Plato.* Translated by F. M. Cornford. New York: Macmillan, 1986.

Pliny, the Elder. *Pliny's Natural History. In Thirty-Seven Books.* London: George Barclay, 1847.

Pollitt, K. *Pro: Reclaiming Abortion Rights.* New York: Picador, 2015.

Potter, J. E., and K. White. "Defunding Planned Parenthood Was a Disaster in Texas. Congress Shouldn't Do It Nationally." *Washington Post,* February 7, 2017.

Prager, J. *The Family Roe: An American Story*. New York: W. W. Norton, 2022.

Ramos, M. "An Interview with a Convicted Abortion Clinic Arsonist." *VICE*, February 24, 2016.

Rankin, H. D. "Plato's Eugenic ΕΥΦΗΜΙΑ and ΑΠΟΘΕΣΙΣ in Republic, Book V." *Hermes* 93, no. 4 (1965): 407–420.

Rankin, L. *Bodies on the Line: At the Frontlines of the Fight to Protect Abortion in America*. Berkeley, CA: Counterpoint, 2022.

Rayasam, R. "The Southern State Where Black Voters Are Gaining in Numbers, but Not Power." Politico, January 2, 2021.

Raymond, E. G., and D. A. Grimes. "The Comparative Safety of Legal Induced Abortion and Childbirth in the United States." *Obstetrics and Gynecology* 119, 2 Pt. 1 (2012): 215–219.

Reagan, L. J. "Crossing the Border for Abortions: California Activists, Mexican Clinics, and the Creation of a Feminist Health Agency in the 1960s." *Feminist Studies* 26, no. 2 (2000): 323–348.

———. *Dangerous Pregnancies: Mothers, Disabilities, and Abortion in Modern America*. Berkeley: University of California Press, 2012.

———. *When Abortion Was a Crime: Women, Medicine, and Law in the United States, 1867–1973*. Berkeley: University of California Press, 2022.

Redden, M. "Pro-Choicers Are Actually Freaked Out About These Planned Parenthood Sting Videos." *Mother Jones*. July 23, 2015.

Regan, M. D. "Court Blocks Mississippi Law That Would Have Shuttered State's Only Abortion Clinic." PBS, March 18, 2017.

Riddle, J. M. *Contraception and Abortion from the Ancient World to the Renaissance*. Cambridge, MA: Harvard University Press, 1992.

Riley, S. "Planned Parenthood Closed After Someone Fires Shotgun at Clinic Doors." *Knoxville News Sentinel*, January 22, 2021.

Risen, J., and J. L. Thomas. *Wrath of Angels: The American Abortion War*. New York: Basic Books, 1998.

Roberts, D. E. *Killing the Black Body: Race, Reproduction, and the Meaning of Liberty*. New York: Vintage, 2021.

Roberts, L. B. (@smartstatistic). "Hi I'm Laurie Bertram Roberts I'm not pro-choice I'm a #Reproductive Justice activist . . ." Twitter, October 8, 2021. https://twitter.com/smartstatistic/status/1446606758223532034.

Ross, L. *Voices of Feminism Oral History Project, Sophia Smith Collection, Northampton, Massachusetts*. Interviewed by J. Follet, November 3–5, 2004; December 1–3, 2004; February 4, 2005.

Ross, L. S., and R. Solinger. *Reproductive Justice: An Introduction*. Berkeley: University of Califronia Press, 2017.

Rowan, C. T., dir. *Searching for Justice: Three American Stories*. Documentary, with T. Marshall. McLean, VA: Gannett, 1987.

Ruttenberg, D., and K. Zeh. "An Ancient Mistranslation Is Now Helping to Threaten Abortion Rights." *Washington Post*, October 12, 2021.

Sanger-Katz, M., C. C. Miller, and Q. Bui. "Who Gets Abortions in America?" *New York Times*, May 3, 2022.

Scherr, M., ed. *Berkeley Barb* 4, no. 12 (March 24, 1967).

Schoen, J. "Living Through Some Giant Change: The Establishment of Abortion Services." *American Journal of Public Health* 103, no. 3 (2013): 416–425.

Schoen, J. *Abortion After Roe: Abortion After Legalization*. Chapel Hill: The University of North Carolina Press, 2017.

Schulder, D. K. F. *Abortion Rap*. New York: McGraw-Hill, 1971.

Seelye, K. Q. "Sarah Weddington, Who Successfully Argued *Roe v. Wade*, Dies at 76." *New York Times*, December 27, 2021.

Sevcik, K. "One Man's God Squad." *Rolling Stone*, August 19, 2004.

Shah, M. *You're the Only One I've Told: The Stories Behind Abortion*. Chicago: Chicago Review Press, 2020.

Shales, T. "The Force of Rowan's 'Justice.'" *Washington Post*, September 12, 1987.

Sherman, L. A. *A Small Town Rises: A Sharecropper and a College Girl Join the Struggle for Justice in Shaw, Mississippi*. Bog Lily Press, 2020.

Silliman, J., Fried, M. Gerber-Fried, L. Ross, and E. R. Gutierrez. *Undivided Rights: Women of Color Organizing for Reproductive Justice*. Chicago: Haymarket Books, 2016.

Simonaitis, J. E. "Spouse's Consent to Sterilization." *JAMA* 228, no. 11 (1974): 1,453.

Singular, S. *A Death in Wichita: Abortion Doctor George Tiller and the New American Civil War*. New York: St. Martin's, 2012.

Smith, J. "Majority of Texas Voters Favor State-Funded Family Planning." *Austin Chronicle*, February 19, 2013.

Smith, M., and B. Aaronson. "Abortion Bill Finally Bound for Perry's Desk." *Texas Tribune*, July 13, 2013.

Society for Humane Abortion. Records of the Society for Humane Abortion, 1962–1979 (inclusive), 1963–1975 (bulk). Container List Box 1: 1–21; Box 2: 22–23, 25–38; Box 3: 39–61; Box 4: 62–63, 65–66, 68–82; Box 5: 83–91, 93–106; Box 6: 107–129; Box 7: 130–147; Box 8: 148–169; Box 9: 170–181. Schlesinger Library, Radcliffe Institute. Cambridge, MA: Harvard University.

Solis, M. "This Is a Story About Abortion, No One Will Read It." Jezebel, September 1, 2020.

Spruill, J. C. *Women's Life and Work in the Southern Colonies.* New York: Norton, 1998.

Stannard, D. E. *American Holocaust: Columbus and the Conquest of the New World.* New York: Oxford University Press, 1992.

Steinauer, J. E., J. K. Turk, T. Pomerantz, K. Simonson, L. A. Learman, and U. Landy. "Abortion Training in US Obstetrics and Gynecology Residency Programs." *American Journal of Obstetrics and Gynecology* 219, no. 1 (2018): 86 e1–86 e6.

Stulberg, D. B., A. M. Dude, I. Dahlquist, and F. A. Curlin. "Abortion Provision Among Practicing Obstetrician-Gynecologists." *Obstetrics and Gynecology* 118, no. 3 (2011): 609–614.

Stumpe, J., and M. Davey. "Abortion Doctor Shot to Death in Kansas Church." *New York Times,* May 31, 2009.

Sweeney, N., dir. *AKA Jane Roe.* TV movie, 1:19. New York: Vice Studios, Monomania, Isotope Films, 2020.

Texas Alliance for Life. "2017 Texas Legislative Scorecard" (website).

Texas Health and Human Services. *A Woman's Right to Know.* Texas Health and Human Services Commission and Texas Department of State Health Services, 2003, revised 2016.

Theobald, B. *Reproduction on the Reservation: Pregnancy, Childbirth, and Colonialism in the Long Twentieth Century.* Chapel Hill: The University of North Carolina Press, 2020.

Tiller, G. R. "George R. Tiller, MD." Physicians for Reproductive Choice and Health. Edited transcript from *Voices of Choice,* January 1, 2003. https://web.archive.org/web/20090605081317/http://www.prch.org/george-r-tiller-md.

Tillman, Z. "A Judge Ruled That Mississippi's 15-Week Abortion Ban Is 'Unequivocally' Unconstitutional." BuzzFeed News, November 20, 2018.

Torpy, S. J. "Native American Women and Coerced Sterilization: On the Trail of Tears in the 1970s." *American Indian Culture And Research Journal* 24, no. 2 (2000): 1–22.

US Congress. "An Act of the Suppression of Trade in, and Circulation of, Obscene Literature and Articles of Immoral Use." Comstock Act of 1873.

US Department of Justice. "Kansas Woman Pleads Guilty to Setting Fires at Two Virginia Women's Health Clinics." Press release, November 4, 1996.

Wall, L. L. "The Medical Ethics of Dr. J. Marion Sims: A Fresh Look at the Historical Record." *Journal of Medical Ethics* 32, no. 6 (2006): 346–350.

Wattleton, F. *Life on the Line.* New York: Ballantine, 1998.

White, K., S. E. Baum, K. Hopkins, J. E. Potter, and D. Grossman. "Change in Second-Trimester Abortion After Implementation of a Restrictive State Law." *Obstetrics and Gynecology* 133, no. 4 (2019): 771–779.

Wilkerson, I. *The Warmth of Other Suns: The Epic Story of America's Great Migration.* New York: Vintage, 2011.

Wolff, J. D. *Ministers of a Higher Law: The Story of the Clergy Consultation Service on Abortion.* New York: Judson Memorial Church, 1998.

Wynn, R. "Saints and Sinners: Women and the Practice of Medicine Throughout the Ages." *JAMA* 283, no. 5 (2000): 668–669.

Zeldovich V. B., C. H. Rocca, C. Langton, U. Landy, E. S. Ly, and L. R. Freedman. "Abortion Policies in U.S. Teaching Hospitals: Formal and Informal Parameters Beyond the Law." *Obstetrics and Gynecology* 135, no. 6 (2020).

Ziegler, M. *Abortion and the Law in America: Roe v. Wade to the Present.* Cambridge, UK; New York: Cambridge University Press, 2020.

———. *After Roe: The Lost History of the Abortion Debate.* Cambridge, MA: Harvard University Press, 2015.

Zutter, H. D. "Group Efforts: Rising Up Angry and the Greasers' Revolution." *Chicago Reader,* September 21, 1989.

INTERVIEWS

Not all of the sources listed here are quoted in this book, but they all contributed to my understanding of the issues herein. Dates have been provided but not locations, for the privacy of the interviewee.

"Ann" (pseudonym): March 30, 2022

"Dani" and "Alex" (psuedonyms): Jan. 15, 2022

"Joan" (pseudonym): Oct. 27, 2021

"Kate" (pseudonym): June 1, 2019; June 11, 2019

"Tamika" (pseudonym): August 30, 2021

Amber Feller: Oct. 26, 2021; Oct. 27, 2021

Amelia Bonow: Jan. 13, 2022; March 25, 2022

Amie (first name only): June 7, 2020

Amy Hagstrom Miller: Feb. 21, 2020

Andrea Shaffar: Oct. 20, 2021

Anna Rupani: March 23, 2022; May 9, 2022

Ashley Brink: Oct. 1, 2021; May 16, 2022
Ashley Coffield: Oct. 25, 2021
Bailey Mack: Jan. 23, 2022
Barbara Ann Luttrell: July 5, 2019
Carl Swinney: Oct. 1, 2021
Carolyn Davis: Oct. 12, 2021
Cathy Torres: Jan. 26, 2022
Chris Ruben: Jan. 12, 2022
Courtney (first name only): May 17, 2020
Diane and Shelley Sherman: Feb. 22, 2021
Donna McNeil: May 30, 2020; Feb. 4, 2021
Dorothy Roberts: Feb. 28, 2022
Dr. Aaron Campbell: Jan. 31, 2022; March 24, 2022; March 31, 2022
Dr. Ghazaleh Moayedi: June 13, 2022
Dr. Leah Torres: August 30, 2021; May 17, 2022
Dr. Nikia Grayson: Nov. 16, 2021
Dr. Sanithia Williams: Oct. 19 2021; July 1, 2022
Dr. Tracy Weitz: June 20, 2022
Elizabeth Nash: Nov. 22, 2021
Emily Berisso: Oct. 26, 2021
Farah (first name only): Jan. 10, 2022
Faye Wattleton: March 3, 2021
Heather Booth: March 31, 2021; Feb. 7, 2022
Imani Gandy: June 1, 2022
Jazmine (first name only): Oct. 20, 2021
Jennifer McCoy: Oct. 1, 2021
Jennifer Pepper: Oct. 28, 2021
Jerri Town: July 3, 2020
Jill Adams: March 26, 2020
Judith Arcana: Nov. 10, 2020
Kari Crowe: June 27, 2022
Kasey (first name only): July 8, 2020
Kat Farris: Oct. 27, 2021
Keli Foster: Jan. 23, 2022
Kirsten Clark: July 14, 2021
Koa Beck: Dec. 21, 2020
Krista (first name only): Oct. 27, 2021
Laura Kaplan: April 16, 2021; April 1, 2022
Laurie Bertram Roberts: June 3, 2019; July 11, 2019; May 18, 2021; March
    12, 2021

Laurie O'Connell: Jan. 17, 2021; Jan. 24, 2021
Lee Ann (first name only): June 7, 2020; Nov. 4, 2020
Lina-Maria Murillo: April 12, 2021
Loretta Ross: March 28, 2022
Lucy Purse: May 18, 2020; May 17, 2022
Madeline Dyer: Jan. 12, 2022
Maria (first name only): Nov. 16, 2021
Mars Wood: Feb. 18, 2022; March 31, 2022
Mary Driscoll: Nov. 12, 2021
Mary Loveless: Oct. 27, 2021
Mary Ziegler: May 20, 2022
Meg Sasse Stern: Noov. 17, 2021
Melissa Tovar: Oct. 1, 2021
Mia Raven: June 27, 2022; June 9, 2022
Mike Hagen: Oct. 1, 2021
Nikiya Natale: Feb. 28, 2022; March 30, 2022
Oriaku Njoku: May 20, 2022; June 1, 2022
Rachael Lorenzo: May 5, 2022
Raeann Williams: Nov. 29, 2020
Rafa Kidvai: Nov. 5, 2021
Rebecca Tong: Oct. 4, 2021
Renee Bracey Sherman: Feb. 22, 2021; March 9, 2021; May 17, 2021; Dec. 3, 2021; May 25, 2022
Rev. Cherisse Scott: Nov. 11, 2021
Rita Sasse: Jan. 12, 2022
Robin Marty: August 30, 2021; Sept. 1, 2021; May 17, 2022; June 28, 2022
Scott Hord: June 24, 2022
Sherry (identified by first name only): May 26, 2020; August 7, 2020
Susan Dodd: June 12, 2020
Taylor (first name only): July 8, 2020
Tori Black: Oct. 27, 2021
Travis Jackson: June 27, 2022
Wendy Davis: July 5, 2022
Zaena Zamora: Oct. 28, 2021
Zamaiya Lowe: Oct. 20, 2021

Index

Becca Andrews is a journalist who covers reproductive health care. Her work has appeared in *Mother Jones*, *Wired*, Jezebel, and the *New Republic*, among others. She is a graduate of Middle Tennessee State University and UC Berkeley's Graduate School of Journalism.

PublicAffairs is a publishing house founded in 1997. It is a tribute to the standards, values, and flair of three persons who have served as mentors to countless reporters, writers, editors, and book people of all kinds, including me.

I. F. STONE, proprietor of *I. F. Stone's Weekly*, combined a commitment to the First Amendment with entrepreneurial zeal and reporting skill and became one of the great independent journalists in American history. At the age of eighty, Izzy published *The Trial of Socrates*, which was a national bestseller. He wrote the book after he taught himself ancient Greek.

BENJAMIN C. BRADLEE was for nearly thirty years the charismatic editorial leader of *The Washington Post*. It was Ben who gave the *Post* the range and courage to pursue such historic issues as Watergate. He supported his reporters with a tenacity that made them fearless and it is no accident that so many became authors of influential, best-selling books.

ROBERT L. BERNSTEIN, the chief executive of Random House for more than a quarter century, guided one of the nation's premier publishing houses. Bob was personally responsible for many books of political dissent and argument that challenged tyranny around the globe. He is also the founder and longtime chair of Human Rights Watch, one of the most respected human rights organizations in the world.

·   ·   ·

For fifty years, the banner of Public Affairs Press was carried by its owner Morris B. Schnapper, who published Gandhi, Nasser, Toynbee, Truman, and about 1,500 other authors. In 1983, Schnapper was described by *The Washington Post* as "a redoubtable gadfly." His legacy will endure in the books to come.

Peter Osnos, *Founder*